Kosovo between War and Peace

Peacebuilding and reconstruction of war-torn societies have increasingly taken the shape of *de facto* trusteeship arrangements, with the ongoing administration of Kosovo being the primary example. This book examines the obstacles to reconciliation and social reconstruction in Kosovo, and discusses the potential and problems of the revived trusteeship institution.

Bringing together international scholars such as Michael Pugh, Mark Baskin and Arne Johan Vetlesen, the book presents the latest empirical knowledge alongside detailed theoretical analysis. After a re-examination of the background factors that continue to hamper the attempt to administrate and reconstruct the society of Kosovo, primarily the nationalist ideologies and the still growing record of ethnic violence, the book analyses the key challenges local parties and the international community have encountered in the country including the ones associated with the reconstruction of local governance, the educational system and the economic sector as well as the question of Kosovo's status.

More generally, the volume asks whether the revived international trusteeship institution is the way forward for international society when faced with reconstruction challenges of the scale of Kosovo, Bosnia, East Timor, Afghanistan and Iraq. In this perspective, it discusses the underlying liberal aspirations as well as the ramifications of the increasing securitization, militarization and great-power domination of international trusteeship arrangements indicated by the examples of Afghanistan and Iraq. Fundamental questions concerning the relationship between trusteeship and sovereignty, national self-determination and the potential of world organization are raised as well.

This book will be of great interest to all students of Balkan politics, peacekeeping, intervention, the UN, international relations and security studies in general.

Tonny Brems Knudsen is Associate Professor of International Relations at the University of Aarhus. He has published a number of books and articles on international intervention and conflict resolution, international law, UN, and IR theory including *Humanitarian Intervention: Contemporary Manifestations of an Explosive Doctrine* and co-edited with Knud Erik Jørgensen *International Relations in Europe: Traditions, Perspectives and Destinations* (both Routledge, 2006). **Carsten Bagge Laustsen** is Associate Professor at the University of Aarhus where he teaches political theory, international relations theory and sociology. He has published numerous articles and books including *The Culture of Exception: Sociology Facing the Camp* (Routledge, 2005) and *In the Shadow of Terror* (Samfundslitteratur, 2004, in Danish), both with Bülent Diken.

The Routledge Series on Peacekeeping

ISSN 1367–9880

General Editor: Michael Pugh

This series examines all aspects of peacekeeping, from the political, operational and legal dimensions to the developmental and humanitarian issues that must be dealt with by all those involved with peacekeeping in the world today.

1 **Beyond the Emergency**
Development within UN Missions
edited by Jeremy Ginifer

2 **The UN, Peace and Force**
edited by Michael Pugh

3 **Mediating in Cyprus**
The Cypriot communities and the United Nations
Oliver P. Richmond

4 **Peacekeeping and the UN Agencies**
edited by Jim Whitman

5 **Peacekeeping and Public Information**
Caught in the crossfire
Ingrid A. Lehman

6 **US Peacekeeping Policy under Clinton**
A fairweather friend?
Michael MacKinnon

7 **Peacebuilding and Police Reform**
edited by Tor Tanke Holm and Espen Barth Eide

8 **Peacekeeping and Conflict Resolution**
edited by Oliver Ramsbotham and Tom Woodhouse

9 **Managing Armed Conflicts in the 21st Century**
edited by Adekeye Adebajo and Chandra Lekha Sriram

10 **Women and International Peacekeeping**
edited by Louise Olsson and Torunn L. Tryggestad

11 **Recovering from Civil Conflict**
Reconciliation, peace and development
edited by Edward Newman and Albrecht Schnabel

12 **Mitigating Conflict**
The role of NGOs
edited by Henry F. Carey and Oliver P. Richmond

13 **Ireland and International Peacekeeping 1960–2000**
A study of Irish motivation
Katsumi Ishizuka

14 **Peace Operations after 11 September 2001**
edited by Thierry Tardy

15 **Confronting Past Human Rights Violations**
Justice vs peace in times of transition
Chandra Lekha Sriram

16 **The National Politics of peacekeeping in the Post-Cold War Era**
edited by Pia Christina Wood and David S. Sorensen

17 **A UN 'Legion'**
Between utopia and reality
Stephen Kinloch-Pichat

18 **United Nations Peacekeeping in the Post-Cold War Era**
John Terence O'Neill and Nicholas Rees

19 **The Military and Negotiation**
The role of the soldier–diplomat
Deborah Goodwin

20 **NATO and Peace Support Operations 1991–1999**
Policies and doctrines
Henning-A. Frantzen

21 **International Sanctions**
Between words and wars in the global system
edited by Peter Wallensteen and Carina Staibano

22 **Nordic Approaches to Peace Operations**
A new nordic model in the making?
Peter Viggo Jakobsen

23 **Kosovo between War and Peace**
Nationalism, peacebuilding and international trusteeship
edited by Tonny Brems Knudsen and Carsten Bagge Laustsen

Kosovo between War and Peace

Nationalism, peacebuilding and international trusteeship

Edited by Tonny Brems Knudsen and Carsten Bagge Laustsen

Routledge
Taylor & Francis Group
LONDON AND NEW YORK

First published 2006 by Routledge
2 Park Square, Milton Park, Abingdon, Oxon, OX14 4RN

Simultaneously published in the USA and Canada
by Routledge
270 Madison Ave, New York NY 10016

Routledge is an imprint of the Taylor & Francis Group, an informa business

Transferred to Digital Printing 2007

Typeset in Times by
GreenGate Publishing Services, Tonbridge, Kent

British Library Cataloguing in Publication Data
A catalogue record for this book is available from the British Library

Library of Congress Cataloging in Publication Data
Kosovo between war and peace : nationalism, peacebuilding and international trusteeship / edited by Tonny Brems Knudsen and Carsten Bagge Laustsen.
p. cm. — (Routledge series on peacekeeping, ISSN 1367-9880)
ISBN 0-7146-5598-8 (hardback)
1. Peacebuilding—Serbia and Montenegro—Kosovo (Serbia) 2. Peacekeeping forces—Serbia and Montenegro—Kosovo (Serbia) 3. Nationalism—Serbia and Montenegro—Kosovo (Serbia) 4. International trusteeships—Serbia and Montenegro—Kosovo (Serbia). I. Knudsen, Tonny Brems. II. Laustsen, Carsten B. (Carsten Bagge), 1970– . III. Series. JZ5584.

Y8K67 2006
949.7103—dc22

2005032971

ISBN10: 0-714-65598-8 (hbk)
ISBN10: 0-415-45958-3 (pbk)
ISBN10: 0-203-96961-8 (ebk)

ISBN13: 978-0-714-65598-7 (hbk)
ISBN13: 978-0-415-45958-7 (pbk)
ISBN13: 978-0-203-96961-8 (ebk)

Contents

Contributors

Tonny Brems Knudsen is an Associate Professor of International Relations at the Department of Political Science, University of Aarhus, Denmark. His publications cover subjects such as international intervention and conflict resolution, international law and the use of force, and international relations theory – especially the international society theory of the English School.

Carsten Bagge Laustsen is an Associate Professor of International Relations and Sociology at the Department of Political Science, University of Aarhus, Denmark. His main areas of research are social and political theory, terrorism and nationalism. He has written or edited eight books, the latest being *Culture of Exception: Sociology Facing the Camp* (2005, with Bülent Diken).

Lene Kühle is an Assistant Professor at the Department of the Study of Religion, Faculty of Theology, University of Aarhus, Denmark, where she teaches sociology of religion. Her list of publications includes articles on secularization, religious pluralism, church-state relations and religion in the public sphere. She is associated with the Centre for Multireligious Studies, University of Aarhus, where she is currently writing a book on the institutionalization of Islam in Denmark.

Arne Johan Vetlesen is a Professor of Philosophy at Oslo University, Norway. He studied in Frankfurt am Main 1985–90 with Jürgen Habermas as supervisor. He has been editor of *Norsk Filosofisk Tidskrift* since1996. Vetlesen has published 13 books, including *Perception, Empathy, and Judgment* (1994), *Closeness: An Ethics* (with H. Jodalen, 1997), and *Evil and Human Agency: Understanding Collective Evildoing* (2005).

Lene Mosegaard Søbjerg is a PhD scholar at the Department of Political Science, University of Aarhus, Denmark. Her academic interests include UN peace operations, trusteeships, humanitarian interventions, development aid and the theory of international society. She has published mainly in Scandinavian journals including *Tidsskriftet Politik*, *Nordisk Østforum* and *Militært Tidsskrift*.

Mark A. Baskin holds a doctorate in Political Science from the University of Michigan and has taught in universities in North Carolina and New York. He is Senior Associate at the Center for International Development at the State University of New York (SUNY) Research Foundation. Earlier, he was a 'Public Policy Fellow' at the Woodrow Wilson International Center for Scholars in Washington, DC, and served as Head of Research at the Pearson Peacekeeping Centre in Canada. He worked as a Civil Affairs and Political Officer for United Nations Peace Operations in Croatia, Bosnia-Herzegovina and Kosovo throughout the 1990s. In Kosovo, in 1999–2000, he served as Deputy Regional Administrator and Municipal Administrator in Prizren. He held Fulbright and IREX fellowships in Yugoslavia and Bulgaria in the 1970s and 1980s. His research has focused on ethnicity and nationalism in socialist Yugoslavia, the economic and political transitions in the Balkans, and the establishment of rule of law and governance in conflict zones. He has published and lectured in North America and Europe.

Wayne Nelles received his PhD in Education in 1995 from the University of British Columbia where he has also been a Senior Associate, Sustainable Development Research Initiative. Currently, he is Senior Research Associate, Centre for Global Studies, University of Victoria. He has consulted for various international agencies and academic institutions while publishing articles on education and security in a number of international journals. Most recently he was editor of *Comparative Education, Terrorism and Human Security: From Critical Pedagogy to Peacebuilding?* (2003), a Palgrave–Macmillan, NY book. As a part of his research, he has visited the Balkans several times.

Michael Pugh is Professor of Peace and Conflict Studies at the Department of Peace Studies, University of Bradford. Previously, he was Professor of International Relations and Director of the Plymouth International Studies Centre, University of Plymouth, UK. He is also the editor of the journal International Peacekeeping. He leads an ESRC-funded research project on the transformation of war economies. His publications include 'Peacekeeping and Critical Theory', *International Peacekeeping*, 11, 1 (2004); with Neil Cooper and Jonathan Goodhand, *War Economies in a Regional Context: the Challenge of Transformation*, 2003; and with Waheguru Pal Singh Sidhu, *The UN and Regional Security: Europe and Beyond*, 2003.

Rasmus Abildgaard Kristensen works as an adviser on business and human rights at the Danish Institute for Human Rights. He has consulted widely on topics related to human rights and corporate social responsibility. His academic interests are in the fields of human rights, corporate social responsibility and the international administration of failed states and contested territories. His current research focuses on implementing corporate social responsibility in global supply chains. He is the author of the report: 'Corporate Codes of

Conduct in Denmark – An Examination of their CSR Contents' (Copenhagen: DIHR, 2005) and several articles on human rights and business in books and academic journals. He received a BA in History and a BSc and an MSc in Political Science from the University of Aarhus, Denmark. In addition, he holds an MSC (Econ) in International Politics (with Distinction) from the University of Wales, UK.

Christopher P. Freeman is currently serving as an Associate Civil-Military and Humanitarian Officer with the United Nations Assistance Mission in Afghanistan (UNAMA). Previously he worked with an Afghan NGO, the Tribal Liaison Office, on issues of tribal policing and political inclusion in the south-eastern border regions. He has also worked in research and programme coordination capacities for Civitatis International, the Pearson Peacekeeping Centre, Canada, and has conducted field research in Bosnia-Herzegovina on 'policekeeping'. Academically, his focus is on the relationship between state-building and rule of law, best practices in peace operations, and the theoretical implications of intervention and governance missions. This work has featured in several journals, and he is currently in the process of co-authoring a book on social transformation.

Preface and acknowledgements

As this book has taken shape, the challenges and pitfalls of the new international trusteeships in Kosovo and beyond have become more and more evident.

In Kosovo, the pattern of nationalism, mythmaking and revenge has taken on a seemingly permanent character. At the same time, the difficulties associated with societal reconstruction in the absence of clarity concerning future status have become all too clear. In addition, there are increasing doubts as to whether the western model of liberal democracy and capitalism can and should be transferred to war-torn societies like Kosovo without damage-controlling measures and a sensibility towards local traditions and circumstances.

In the more recent examples of Afghanistan and Iraq, the revival of international trusteeship has become securitized to a hitherto unseen degree: military trusteeships designed for an imposed liberal-democratic transformation of dictatorships as a means in the 'war on terror' instead of United Nations (UN) trusteeships which – although hardly innocent when it comes to purposes of ideology and security – have been designed as a follow-up to humanitarian intervention as in Kosovo and East Timor. Finally, the return to international trusteeship has given rise to some critical political, normative and theoretical questions concerning the consistency of the institutional framework of international society.

In critical and constructive analyses of the return to trusteeship in Kosovo and beyond, the essays in this book shed further light on these specific and general challenges in an attempt to uncover their causes and point to possible ways forward for international administrators, local authorities and international society as a whole. It is our hope that these endeavours will prove to be of value to the practician as well as the theorist, to the student as well as the researcher.

It has been a great pleasure to work with the contributors who have taken on board several rounds of our comments, in spite of the fact that their contributions were already skilled and inspiring as first drafts. We would also like to express our warmest thanks to general editor Michael Pugh for supporting this project, and to secretary Helle Bundgaard for invaluable assistance with the manuscript. Our biggest debt is to Chris Freeman, who has provided strong linguistic assistance and many helpful comments on the book as a whole as well as on a number of draft chapters including the opening one.

Tonny Brems Knudsen and Carsten Bagge Laustsen

Acronyms and abbreviations

AAK	Alliance for the future of Kosovo
UNAMA	United Nations Assistance Mission in Afghanistan
CoE	Council of Europe
CIM	Chief of the Implementation Mission
DESK	Developing an Education System for Kosovo
DOS	Democratic Opposition
DSR	Deputy Special Representative
EU	European Union
EUA	European University Association
FRY	Federal Republic of Yugoslavia
ICG	International Crisis Group
ICTY	International Criminal Tribunal for the Former Yugoslavia
IDEA	International Institute for Democracy and Electoral Assistance
KEWR	Kosovo Early Warning Report
KLA	Kosovo Liberation Army
KFOR	Kosovo Force
LDK	Democratic League of Kosovo
MEST	Ministry of Education, Science and Technology
NATO	North Atlantic Treaty Organization
NDI	National Democratic Institutions
NGO	Non-Governmental Organizations
OHR	Office of the High Representative
OSCE	Organization for Security and Cooperation in Europe
PDK	Democratic Party of Kosovo
PIC	Peace Implementation Council
PISG	Provisional Institutions of Self-Government
RAE	Roma, Ashkallia and Egyptians
SCR	Security Council Resolution
SMES	Serbian Ministry of Education and Sports
SRSG	Special Representative of the Secretary-General
UNAMI	United Nations Assistance Mission for Iraq
UNDP	United Nations Development Programme
UNESCO	United Nations Educational Scientific and Cultural Organization
UNHCR	United Nations High Commissioner for Refugees
UNICEF	United Nations Children's Fund
UNMIK	United Nations Interim Administration Mission in Kosovo
UNMIK-DoES	UNMIK Department of Education and Science
UNTAET	United Nations Transitional Administration in East Timor
UNTAES	United Nations Transitional Administration in Eastern Slavonia
USAID	United States Agency for International Development

1 The politics of international trusteeship

Tonny Brems Knudsen and Carsten Bagge Laustsen

At the beginning of the twenty-first century, the practices of international intervention, peacebuilding and the reconstruction of war-torn societies have reached a stage of ambitious *de facto* trusteeship arrangements with the ongoing international administration of Kosovo as the primary, but by no means exclusive, example.[1] This book examines the obstacles to reconciliation and social reconstruction in Kosovo in the context of what is neither war nor substantial peace. It also discusses the potential and problems of the revived trusteeship institution more generally, as well as its ramifications for the institutional machinery of international society. The resultant collection of essays is thus an attempt to combine practical knowledge and theoretical analysis.

At the practical level, the book discusses a number of the major problems, challenges and dilemmas that the local parties and the international community have encountered in Kosovo including how to develop effective, inclusive and accountable local government; how to construct an educational system capable of stimulating integration and development instead of ethnic separation and exclusion; how to accomplish the partly opposed goals of reconstructing the province while avoiding renewed ethnic and international strife over its future; how to counter crime and the dysfunctional aspects of liberal economic reform, and how to handle the specific challenge of Kosovo's future status. The book also re-examines the background factors that continue to influence and hamper the attempt to administrate and reconstruct the province, most importantly the nationalist ideologies, the myths and the record of ethnic violence.

At the more general and theoretical level, the book asks whether international trusteeship is the way forward for the international community, when faced with reconstruction challenges of the scale of Kosovo, Bosnia, East Timor, Afghanistan and Iraq. In perspective, it also discusses the ramifications of the increasing securitization, militarization and great-power domination of international trusteeship arrangements indicated by the examples of Afghanistan and especially Iraq. The book thus contains discussions that span two markedly different periods and contexts of international trusteeship arrangements, namely the internationalism of the 1990s on the one hand, and the 'war on terror' following 11 September 2001 on the other.

Finally, the book asks how the institution of international trusteeship – a set of principles and practices which are highly interventionist and ambitious in their political nature and strongly solidarist in their moral aspiration – can be incorporated into the still predominantly Westphalian institutional foundations of international society. With its temporary transferral of authority from the national to the super-national level and with its almost inevitable opening of the question of self-rule, international trusteeship cannot be separated from difficult questions of state sovereignty and national self-determination. In the present collection of essays, these more fundamental and institutional aspects of the move from comprehensive peacebuilding to international trusteeship are addressed in terms of the specific problem regarding Kosovo's future status, and the general question of trusteeship as a midway-station to independence for secessionist nations and territories.

These questions and ambitions are reflected in the structure of the book which includes: two chapters on the importance of nationalism, myths and atrocious conduct as the seemingly almost inescapable background and context of the peacebuilding endeavours of the UN-trusteeship in Kosovo; four chapters on key aspects of the ongoing reconstruction of the province including the performance of UNMIK, local governance and democracy, the educational system and crime and capitalism; and three chapters on key issues regarding the relationship between international trusteeship and international society including the regulation of sovereign membership of international society, national self-determination and future status and the role of liberal ideology in contemporary international trusteeship arrangements.

This introductory chapter opens with a general discussion of trusteeship as an emerging institution of international society before moving on to a brief presentation of the main themes covered by the contributors.

Trusteeship as an institution of international society

The tendency that agents acting in the name of international society – most notably the UN but also other international organizations like the EU, NATO and the OSCE, non-governmental organizations and states – take on a far-reaching responsibility for war-torn societies can be traced at least as far back as UN Secretary-General Boutros Boutros-Ghali's ambitious plan for a comprehensive reconstruction of war-torn, starving and generally failed Somalia in his report to the UN Security Council of 3 March 1993, and the ensuing UN Security Council Resolution 814 of 26 March. In the latter, a number of tasks were defined for the UN operation including humanitarian relief, the maintenance of peace, stability, law and order, and assistance with respect to political reconciliation and the re-establishment of a national police force and civil administration throughout the country.[2]

Although the humanitarian intervention in Somalia has generally been seen as a failure,[3] the UN was soon engaged in other comprehensive peacebuilding activities, some of them amounting to *de facto* international trusteeships. The clearest examples of such operations include Bosnia (1995) and Eastern Slavonia (1996) following the Balkan Wars; East Timor following the vote for independence in the 1999 referendum and the ensuing international intervention to bring an end to the anti-secessionist atrocities and ensure that the Indonesian government would stick to its promise regarding independence; and Kosovo following the uprising, the atrocities and the NATO intervention in 1998–9.[4]

For a number of reasons, it is useful to dwell a moment on other less obvious cases, which can and should be considered in the debate over the revival of international trusteeship as well: Afghanistan following the US-sponsored toppling of the Taleban regime in 2001 and, more controversially and problematically, Iraq following the US-led attack on and occupation of the country in 2003.[5] As for the international involvement in the reconstruction of Afghanistan, it seems to be more correct to say that this has taken the character of a strong 'helping hand' rather than an international trusteeship or protectorate. This distinction was made by the International Crisis Group (ICG) at an early point in the debate, but with reference to Bosnia and Kosovo respectively.[6] However, given the far-reaching powers of the UN High Representative in Bosnia not only to guide, but also to overrule the Bosnian authorities, and considering also the increasing will of the High Representative to use these powers from 1998 onwards, it is more correct to characterize Bosnia following the 1995 Dayton Peace Agreement as a *de facto* trusteeship, although Kosovo remains the clearest example along with East Timor. In contrast, the UN-sponsored peacebuilding assistance to post-Taleban Afghanistan, following the December 2002 Bonn meeting, with respect to security, the formation of a new government, and technical, humanitarian and financial assistance could adequately be seen as a helping hand, or as something in between 'partnership' and 'control' to use the categories that have been proposed by Jarat Chopra.[7]

This restricted level of engagement compared to cases like Bosnia, Kosovo and East Timor have prompted writers like Roland Paris and Richard Caplan to ask whether the UN involvement in the reconstruction of Afghanistan should in fact be interpreted as a retreat to the model of a 'light footprint'.[8] However, as also indicated by these writers, the main reason for the less ambitious and more cautious UN approach in Afghanistan (as well as in Iraq) might very well be found in the colossal operational challenges involved and in the internationally controversial backgrounds of full-scale war in these two cases rather than in a retreat from the trusteeship model as such. It should be added, in any case, that neither Paris nor Caplan seem to believe that the light UN footprint and the associated great-power unilateralism is the way forward for international society in complex peacebuilding.

Turning to the administration of Iraq following the fall of Saddam Hussein, this has a background of full-scale war and a highly doubtful legal justification as evident from the widespread resistance to the resort to force in and beyond the UN Security Council in the winter and spring of 2003.[9] Since the post-war administration of Iraq has, on top of that, involved great-power dictate, occupation (which formally ended 30 June 2004)[10] and the temporary rule of a US governor, it might preferably be referred to as a 'military trusteeship' or a 'military governorship' to underline the differences compared to trusteeship arrangements authorized, orchestrated and run by the UN.

Given the relatively modest involvement of the UN and other representatives of the international community in Iraq, there is also a justification for arguing that such cases are not examples of any kind of international trusteeship or protectorate at all.[11] The preamble of UN Security Council resolution 1483 of 22 May 2003 formally and expressively stipulated that the US and the UK had the status of occupying powers under international law (formulated as a statement of a fact and not as an authorization), and the role, or anticipated role, of the UN since then has been one of supporting the occupying authorities and the new Iraqi authorities rather than one of administrating the country on a mandate from the international community.

On the other hand, UN Security Council resolution 1483 (paragraphs 8 and 9) also envisaged a potentially far-reaching UN-organized assistance to the reconstruction of Iraq (and so did resolution 1511 of 16 October 2003) including civilian administration, police and law. As argued by the UN Secretary-General's Special Representative to Iraq at the time, Sergio Vieira de Mello, who was killed in the terrorist attack on the UN headquarters in Baghdad on 19 August 2003, resolution 1483 was sufficiently unclear to allow the UN's role in Iraq to develop with the situation.[12] Although de Mello added that the UN could not replace the Coalition Provisional Authority it is not inconceivable that the UN could have assumed administrative functions and authorities approximating a *de facto* international trusteeship for a transitional period, if the position of the Authority (meaning essentially the US) and the security conditions in the country had been more conducive.

It did not turn out this way, but there is a point in reserving the terms of a military trusteeship or a military governorship to describe Iraq following the war in 2003 (at least until the formal end of occupation on 30 June 2004)[13] in order to bring attention to the risk that the revived trusteeship institution associated with UN-sponsored examples like especially Kosovo and East Timor will increasingly be taken over and run by great powers: actors who will be motivated more by security concerns than by humanitarian concerns, who will be thinking and acting more along unilateral than along collective lines, and who will be organizing their presence more as an occupation preparing the society in question for the 'right' kind of rule than as a transitional administration preparing a people for self-rule or self-determination. In the present volume, this actual and potential development in the contemporary revival of international trusteeship is put into critical perspective by Michael Pugh (Chapter 7), who sees some of these tendencies already in the case of Kosovo as for the economic and the ideological aspects, and Chris Freeman (Chapter 10), who discusses the securitization of the trusteeship institution as such with a number of examples, and also including Afghanistan and Iraq.

This is a timely and highly relevant critique since cases like Kosovo, Afghanistan and Iraq have demonstrated that there is not necessarily any entirely clear and consistent line[14] between unauthorized war and occupation on the one hand and UN-authorized intervention and trusteeship arrangements on the other, just as it is sometimes very difficult to separate the goals of humanitarianism and international order from the goals of national security and national interest. UN-authorized trusteeship and peacebuilding arrangements may follow upon an unauthorized resort to force (no matter whether force was used for humanitarian reasons as in the case of Kosovo or for a mixture of national and international security as in the case of Afghanistan) and military occupation may continue alongside a UN-authorized and UN-orchestrated peacebuilding operation which could possibly even amount to an international trusteeship, although the foreign presence in Iraq has not been taken that far into grey-zone complexity.

These reflections may lead to the following observations concerning the politics of the revived trusteeship institution: First, it is helpful to distinguish between military trusteeships (or governorships) in which the governance and reconstruction of the society in question is dominated by (formally or *de facto*) occupying powers as in the case of Iraq, and UN trusteeships where these tasks are in the hands of UN administrators and (in varying degrees) their local, organizational and state partners as in the cases of Bosnia, Eastern Slavonia, Kosovo and East Timor.

Second, in their ideal forms both of these models of outside administration are unlikely to be found very often in reality. On the one hand, great powers are also likely to play a central role in UN trusteeship arrangements as evident in the case of Kosovo. On the other hand, great powers will rarely want to do completely without the expertise, the resources and the legitimacy of the UN in the administration of war-torn or contested societies as indicated even in the divisive case of Iraq, where the US asked the UN to take part in the reconstruction of the country despite the fact that the invasion had been widely deplored in the UN Security Council and the General Assembly, and by Secretary-General Kofi Annan.

Third, although each case is unique, most academic and political observers would presumably agree that all other things being equal, the legitimacy of an international trusteeship is going to be higher, the greater the involvement of the UN, the clearer the original legal case for interventionist measures, and the clearer the humanitarian and international security concerns. If this is a correct observation, we are likely to witness bigger legitimacy problems concerning the establishment and running of trusteeship arrangements under the current anti-terror agenda than under the neo-internationalist agenda associated with the 1990s.[15] Since '9/11', the 'war on terror' has conquered ground from the doctrines of human rights and humanitarian intervention, and in spite of some Third World scepticism towards the latter, the former is likely to be seen as a more controversial point of departure for peacebuilding and trusteeship projects, unless the case for intervention is, at the very least, as legally and politically clear as in Afghanistan following the attacks on New York and Washington on 11 September 2001.

Arguably, an anti-terror case for military intervention and political reconstruction like the one of Afghanistan in 2001 is likely to enjoy as much support as a humanitarian case like the one of Kosovo in 1999. However, in the context of the 'war on terror', the US has launched and so far not withdrawn two doctrines that remain unlikely to command widespread international support and approval, namely the doctrine of preventive use of force and the doctrine of the coalition of the willing as the heart of multilateralism.[16] Whereas humanitarian intervention is by definition a matter of extreme urgency and necessity (unless the right is simply abused), any preventive use of force is bound to attract international resistance on the grounds that it was not required and thus not justified. Consequently, trusteeship arrangements are likely to have a better start with respect to international legitimacy and backing, no matter whether the initial resort to force has been authorized by the UN or not, if it grows out of a humanitarian intervention (or a response to a clear and imminent threat to peace and security) instead of a preventive attack. This is at least the message that follows from a comparison of Kosovo (1999) and Afghanistan (2001) on the one hand and Iraq (2003) on the other. To this it must be added, that no imposed international trusteeship arrangement is likely to be seen as legitimate in international society, unless it rests upon a mandate from the UN Security Council. However, when the case for intervention is doubtful, a mandate basis for the reconstruction is not always enough, as illustrated by the widespread international reluctance to offer the ongoing reconstruction of Iraq wholehearted support.

Definitional and institutional aspects

As evident from this preliminary discussion of relevant cases and their political implications, a number of terms have been applied and suggested for the extension of international responsibility and administration of war torn-societies since the early 1990s. Some scholars prefer the terms that have become the UN's own in cases like Kosovo, namely 'interim administration' and 'transitional administration'[17] referring to the temporary assumption of governmental functions by the UN and its state and organizational partners over territories and peoples that have been left in a potentially fatal political vacuum, for instance because of civil war, systematic crimes against humanity, state failure, territorial disputes or outside military intervention.[18]

Others refer to 'comprehensive peacebuilding' which, following former UN Secretary-General Boutros Boutros-Ghali's 1992 'Agenda for Peace', can be defined as 'efforts to identify and support structures which will tend to consolidate peace and advance a sense of confidence and well-being among people'.[19] This term captures a number of the activities involved in subsequent examples of ambitious administration of war-torn and contested territories such as Kosovo and East Timor including the reforming of governmental institutions as suggested already by Boutros-Ghali in 1992. Consequently, the term also signifies the readiness of the UN to take on increasing responsibilities in such complicated operations through the 1990s as is evident from the gradual drift from traditional peacekeeping to wider peacekeeping, peace-enforcement, humanitarian intervention and, ultimately, the civil, political, social and economic reconstruction of entire societies.[20]

However, some observers, among them a number of the contributors to this volume, find that there is more to it than the assumption of more and more responsibilities in the work for peace. As stated by Lene Mosegaard Søbjerg (chapter 4), peacebuilding means that the UN takes on far-reaching responsibilities for the society in question, but it does so working with the government of that society. In cases like Kosovo, the UN *becomes* the government as evident from UN Security Council Resolution 1244 of 10 June 1999 which provided for the establishment of the 'United Nations Interim Administration Mission in Kosovo' (UNMIK) with responsibility for promoting substantial autonomy, carrying out basic civilian administration, organizing the establishment of democratic institutions, supporting the reconstruction of infrastructure and the provision of humanitarian aid, maintaining law and order, protecting human rights and assuring the safe return of refugees.[21]

Clearly, the assumption of such powers and authorities by representatives of the international community amount to a qualification or cancellation of state sovereignty, meaning that both its internal and external aspects are affected:[22] Internally, the supreme right of a state to govern itself is temporarily annulled. Externally, the mutual recognition of state sovereignty – which has for centuries been the basis of coexistence and participation in international society with all rights and duties under international law – becomes less clear-cut, since the outside administration temporarily brings a hybrid political actor into play. Furthermore, judging from recent examples, this typically happens as a consequence of a military intervention which the former sovereign authorities would, at a minimum, have preferred to avoid. At the same time, arrangements like the ones in Kosovo and East Timor inevitably reopen sensitive questions concerning national self-determination and the potentially super-national authority of world organization. The political, legal and institutional machinery of international society is affected at a fundamental level.

For these reasons, Kosovo and similar cases of comprehensive international administration of war-torn and contested territories should be discussed in terms that capture this fundamental institutional dimension and its historical precedents: (1) International *protectorates* referring especially to the institutionalized practice under the League of Nations of entrusting a dependent area to an advanced state which was in turn responsible to the League and on whose behalf it was to administer the mandate, either relatively permanently (type B and C) or temporarily until the mandate was ready to gain full independence as foreseen at the outset (type A).[23] (2) International *trusteeships* referring to the International Trusteeship System and Council (established under Chapter XII and XIII of the UN Charter) under whose supervision the state entrusted with the task took it upon itself to prepare the territory in question for the explicit goal of self-government or independence.[24]

Although both terms and the associated principles, institutions and practices are, to varying degrees, burdened with colonial connotations they seem to capture much of the content of present-day governing arrangements including to a considerable degree the institutionalized element, as the UN – led by the UN Security

Council and the Secretariat – has taken it upon itself to authorize, establish, run and oversee such arrangements. Admittedly, the supervisory powers and mechanisms of the redundant Trusteeship Council are more clearly defined than the ones that are evolving from the case-by-case initiatives taken by the Security Council since the middle of the 1990s, and the will and ability of the Security Council and the Secretariat to oversee trusteeship arrangements like the ones in Kosovo and East Timor can also be questioned.[25] However, the Security Council and the Secretariat provide a legal framework and a degree of political accountability, supervision and control which, in a number of respects, resemble the earlier protectorate and trusteeship institutions in spite of the fact that today, the world organization is no longer supervising administrating states, but its own agencies, representatives and partners.[26]

First, the composition of the Security Council resembles the one of the Trusteeship Council, which was supposed to include the five veto-powers as well as a balanced representation of trusteeship powers and states without such responsibilities.[27] The five veto-powers are also represented in the Security Council which is at any time likely to include states that take active part in a trusteeship arrangement and states which do not. Furthermore, the Third World is always represented. Second, the Security Council has the necessary authority and legitimacy to put a territory under international administration, and to create a legal basis and framework for the exercise of it, as evident from the adoption of resolutions like 1244 on 10 June 1999 on the governance and reconstruction of Kosovo. Third, there is an element of control and accountability in today's trusteeship arrangements in so far that the Special Representatives report to the UN Secretary-General, who in turn reports to the Security Council. The Security Council and the Secretary-General may furthermore decide to launch investigations or fact-finding missions, and new resolutions or directions may be adopted. This element of supervision and accountability is further strengthened by the participation of a range of other international and non-governmental organizations whose presence increases the likelihood that misrule and failures will come to the critical attention of the international public. Kosovo, to take the primary example of this book, is in fact administrated by a veritable network of international organizations, arranged in and around the four pillars of UNMIK.[28] For all its shortcomings, stemming from its incremental evolution and pragmatic nature, the potential of the current informal trusteeship machinery might not be as weak as one might think, when compared to the formal one of the Trusteeship Council.

What terms like 'international protectorates' and 'international trusteeship' emphasize in particular, however, is the authoritative decision by representatives of international society to resort to institutional arrangements which depart from the strict Westphalian model of international order in which states are the only bearers of rights and duties under international law. It is not least in these respects that present-day governing arrangements like the one in Kosovo amount to 'an international trusteeship in everything but name' as it has – with concern and a call for caution – been formulated by Robert Jackson, a leading defender of Westphalian or 'pluralist' international society.[29] In Kosovo, East Timor, Eastern

Slavonia and Bosnia, the international administration has (more or less completely) been entrusted not to a particular state, but to the United Nations acting through the special representatives of the Secretary General in cooperation with a number of organizational and state partners. Like before, the relevant territories and societies are placed under the protection of the international community with the promotion of the well-being and self-governance or independence of the people in question as the declared goal. But in the openness towards a variety of territories and societies as potential candidates for temporary administration, in the strong role of world organization and in the implicit or explicit assumption that the international administration cannot go on permanently (and certainly not along colonial lines), but must give way to self-determination or independence, the post-Cold War revival of outside administration of war-torn and contested territories comes closer to the UN trusteeship system than to the protectorates of the League of Nations.

Consequently, we prefer the term ‘trusteeship’, which can be defined as the temporary (although sometimes relatively permanent) assumption of governmental authority over a territory and its population by the UN or other representatives of the international community based on a relatively stable and institutionalized set of habits and practices shaped towards the comprehensive reconstruction of war-torn societies and the management of contested territories with the declared aim of promoting the (re)establishment of orderly and just affairs in domestic society, the normalization of its international relations, and a progression to self-rule or, sometimes, independence from the former sovereign authorities.

Following the vocabulary, though not the listing of examples, of Hedley Bull and the English School, international trusteeship can thus be seen as a fundamental or semi-fundamental institution of international society: a set of principles, practices and habits ‘shaped towards the realization of common goals’.[30] This institution may not be as fundamental as to be indispensable to international society as implied by Hedley Bull’s (but to a lesser extent his source of inspiration, Martin Wight’s) historical and sociological usage of the term ‘fundamental institutions’. It is, as already indicated, also as open to abuse and malfunction as other fundamental institutions like war and the balance of power. However, the resort to international trusteeship arrangements can in some, although not in all, situations be seen as a reflection of concerns for international order and international justice. In Bosnia, Kosovo and East Timor, the former sovereign authorities had demonstrated a lack of will or ability to provide for orderly and just conditions. At the same time, atrocities, civil war, outside intervention and territorial disputes had left a political vacuum which for reasons of international stability called for a temporary international governance of these areas. In some cases, international trusteeship is therefore first of all a pragmatic response to the breakdown of order and justice, and at a moment in world history where it is increasingly difficult to separate domestic from international sources of disorder, it would be a loss for the international community if private great-power ambitions, value-imperialism or a lack of resources should eventually lead, once again, to an abandonment of this institution.

The potentially positive effects of international trusteeships on regional stability and international order should be taken into account on the positive side when considering the relevant, but not necessarily decisive, concerns raised by 'pluralist' writers like Robert Jackson and Will Bain that a revival of international trusteeship is at odds with fundamental organizing principles of international society, not least those relating to sovereignty, and that this has profound political and moral implications for questions of freedom and self-determination.[31] The pluralist calculation should weigh the potentially negative effects of trusteeship arrangements against what can be gained in terms of the prevention of further war, conflict and atrocities. To 'solidarist' writers, there is, potentially, even more to gain from international trusteeships than order.[32] Given that trusteeships are in their ideal form expressions of collective management, global responsibility for peoples at risk, and the belief in the capacity of international society to govern, it is also a strong project of international solidarity and global governance. Moreover, as long as the UN and leading quarters in the international community are from time to time prepared to prevent crimes against humanity and genocide by the use of force, they can hardly do without international trusteeship as a part of the international institutional machinery when intervention gives way to reconstruction.

In the institutional and political perspective on international trusteeship unfolded in this book, it means less that as a part of his 'In Larger Freedom' reform program, UN Secretary-General Kofi Annan has proposed that Chapter XIII of the UN Charter should be deleted (meaning that the Trusteeship Council will be formally closed rather than just suspended), and that the member states seem to have agreed on this at the high-level plenary meeting of the UN General Assembly in New York 14–16 September 2005 (the September World Summit). For historical and especially colonial reasons, it would have been very difficult to reopen this organ in any case. It is worth noting, however, that Annan has also proposed – and obtained support for this at the World Summit – the establishment of two new peacebuilding units, namely a Peacebuilding Commission and a Peacebuilding Support Office (to be situated in the Secretariat).[33] The rationale of the member states for taking this decision was 'the need for a dedicated institutional mechanism to address the special need of countries emerging from conflict towards recovery, reintegration and reconstruction', and the purposes of the Peacebuilding Commission will be 'to bring together all relevant actors to marshal resources and to advise on and propose integrated strategies for post-conflict peacebuilding and recovery' with 'attention on the reconstruction and institution-building efforts necessary for recovery from conflict'.[34]

Although the language is expressed in the less explosive terms of post-conflict peacebuilding, the new commission and its support office are likely to get involved in the full range of peacebuilding activities also including at times genuine trusteeship arrangements comparable to the one in Kosovo. Moreover, the dual structure of the new commission means that it is going to be preoccupied with the general and organizational aspects of peacebuilding as well as country-specific reconstruction. The first-mentioned tasks are in the hands of the standing

Organizational Committee itself, which is to be comprised of permanent and other members of the UN Security Council, members of the Economic and Social Council, and UN top providers of financial contributions, military personnel and civilian police. To this committe come country-specific settings organized as a series of meetings bringing together the country under (consideration for) post-conflict reconstruction, regional participants in this process including both states and organizations, the major financial, troop and civilian police contributors involved in the specific recovery effort, the relevant UN representatives in the field and beyond, and other relevant institutions.[35]

With this dual structure, the Peacebuilding Commission and its Support Office will have the potential of contributing not only to the improvement of vital reconstruction elements like multilateral coordination, the collection of financial, military and civilian resources, and the development of best practices, but also to the stronger involvement of the country or society under reconstruction and a higher degree of international accountability as called for by a number of observers in cases like Kosovo and East Timor, for instance by means of periodic reviews of progress and direct follow-up involvement of the Security Council and the Economic and Social Council as proposed by Kofi Annan.[36]

It seems, in other words, that the Secretary-General and the September 2005 World Summit has formally closed down the redundant Trusteeship Council with one hand, while at the same time it has prepared for a further institutionalization of the *de facto* post-Cold War trusteeship machinery with the other, as a part of the broader peacebuilding agenda. It should also be noted that the World Summit has not eliminated the UN Trusteeship System as provided for in Chapter XII of the UN Charter, but only the Trusteeship Council. This means that (some of) the provisions regarding the trusteeship system might be directly or indirectly relevant for the *de facto* trusteeship arrangements established by the UN Security Council, and that the new peacebuilding units might be activated as supportive instruments for a *de facto* UN trusteeship system.

In an ideal formulation – meaning, first, that that we are not talking about military trusteeships applied strategically in the 'war on terror', and second that we refer to the potential rather than the recent practice of UN trusteeship – the contours of this evolving system can be envisaged as follows: (1) The UN Security Council may decide to put war-torn or contested territories under temporary international administration and thereby turn them into *de facto* trusteeships, either with or without the consent of the sovereign authorities as in the cases of East Timor and Kosovo respectively. (2) The main goals of such temporary administrations should be the ones stipulated for the UN Trusteeship System in Article 76 of the UN Charter including especially 'to further international peace and security', 'to promote the political, economic, social and educational advancement of the inhabitants of the trust territories, and their progressive development towards self-government or independence', and 'to encourage respect for human rights and fundamental freedoms for all'. (3) Such temporary trusteeship arrangements should preferably be supervised and run by a number of UN agencies – including the Security Council; the Secretary-General, his

Secretariat, and his special representatives; the UN missions and the new Peacebuilding Commission and Support Office – in cooperation with a network of organizational (governmental and non-governmental) and state partners. (4) The legal basis of these *ad hoc* trusteeship arrangements will be the UN Security Council resolutions by which they are established and the Charter provisions on which these authoritative decisions rest, namely those regarding the maintenance of international peace and security, and, arguably, those relating to the UN trusteeship system in Chapter XII of the UN Charter, some of which remain relevant to the legitimacy and goals of contemporary trusteeship arrangements in spite of their *ad hoc* and partly informal nature.

However, the need for improvements in the legal and institutional machinery of international trusteeship and guarantees against further securitization are only some of the many challenges that have come with the post-Cold War revival of this practice. In what follows, some of the other main challenges discussed in this book, with Kosovo as the principle (but not the exclusive) object of attention, will briefly be introduced.

Kosovo as an international trusteeship: challenges and implications

With the adoption of UN Security Council Resolution 1244 of 10 June 1999 and the establishment of UNMIK, the UN and its partners, including among others NATO, the OSCE and the EU, became responsible for the territory, the people and the society of Kosovo. This means not only taking responsibility for security, the rule of law, education, and civil administration for a period of time, but also for the reconstruction of the institutional preconditions of these essential elements of domestic society. The standard of success becomes, virtually, to provide for the introduction of 'the good life' in a place where this has not been a part of reality for long periods of time. This is a heavy burden to put on the shoulders of international society.

In the present book, some of the associated challenges have been singled out for deeper analysis in individual contributions on the international administration of Kosovo and, secondarily, other recent examples of international trusteeship. These challenges can be grouped together under the following headings: nationalism and revenge; local governance and education; crime, capitalism and securitization; self-determination, future status and the dual function of trusteeship.

Nationalism and revenge

As argued above, international trusteeship arrangements typically come about under or immediately after circumstances that are likely to give them a highly difficult start, for instance civil war, crimes against humanity, outside intervention and territorial disputes. The ability to understand and deal with negative patterns of interaction, and the ability to initiate or take advantage of positive ones, is therefore essential to the chances of success. Ethnic cleansing, for instance, must to some extent be seen as a product of the attempt by ethnic groupings to stereotype and devalue groups they see as their enemies. Consequently, national and international efforts to bring about reconciliation can hardly be successful, if they do not attempt to reverse these xenophobic images and the habit of identity formation by means of exclusion. Such considerations are at the heart of the contributions by Lene Kühle and Carsten Bagge Laustsen (Chapter 2) and Arne Johan Vetlesen (Chapter 3) who discuss the consequences of nationalism, mythmaking and atrocities for the reconstruction of Kosovo.

Vetlesen starts out from the observation that the Serb attacks on the Kosovar Albanian population in 1998–9 constituted acts of genocide. Although the hostilities started as a targeting of the KLA (Kosovo Liberation Army) who had attacked and killed Serbian police officers, it culminated in what has become known as 'Operation Horseshoe'. Ninety per cent of the Kosovar Albanian population, that is more than one million, were forcefully deported or internally displaced, and an estimated 10,500 Kosovar Albanians were killed in the campaign.[37] The aim was to counter what was seen as an imminent danger to the Serb community in Kosovo presented by the rebellion as well as the long-term suppression of Serb culture, discrimination, and a steady Serb and Montenegrin emigration from the province for which the Albanian community was held responsible. Without excluding discrimination and fear as factors explaining Serb emigration (along with poverty), other sources have found that the growing tension between the two main segments of the population from the early 1980s and onwards had more to do with the recurrent obstruction and prevention of teaching in Albanian, the removal (1989) and revoking (1990) of Kosovo's autonomy and the ensuing Serb resort to a number of highly discriminatory initiatives.[38]

But why did these tensions escalate into war and atrocities? According to Vetlesen, the most important background factor was Serb nationalism and the mobilization of it as a legitimizing device for former President Slobodan Milošević's reign. Unfortunately, the nationalist rhetoric and sentiments did not only help Milošević to seize more power and to hold on to it. It also created an atmosphere of mutual suspicion between the republics, the provinces and the various populations of the former Yugoslavia, and it certainly made the package of war, atrocities and displacement of populations more likely to occur. According to Laustsen and Kühle, this nationalist factor and the use of it must be considered in close connection with the role played by mythology. In their investigation of the 'Kosovo myth', Kühle and Laustsen pay particular attention to the Serbian ideas of an elected people, a cultural and religious vanguard, and a historical role as victims. Special emphasis is thereby put on the twinning of nationalism and Christianity, which turned out to be a deadly cocktail capable of legitimizing war and atrocities in, successively, Croatia, Bosnia and Kosovo even at the end of twentieth century, and which continues to impede the process of reconstruction and reconciliation in the former Yugoslavia.

However, there are myths and memories among the Kosovar Albanian population as well and, sadly, also a recent record of recurrent revenge against the Serb population, which is now at great risk in the province. What the chapters by Vetlesen, Laustsen and Kühle show most of all is a vicious and tragic circle of myth, atrocities and revenge with the March riots of 2004 as a major example.[39] Their thoughts on co-existence and reconciliation are greatly needed.

Local governance and education

As stressed by Mark Baskin (Chapter 5), local governance is the tier of public authority that citizens first look to, to solve their immediate social problems. It is also the level of democracy in which the citizen has the most effective opportunity to actively and directly participate in decisions made for all of society. However, in ethnically divided societies like Kosovo, local elections are bound to confirm the ethnic distribution of the given community and to transform such patterns into legitimate structures of authority: in other words, majorities dominating minorities with a democratic mandate. On the other hand, local elections make it possible for minorities to have a voice in local government as well, if they can be persuaded to participate.

Local democratic governance is thus a dual sword. The same can be said of the powers of international administrators to overrule the local authorities. On the one hand, this is a means by which nationalistic and xenophobic measures taken by the majority can be annulled. On the other hand, it complicates and potentially destructs a key element of local democratic governance, namely the belief in the minds of politicians as well as their constituencies that those who get elected are fully responsible for decisions taken, and that they are therefore to be held fully accountable for their choices at the next election. In the absence of such clarity, it is too easy for nationalist forces to blame external administrators and internal opponents for all societal problems. However, as argued by Baskin, local democratic governance is not hopeless under trusteeship conditions, and his points regarding further decentralization and constitutional clarification deserve close attention.

Education is another key element in the reconstruction of Kosovo. As argued by Wayne Nelles (Chapter 6), the separation of ethnic groups by education must be reversed. The various ethnic and national communities have long remembered and taught different histories reflected in diverse educational systems. This is also a reality today since the Albanian dominated authorities in Pristina support one (Albanian) educational system while Belgrade sponsors another (Serb) system for northern Kosovo. Parallel educational systems reflect and confirm parallel societies. However, seen from the perspective of the Serb minority, whose survival in the province is now at stake, parallel systems are better than having an Albanian system only. To Nelles, educational reform is therefore a matter of minority protection in the short run, while in the longer run it is a precondition for the hopes of co-existence and integration.

Crime, capitalism and securitization

In a critical review of the attempt by the western-led international administrators to transform Kosovo's economy into a hard version of liberal capitalism, Michael

Pugh (Chapter 7) warns against ignoring the social functions of crime, especially forms of illegal activity that make it possible for ordinary people to sustain life in severe conditions stemming from the introduction of tough neo-liberal economic reform. The shadow economy is a life line for many people, so it would be dysfunctional to try to remove it. Removing shadow economies should be seen as an accompanying bonus of a successful restoration of the economy and of social security, not as a means to it. The dilemma is sharply presented in Pugh's analysis: on the one hand, the external agencies have attempted to impose a neo-liberal economic model rooted in the 1989 Washington consensus on developmentalism. On the other hand, the Kosovars have clung to clientism, shadow economic activities and resistance to centrally audited exchange. Neo-liberal economic ideology and reform must therefore be mixed with other economic philosophies and initiatives.

Behind this recommendation lies the fear that the revived practices of UN-sponsored trusteeship have been turned into a project of liberal trusteeship in Kosovo and beyond. As indicated above, Christopher Freeman (Chapter 10) discusses how this liberal model of international trusteeship has furthermore been securitized, possibly already from the beginning although the picture varies from case to case. The central question asked by Freeman with reference to the cases of Bosnia, Eastern Slavonia, East Timor, Kosovo, Afghanistan and Iraq is whether the liberal theory that domestic democracy leads to international (and arguably inter-ethnic) peace has been seized by the western world, so that the reconstruction of war-torn societies becomes an element in its national security strategies. Clearly, such a development is bound to have critical implications for questions of success, exit and legitimacy, not least when the context is the so-called 'war on terror', as in Afghanistan and Iraq.

Self-determination, future status and the dual function of trusteeship

Under the current international normative framework, trusteeships like the one in Kosovo may, as argued by Rasmus Abildgaard Kristensen in Chapter 8, at times find it difficult to reconcile its two main functions: to fill a governance vacuum and to solve a territorial dispute meaning in most cases a problem of secession, or a problem of competing claims for the same territory. However, to the majority of international society the solution to the latter problem must preferably not involve an outright or open violation of the fundamental principles of sovereignty, non-intervention and formal interstate equality. These conflicting concerns and principles of human government and state sovereignty are clearly evident in UN Security Council resolution 1244 of 10 June 1999 which turned Kosovo into a *de facto* international trusteeship designed for the dual purpose of governing the province and suppressing the territorial dispute, but without deciding the delicate question of future status and self-determination. The dilemma of sovereignty and national self-determination has been built into the trusteeship arrangement, but it has not been solved by it.

To Kristensen, therefore, the main problem in Kosovo is not that UNMIK and its partners have been guilty of bad management. Rather, the problem is to be found in the lack of consistency in the legal and normative framework of international society. The challenge, for Kristensen, is to point to ways in which renewed consistency can be added to this framework without giving up the revived trusteeship institution. The challenge for the international community, the administrators, and the opposed parties in Kosovo will be to work out a solution to the question of future status in the absence of such consistency. As argued by Knudsen in Chapter 9 (and as recognized, finally, by the great powers and the administrators), it is imperative that a final solution to the future status of Kosovo is found quickly in order to prevent renewed setbacks like the 2004 March Riots which were more than anything fuelled by Kosovar Albanian frustration and uncertainty. The case is made for independence, but with political conditions and legal qualifications designed for a preservation and protection of the Serb and other minorities in Kosovo, which also remains a legitimate concern for Serbia and Montenegro.

Such a solution can only work, if elements of the trusteeship arrangement continue: to begin with as a still required means of securing the transition to orderly, just and effective self-government; later as a means of institutionalized surveillance and guarantee.

Notes

1 Other contemporary examples of international peacebuilding operations resembling the protectorates of the League of Nations and the trusteeships of the United Nations in terms of outside assumption of administrative powers and sovereign authority include Bosnia, Eastern Slavonia and East Timor (see below).

2 See Boutros Boutros-Ghali, 'Report of the Secretary-General', 3 March 1993 (S/25354), and UN Security Council Resolution 814, 26 March 1993.

3 See for instance Jeffrey Clark, 'Debacle in Somalia: Failure of the Collective Response', in Lori Fisler Damrosch (ed.), *Enforcing Restraint: Collective Intervention in Internal Conflicts* (New York: Council on Foreign Relations Press, 1993), pp. 205–239.

4 For analyses of these cases as examples of a de facto revival of the nineteenth and twentieth century protectorate and trusteeship institutions see William Bain, *Between Anarchy and Society: Trusteeship and the Obligations of Power* (Oxford: Oxford University Press, 2003), pp. 140–154; Richard Caplan, *International Governance of War-Torn Territories: Rule and Reconstruction* (Oxford: Oxford University Press, 2005), esp. pp. 16–41; Jarat Chopra, 'The UN's Kingdom of East Timor', *Survival*, 42.3, Autumn 2000, pp. 27–39; International Crisis Group, 'The New Kosovo Protectorate', ICG Balkans Report No. 69, Sarajevo, 20 June 1999, Crisis Webnews (www.crisisweb.org), pp. 1–7; and Robert Jackson, *The Global Covenant: Human Conduct in a World of States* (Oxford: Oxford University Press, 2000), pp. 294–315. See also the 'Special Issue on the Politics of International Administration' (eds. Mats Berdal and Richard Caplan), *Global Governance*, 10.1, Jan–Mar. 2004.

5 Some scholars have considered an even broader list of cases. See Edward Mortimer, 'International Administration of War-Torn Societies', *Global Governance*, 10.1, Jan–Mar. 2004, pp. 7–14 (see pp. 8–10).

6 International Crisis Group (ICG), 'Kosovo: Let's Learn from Bosnia. Models and Methods of International Administration', ICG Balkans Report No. 66, 17 May 1999, pp. 1–24.

7 Jarat Chopra, *Peace-Maintenance: The Evolution of International Political Authority* (London: Routledge, 1999), p. 16. See also Jarat Chopra, Jim McCallum and Alexander

Their, 'Planning Considerations for International Involvement in Post-Taleban Afghanistan', paper, US Army Peacekeeping Institute, Pennsylvania, 14 November 2001.

8 Roland Paris, *At War's End: Building Peace after Civil Conflict* (Cambridge: Cambridge University Press, 2004), pp. 225–226; Caplan (n. 4 above), pp. 26, 256.

9 Tonny Brems Knudsen, 'Denmark and the War Against Iraq: Losing Sight of Internationalism?', *Danish Foreign Policy Yearbook 2004* (eds Per Carlsen and Hans Mouritzen) (Copenhagen: Danish Institute for International Studies, 2004), pp. 49–90.

10 See UN Security Council Resolution 1546, 8 June 2004, preamble and paragraph 2.

11 This is the position of Caplan (n. 4 above), pp. 3–4. Similarly, Roland Paris (n. 8 above) largely leaves out Afghanistan and Iraq from his study of ambitious peacebuilding with the argument that the challenges of peacebuilding after conquest are quite different.

12 See Sergio de Mello's address to the UN Security Council at its 4,791st meeting, 22 July 2003 (S/PV.4791), p. 8.

13 The governance of Iraq following the formal end of the war can be divided into the following phases: 1. Occupation not regulated by the UN Security Council until the adoption of resolution 1483 of 22 May 2003. 2. Occupation by the so-called Coalitional Provisional Authority recognized (but not authorized) in resolution 1483 which, however, provided for a UN-role and military contributions by non-occupying states (22 May 2003 – 16 October 2003). 3. Continued occupation alongside UN assistance, but now with an explicit mandate for the presence of the multinational forces as stipulated in resolution 1511 of 16 October 2003 (16 October 2003 – 30 June 2004). 4. Formal end of occupation and resumption of full Iraqi sovereignty by the Interim Government, but with the continued presence of the multinational force and the UN as stipulated by UN Security Council Resolution 1546 of 8 June 2004 (30 June 2004 – December 2005). 5. Full independence following the formation of a constitutionally elected government foreseen for December 2005. Iraq has thus been a military trusteeship in phases 1–3 and it arguably remains so de facto in phase 4 (the time of writing) and beyond.

14 For attempts to make such a clear-cut distinction see Caplan (n. 4 above), pp. 3–4 and Paris (n. 8 above), pp. 4–5, 212.

15 On the distinction between the neo-internationalist agenda of the 1990s and the anti-terror agenda following 9/11, see Knudsen 2004 (n. 9 above).

16 White House, 'The National Security Strategy of the United States of America', Washington, September 2002. For a discussion, see Knudsen 2004 (n. 9 above), pp. 69–73, 80–85.

17 See UN Security Council Resolution 1244 (esp. paragraph 10) of 10 June 1999 which provided for the establishment of 'The United Nations Interim Administration Mission in Kosovo' (UNMIK).

18 See for instance Caplan (n. 4 above), pp. 16–17, where the term 'international administration' is explicitly preferred over 'trusteeship' and 'protectorate'. 'International administration' is also preferred by Berdal and Caplan (n. 4 above).

19 Boutros Boutros-Ghali, *An Agenda for Peace* (2.ed) (New York: The United Nations, 1995), p. 61. In his recent study, Roland Paris (n. 8 above) prefers the term peacebuilding as well.

20 On this development, see Michael Pugh (ed.), *The UN, Peace and Force* (London: Frank Cass, 1997).

21 Arguably the administration of East Timor from 1999 to 2002 is an even clearer example of the temporary assumption by the UN of full sovereign authority (and legal personality) over a territory and its population. See Chopra (n. 4 above).

22 On the institutional aspects of sovereignty see Martin Wight, *Systems of States* (Leicester: Leicester University Press, 1977), pp. 129–136 and Alan James, *Sovereign Statehood: The Basis of International Society* (London: Allen and Unwin, 1986).

23 James N. Murray Jr., *The United Nations Trusteeship System* (Urbana: The University of Illinois Press, 1957), pp. 7–19.

24 Ibid., pp. 43–45. See also Søbjerg's chapter in this volume.

25 Mortimer (n. 5 above), pp. 10, 12–14; Chopra (n. 4 above).

26 Actually, the UN (and before it the League of Nations) has been directly in charge of the administration of territories and peoples before the post-Cold War revival of this phenomenon. See Ralph Wilde, 'From Danzig to East Timor and Beyond: The Role of International Territorial Administration', *American Journal of International Law*, 92 (July 2001), pp. 583–606.

27 For an analysis of the trusteeship system see Murray (n. 23 above).

28 See chapter 4 by Lene Mosegaard Søbjerg.

29 Jackson (n. 4 above), p. 307. See also Robert Jackson, 'International Engagement in War-Torn Countries', *Global Governance*, 10, 1 (Jan–Mar 2004), pp. 21–36. The term trusteeship is also preferred by Bain (n. 4 above, p. 154), while International Crisis Group compares Bosnia, Eastern Slavonia, East Timor and Kosovo to the international protectorates in the pre-war and League of Nations periods.

30 Hedley Bull, *The Anarchical Society* (London: Macmillan, 1977), p. 74 and further Barry Buzan (2004), *From International to World Society? English School Theory and the Social Structure of Globalisation* (Cambridge: Cambridge University Press, 2004); Tonny Brems Knudsen, *Humanitarian Intervention* (London: Routledge, forthcoming 2006).

31 For the works by Jackson and Bain, see notes 4 and 29 above.

32 The distinction between the pluralist (focussing on international order, interstate diversity and the freedom of states) and the solidarist (focussing on collective action, international governance and human rights) conception of international society goes back to Hedley Bull, 'The Grotian Conception of International Society', in Herbert Butterfield and Martin Wight (eds), *Diplomatic Investigations* (London: Allen and Unwin, 1966), pp. 51–73. See also the chapters by Søbjerg, Kristensen and Knudsen.

33 On these proposals and decisions regarding the closure of the Trusteeship Council and the creation of new peacebuilding organs, see Kofi Annan, *In Larger Freedom: Towards Development, Security and Human Rights for All*, Report of the Secretary-General, A/59/2005 (New York: The UN General Assembly, 21 March 2005), pp. 46–7, 52, 58–9 (and addendum 2 of 23 May 2005 on the Peacebuilding Commission), as well as the '2005 World Summit Outcome' document (New York: The UN General Assembly, A/60/L.1, 20 September 2005), articles 97–105 and 176.

34 '2005 World Summit Outcome' document (see n. 33 above), articles 97 and 98.

35 Ibid., articles 100–101.

36 See Annan (n. 33 above), addendum 2, pp. 3–4. As for the academic critique of contemporary trusteeships, the establishment of the Peacebuilding Commission might lead to a stronger involvement of the UN Security Council regarding the supervision and direction of UN administrators as called for by Mortimer (n. 5 above, pp. 13–14). The Peacebuilding Commission can also be seen as a strong institutional answer to Chopra's (n. 4 above, pp. 35–36) call for a 'contact-group' concept coupled with the involvement of all relevant governmental and non-governmental actors holding the necessary expertise and capacity.

37 The figures are those estimated by the Independent International Commission on Kosovo, *The Kosovo Report* (Oxford: Oxford University Press, 2000), Annex 1. The Kosovo Report does not claim with full certainty that there was a plan called 'Operation Horseshoe', but it refers to a systematic and planned mass expulsion of Kosovo-Albanian civilians accompanied by the killing of more than 10,000 people.

38 Independent International Commission on Kosovo, *The Kosovo Report* (Oxford: Oxford University Press, 2000), pp. 33 ff.

39 On the riots and their consequences see also Human Rights Watch, *Failure to Protect: Anti-Minority Violence in Kosovo, March 2004*, 16, 6 (D) July 2004.

2 The Kosovo myth

Nationalism and revenge

Lene Kühle and Carsten Bagge Laustsen

> When we first heard people talk of political myths, they seemed to us so raw, so comical, so crazy and senseless that we found it hard to take them seriously. Now we know that this was a grave mistake. We must not make it a second time. For this reason it is necessary to undertake painstaking research into the origin, structure and techniques of political myths.[1]

Some aspects of the 1998–99 conflict over Kosovo call for further discussion. Why was it so important for Serbians to hold on to what they considered part of their territory? There appeared to be something fundamentally irrational about the way the Serb government hung on to Kosovo, a tiny and relatively poor area, primarily occupied by Albanians, even under the threat of a disastrous confrontation with a powerful international military force. This chapter will attempt to cast light on the conflicts over Kosovo with reference to the existence of a Serbian national myth, which helped to make an alleged Albanian demographic takeover of Kosovo problematic in the first place and then helped to legitimize armed conflict and even acts of genocide.

The argument is not that the existence of a national myth, focused on the fourteenth century Battle of Kosovo, *caused* the wars in Slovenia, Croatia, Bosnia and finally in Kosovo, but rather that it was most *useful* in legitimizing the rule of Slobodan Milošević and the brutal conduct of regular and paramilitary forces loyal to the 'Serbian cause'. Milošević's speech on the 600th anniversary of the battle of Kosovo Polje, on 28 June 1989, played an important part in paving the way for the wars against the now former Yugoslavian republics. In front of an audience of at least half a million Serbs, Milošević stressed that Serbia was under pressure and that war might be ahead. Milošević himself had legitimized his reign in accordance with the nationalist and mythic credo before, but the speech at Kosovo Polje was its most explosive manifestation. Then, when the war of words paved the way for a war of bodies, myth became a reality which was lived and suffered. It is to some extent with us even today, making reconciliation between the 'former' enemies slow and difficult.

The myth of the battle of Kosovo is a story of a military defeat and moral victory. An earthly kingdom was lost to the Ottomans, the Turks, and a heavenly kingdom was gained and came to live on in the mind and soul of the Serbian people, now suffering the hardship of an occupation. According to the myth, the Serb commander in chief, Prince Lazar, was offered a choice by God between the two kingdoms, and, in choosing the heavenly kingdom, the Serbs became a chosen people. Throughout the centuries, the event gained importance and finally it came to be seen as the birth of (modern) Serbia. Since this event unfolded on Kosovo Polje, this hill came to be seen as the cradle of Serbia, one of the Serb nation's most 'holy' places.

The Kosovo myth was used by the Milošević government and the Orthodox Church to create a narrative of an existential and morally superior 'Serbdom' which was seriously threatened by barbaric forces. The distance between accusations and action shortened as myth and security politics intertwined. Violent actions were legitimized as an attempt to counter the enemy's wicked plans. Pre-emption was necessary considering the deeds of past generations and the plan of their present followers. The *actual* deeds and beliefs of the opponent became irrelevant as 'past became present'.

However, the causes of the Kosovo war are complex and cannot be reduced solely to political entrepreneurs' usage of nationalist myths. Even though Kosovo is the poorest area of Yugoslavia, there are still some important interests in the northern part, which Belgrade might have been ready to fight for. A Serb minority remains to be protected and there are also important churches and monasteries (including the one hosting Lazar's saintly remains). Moreover, there is the always troubling question of who is next – where does secession end? Slovenia, Croatia, Bosnia, Kosovo ... ? All these factors pushed in the same direction – towards war. However, there were also factors and voices pulling the other way: an anti-nationalist opposition, factions within the church and numerous people of reason. In speaking about a *Serb* myth, about the *Serbs*, about the *Serb* government, we are not paying tribute to these dissident groups. In explaining an important aspect of the Kosovo war, the mythic aspect, this might be justified, but in looking for social forces to vanguard the process of reconciliation, this methodological bias is of course problematic. Thus, the perspective necessarily shifts towards the end of the chapter when we discuss how myth and the desires it mobilizes are best dealt with.

Methodically speaking, the argument is a constructivist one: ideas and narrative content are analysed as political constructions. Myths are in this view both structuring and structured: they condition beliefs and behaviour but never in an essentialist and mono-causal way. Myth is shaped and transformed through practice. This also means that today the task is to rework the mythical space to make it allow for reconciliation or at least for a less violent communal life. However, an inquiry into the content and function of myth and its actual use in the Yugoslavian war(s) is needed before articulating such hopes. Thus, this chapter opens with an investigation of the narrative content of the Kosovo myth and the way it came to be used by the dominant political players in Serbia. The analysis is then paralleled by a short enquiry into the Albanian 'counter-myth' – a story which is structurally similar to the Serb version, that is to say, the only difference is that the Albanians are constructed as the true inheritor of the Kosovo Plain.

The power of myth

While some scholars stress the connection between religion and myth – for instance, evidenced by William Paden's definition of myth as 'the world-building, world-shaping language of religion'[2] – others do not make this connection. The well-known religious historian, Russell McCutcheon, thus emphasizes that 'myths' can be related to all situations where people, 'construct, authorize and contest their social identities' and therefore cannot be of significance only for the historian of religion.[3] Rather than being related by necessity to gods and non-empirical powers, McCutcheon suggests that myths should be regarded as 'the vehicle whereby any of a variety of possible social charters is rendered exemplary, authoritative, singular, unique, as something that cannot be imagined differently.'[4]

Myths can be understood as a second order semiological system that 'freezes' and naturalizes narrative content.[5] Myth delimits the free play of signifiers and makes acts and beliefs seem natural, right, just, inevitable and innocent. Through myth the world becomes less chaotic and dangerous. It turns history into nature.[6]

> In passing from history to nature, myth acts economically: it abolishes the complexity of human acts, it gives them the simplicity of essences, it does away with all dialectics, with any going back beyond what is immediately visible, it organizes a world which is without contradictions because it is without depth, a world wide open and wallowing in the evident, it establishes a blissful clarity: things appear to mean something by themselves.[7]

Myths differ from other discourses in explicitly thematizing a 'founding act' (in other words, the narrative of an origin is the mythical part of a discourse).[8] The distinction between a diffuse pre-historical and historical time (the history of Serbia) is marked by a moment of decision, a challenged or similar founding act (in Serb mythology the choice between the two kingdoms); this moment then explains why there is something (Serbdom) instead of nothing. In choosing oneself, in listening to a divine call, and so on, one truly achieves one's self. The French philosophers Jean-Luc Nancy and Philippe Lacoue-Labarthe have coined the term 'immanentism' to describe this idea of auto-affection.[9] A counter-position of 'speech' and 'writing' could be used in illuminating the term. For instance, Barthes describes myth as a form of depoliticized *speech*[10] and Jean-Luc Nancy as a 'unique' *speech*.[11] Writing is what allows for interpretation, play and ambiguity, while speech is considered to be given and received without deferral. Hence the importance of wonders, revelations, and the inner voices of mythical figures through which God makes himself known without ambiguity.[12] Whatever is communicated is communicated without loss. Thus, myth is not just a culture: 'it is transcendence (of gods, of man, of speech, of the cosmos, and so on) presented immediately, immediately immanent to the very thing it transcends and that it illuminates or consigns to its destiny.'[13]

Myth is the pact of its own recognition and thus tautological: it communicates nothing except itself. It produces the consciousness in which it is located.[14] Community and myth engender one another, which is why the actual content of the myth is often less important.[15] To listen to and to tell a myth is a form of communion.[16] The narrative is also that of commonness and sharing – even with the dead and those who are not yet born. Myth explains why we are here, and more fundamentally, why we are in fact a 'we'. The myths, are not really about a distant past, about forefathers and their heroic deeds, but stories about us, about our identity and being, which is also the reason why we are so eager to tell and live them.

Another important aspect is the geopolitics of myth. Myths are associated with spaces of gathering, and this is evidently so in Serb mythology. Space is also crucial in another sense. Pilgrimage to mythic sites aim to establish the form of 'full' or 'unique' speech mentioned earlier. It is as if these places reverb with power. There is also a time for myth just as there is a space. To increase its toxicality, the mythical experience is enabled only for certain days or months. These days or months are then linked through repetition, turning time into an eternal present. To participate in myth is thus basically to repeat an original choice of an essence, perhaps even a divine essence as it is in the case in the choice of a heavenly Serbia.

> Thanks to the procedures of emplotment, it is possible to establish apparently logical connections between what are otherwise unconnected, contradictory and ambivalent political events, ideas and figures. Transformed into sequences of narrative time, national history can develop without deviation or discontinuity. Thanks also to specific steps in the development of narrative time, it is possible to set up a direct, living connection with the past. The use of the historic present gives the impression that past events are unfolding before our eyes. Similarly, through the use of the traditional epic style ... to tell the story of contemporary events, those events acquire the patina of a distant and glorious past. This in turn suggests that it is in the past that we should seek the key to their only correct interpretation.[17]

'Myth' is, as most other important terms, of Greek origin. 'Mythos' was seen by Plato as a threat to 'logos', which was why he disbanded the poets from the polis. Their myths were lies about the divine he claimed.[18] Since then, myth has been seen as the hyperbolic; as unreason per se, and not just unreason but also that which fuels and lives by desire – that is in fact how they are still understood. Myth works in an affective mode. Its power leads people astray – away from the path of reason. There exists a will and a desire for myth, perhaps even a demand for it, which is why it is such a great mobilizing force. However, this still allows for a considerable variation in the narrative content of the myths and in the ways they can be used politically. Myths and the energies they activate can be used both as a means of oppression and a weapon against it. Before focusing on the actual use of the Kosovo myth, on the *politics* of this specific myth, we should first describe its narrative content.

Battle of Kosovo Polje

The 1389 battle of Kosovo Polje – or the Field of Blackbirds – is central to Serbian national self-image. According to the myth, in the fourteenth century

Serbia was the centre of a rich and large empire, the ambitions of which were challenged by the Ottoman Empire. When the Ottoman Sultan Murad tried to force the Serbian Prince Lazar to submit to his powers, this resulted in war. The highpoint of this conflict, the Battle of Kosovo Polje, ended in Serbian defeat and the death of Prince Lazar, beheaded by the Turks. Yet the Turk victory had its price as the Sultan Murad also died, ingeniously killed by the Serb Miloš Obilić, who had obtained an audience with the sultan and attacked him with a knife, cleverly hidden in his clothes. This assassination was Obilić's answer to the accusation of disloyalty towards Lazar which was raised against him the night before the battle. The allegation against Obilić was raised by Lazar at the common dinner table, but the source of the lie was Lazar's jealous son-in-law, Vuk Branković. It was he who betrayed Lazar in withdrawing his troops after agreement with the Turks.

But Branković was in some sense just part of a greater divine plan. A falcon representing Saint Elijah and a swallow representing Virgin Mary thus come to Lazar at the battlefield and offer him a choice. He can choose the Kingdom of Earth and attack the Ottomans immediately and he will win; or he can chose the Kingdom of Heaven and build a church in Kosovo and call his men to communion, in which case he loses the Kingdom of Earth, but wins an eternal kingdom.[19] Evidently, as Prince Lazar was defeated, he had chosen the Kingdom of Heaven instead of the Kingdom of Earth, which the presence of the Serbian-Orthodox monastery of Gračanica, outside Priština is said to confirm.[20] Through the eyes of the Serbian tradition, the death of Lazar and the defeat at Kosovo Polje marked the end of a glorious empire and the beginning of centuries of slavery under Ottoman rule.[21] Simultaneously, the main characters of the story: Prince Lazar, Branković, Obilić, the Kosovo maiden, who tends the wounded warriors and the mother of the Jugovići, who lost nine sons in the battle, become 'archetypes of the Serbian virtue and villainy.'[22]

The story of Lazar's defeat is clearly modelled over the well-known Christian symbols. Lazar is Jesus who is given a choice between heavenly and earthly kingdoms, and Branković is Judas who betrays him in a scene resembling the Last Supper. Kosovo Polje is the Serbian Golgotha, where Lazar is killed and the Kosovo maiden and the mother of the Jugovići play the part of Mary Magdalene and the Virgin Mary mourning the dead. The framework of the Serbian national self-understanding is thus well-known Christian stories, though they tend to have a specific twist. The story of the Battle of Kosovo has, strikingly, been called a 'nationalized Christiad,' where Christianity and nationalism have become one.[23]

Historically, it is impossible to verify the scenario presented above. It has been argued that there is no evidence that Branković betrayed Lazar or even that Obilić is a historical figure,[24] but more crucially, it is possible the Serbs were not even defeated. In fact, a majority of the preserved sources assign this loss to the Ottomans.[25] Other military events, in particular the Serbian defeat in the Battle of Marcia in 1371 were much more important for the fate of the Serbian empire.[26] The significance of the Battle of Kosovo Polje lies therefore not in the fourteenth century but in the way it has shaped later Serbian history.

In the centuries after the Battle, Lazar was proclaimed a martyr by the Orthodox Church,[27] but, as a minority faith within the *millet* system of the

Ottoman Empire, the Church could not overtly rejoice in the memory of the past glory. By the seventeenth century only the Monastery of Ravenica, where Lazar was buried, still celebrated a cult for Lazar.[28] Stories of the breakdown of a great empire lived on in folk tales and songs, but it was only with the advent of modern nationalism that it condensed into a coherent and comprehensive story. It is thus the nationalistic Serbian literature and art of the nineteenth century that gives the Battle of Kosovo its present importance. In the mid-nineteenth century, Vuk Karadižić (1787–1864), a collector of folk tales and songs, was crucial in his efforts to compile folk tales into coherent stories[29] and in pointing to the central position of the story of Lazar and the battle of Kosovo.

It is in the literature and art of the second half of the nineteenth century that the transformation of Lazar into an 'explicit Christ figure' is completed.[30] In a painting by Adam Stefanović from the 1870s, Lazar and his men are depicted resembling Christ and his disciples at the Last Supper, and various pictures show the suffering Lazar being nurtured by the 'Maiden of Kosovo' in a situation strikingly similar to the way Michelangelo placed the dead Christ in the arms of the Virgin Mary in his famous marble sculpture *Pieta* (1499). With the famous *Mountain Wreath* of Petar Petrović Njegoš (1813–51), 'a masterpiece in Serbian and Montenegrin literature' as well as 'an emblem' of Serbian identity,[31] the final step in the process from an incoherent and unfocused folk tale to a comprehensive, consistent national myth was taken. From a myth-theoretical standpoint the importance of enscribing the myths is crucial. When myths are written down their status changes. The written form means that the content of the myth becomes stabilized, enhancing its power.[32]

Njegoš clearly represents Miloš Obilić, Vuk Branković and Prince Lazar as universal archetypes that every Serb has to make a choice between: should one give in to the Turks like Vuk Branković or should one fight them like Miloš Obilić.[33] Through this actualisation of the Kosovo myth the *Mountain Wreath* in fact provides the first major example of 'Kosovo in the Active Mood', in other words a situation where the myth triggers revolutionary acts.[34] In the nineteenth century, the Kosovo myth was thus instrumental in the Serbian uprisings which ended with the attainment of Serbian sovereignty in 1878. But the Serbian independence did not mean the abolishment of the myth, but rather its institutionalisation.

The nineteenth century artistic reconstruction of the Kosovo legend as a nationalist founding myth was accompanied by the introduction of the national celebration of rituals of remembrance, most importantly 'Vidovdan' – St. Vitus' Day or Vid's Day on 28 June – the same date as the battle of Kosovo. According to some sources the day refers to St. Vitus, a southern Italian martyr who had been celebrated by the Serbian Orthodox Church for centuries,[35] while others claim that the day refers to the pagan sun god Vid.[36] Regardless of the background of Vidovdan it was only with the 'national renaissance' of the late nineteenth to the early twentieth century that it came to be a day of national remembrance dedicated to glorious events in national history.[37]

From the first public political celebration of Vidovdan in 1851, the celebration of the defeat of Lazar rapidly became an important symbol in the struggle for

Serbian independence from Ottoman rule.[38] Coincidentally, or perhaps intentionally, the importance of Vidovdan has grown since to become the most important day in Serbian history. It was on this day in 1876 that the war of independence against the Ottomans was declared and on this day in 1881 that a Secret Convention with Austria-Hungary was signed. Furthermore, on Vidovdan 1914 a Serbian nationalist killed the heir to the Austro–Hungarian throne, Archduke Franz Ferdinand thereby initiating the First World War and, importantly, Vidovdan was also chosen to sign the Versailles Peace Treaty in 1919, which was to end the War.[39] Moreover, it was on Vidovdan that the 1921 Yugoslav Constitution was proclaimed, and the 1948 resolution of the Cominform was declared. However, it was only with the reign of Milošević that Vidovdan became the occasion for yearly celebrations of national identity coupled with 'an appeal to Serbian leaders never again to permit the defeat of Serbian arms'.[40]

The Kosovo question as seen from Serbia in the 1980s

The celebration of Vidovdan in 1989 was the first public celebration since the communist era.[41] 1989 was something special as the Serbs celebrated the 600th anniversary of the Battle of Kosovo. The scene was certainly set for something extraordinary. Two years previously, the relics of Prince Lazar had been carried in a religious procession followed by thousands of spectators through what was considered to be sacred and eternal Serbian territory. Until 1401 these remains had rested in Priština, from where they were removed to the convent Ravenica. In 1690 the relics were moved to Szentendre (Sent Andreja) close to Buda (Budapest), in 1697 to a monastery in Srem, Sremska Ravanica, and then in 1942 to the Orthodox Cathedral of Belgrade.[42] The 600th anniversary of the Battle of Kosovo meant the return of the relics to Kosovo Polje and the monastery Gračanica which was said to be built by Lazar himself. The anniversary was the culmination of a period of growing interest in national history and a revival of national symbols, like the four Cyrillic c's (equivalent to s) *samo sloga Srbina spagava*: 'solely solidarity saves the Serbs', in combination with the Kosovo maiden and the double-headed eagle.[43] Simultaneously there was a renewed interest in Njegoš as the national poet[44] and an 'outburst' of publications emphasizing the suffering of the Serbs.

Milošević's presence at the place where Lazar had been defeated 600 years previously seemed to be a spectacular attempt to unite the Serbian people in a common cause. By posing as the heir of Prince Lazar, Milošević urged the Serbian people to not behave like Vuk Branković and give in to their enemies, but instead to choose the role of Miloš Obilić and be loyal to their country and their leader.[45] Milošević wanted to draw a parallel between the fragmentation of the Serbian forces in 1389 and the present state of affairs. The speech is thus a warning to those who want to tear the republic apart. It is time to break the 'evil fate' of the Serbian people, Milošević said.[46]

The 'vassal mentality' among former leaders had led Serbia astray, a situation which had lasted for decades, but was now to end.[47] Serbia was facing a new battle and this time they were going to be victorious: 'Six centuries later, now, we are again being engaged in battles and are facing war. They are not armed battles, although such things cannot be excluded'.[48] This sentence was of great significance. It addressed two audiences: the Serbs, who should prepare themselves for war, for making sacrifices, and the other republics, who should be aware that succession would imply war with a Serbia unflinching in its commitment to territorial sovereignty.

There is however also a more specific context for Milošević's speech. During the 1980s, numerous rumours of Muslim attacks on Serbs in Kosovo were fabricated and several of these concerned acts of rape. The first case to have political consequences was the reported rape of the 56-year-old peasant Djordje Martinović on 1 May 1985. Martinović claimed that Albanian men had sexually abused him with a bottle. However, the validity of the story remains disputed.[49] Some claimed that he was raped, while others said that it was an unfortunate sexual experiment gone wrong. Martinović added to the confusion when he confessed to inflicting his own wounds, but later claimed that the confession was coerced.[50]

The questionable validity of the story was no hindrance to its use for propaganda. In fact, its disputed character served to keep the story alive for years. Actual responsibility for the deeds became irrelevant as the name Djordje Martinović came to stand as a symbol for the Serb suffering in Kosovo.[51] A petition signed by Serbian intellectuals thus read: 'the case of Djordje Martinović has become that of the entire Serb nation in Kosovo'.[52] As Martinović was raped, so was the Serbian nation. In *Politika*, a Belgrade daily which functioned as a loyal organ to the government during the wars, it was claimed that Albanian men had tried to buy Martinović's land but that he refused and was punished for his 'stubbornness'. The underlying message was clear: the Martinović case was part of a 'Turkish' conspiracy to force Serbs out of Kosovo.

In 1985, a petition was handed over to the Serbian government begging it to stop the Serbian exodus in Kosovo and the *Memorandum* appeared the following year. These petitions offered arguments for stripping Kosovo of its autonomous status and retrieving a 'Greater Serbia'.[53] The Kosovo question was Milošević's 'claim to fame'. On a visit to Kosovo on the 24 April, he made an impromptu speech in front of angry Kosovo Serbs complaining about harassment from Albanian dominated authorities. This speech, of which the most well-known sentence, 'nobody should dare to beat you', rocketed his political career.[54] Here is a longer extract from the speech:

> First I want to tell you, comrades, that you should stay here. This is your country; these are your houses, your fields and gardens, your memories. You are not going to abandon your lands because life is hard, because you are oppressed by injustice and humiliation. It has never been a characteristic of the Serbian and Montenegrin people to retreat in the face of obstacles, to demobilize when they should fight, to become demoralized when things are difficult. You should stay here, both for your ancestors and your descendants. Otherwise you would shame your ancestors and disappoint your descendants. But I do not suggest you stay here suffering and enduring a situation with

which you are not satisfied. On the contrary! It should be changed, together with all progressive people here, in Serbia and in Yugoslavia ... Yugoslavia does not exist without Kosovo! Yugoslavia would disintegrate without Kosovo! Yugoslavia and Serbia are not going to give up Kosovo.[55]

In January 1986, the infamous *Memorandum* appeared, signed by some 200 intellectuals from Belgrade and it had the national assemblies of Serbia and Yugoslavia as its addressee. It was not officially released but gained importance through successive leaks to the press. *The Memorandum* speaks of the 'unbearable condition of the Serb nation in Kosovo' and claims a right to resist the ethnic purge of Serbs in Kosovo, an 'expulsion' which was claimed to have been going on for three centuries: 'The new Deacon Avakum [a victim of the Ottoman era] is called Djordje Martinović'. He symbolizes 'the predicament of all Serbs in Kosovo'.[56]

The Martinović case was seen in the *Memorandum* as 'remiscent of the darkest days of the Turkish practice of impalement'.[57] Impalement was a technique used for killing Serbs during Turkish oppression. A stake was inserted running from rectum to neck avoiding contact with vital organs. This was a particulary barbaric form of 'crucifixion': the victim suffered a slow and most painful death.[58] 'Impalement by a beer bottle' thus became 'a metaphor for five centuries of real, but also mythical Turkish acts of impalement'.[59] The name of Martinović was continuously invoked reminding the public of the barbaric nature of the Albanian oppressors occupying Kosovo.

The rape of Djordje Martinović is one of the many stories from the 1980s shaped by the Kosovo myth. The recurring theme is that Kosovo is an ancient Serbian land marked by the heroic suffering of its heirs. For instance, the President of the Serbian Union of Authors, Matija Bekovic, claimed that Kosovo was the equator on the Serbian planet and on another occasion, also in 1989, that 'Kosovo is Serbia ... there is so much Serbian blood and so many Serbian shrines there that it will still be Serbian land even if not a single Serb remain there'.[60] Graves are thus the natural frontier of Serbia.[61] Not just Lazar but several bodies of Serbian victims of the Second World War were exhumed and reburied. Counting and memorizing the dead became 'a national hobby'.[62]

Likewise, the Kosovo Albanians are considered to be the heirs of former enemies of Serbia which explains their barbarism and excesses. They are jihad fighters, mujahidin, janissaries, brothers in fez, and so on.[63] An illustrative quote from the *Memorandum*: 'Old women and nuns are raped, frail children beaten up, stables built with gravestones, churches and historic holy places desecrated and shamed, economic sabotage tolerated, [and] people forced to sell their property for nothing'.[64] The Kosovo-Albanian desire for independence was seen as a part of a strategy aimed at recreating an Ottoman empire which in turn explains the barbaric violence involved. When the war came, Serbian forces noticeably targeted Islamic religious institutions. A total of 218 mosques were destroyed, the homes of 302 *imams* devastated and 16 of these killed.[65]

A Serbian Jerusalem?

The question remains whether the content of the Serbian national myth of Kosovo and thereby of the conflict can be regarded as religious. For some observers, the conflicts in the Balkans were fundamentally religious. Most well-known is probably Samuel Huntington's explanation of the Balkan conflict as an expression of a clash of civilisations.[66] Another – but in some sense nevertheless similar – explanation is provided by Anzulovic who understands the brutality of the Serbian warfare to be a consequence of a non-Christian heritage. The presence of ideas of revenge, slaughter and offering of sacrifice signify the 'triumph of the Dinaric pan-heroic ethos and a marriage of this ethos to imperial ambitions'[67] and reflect the influence of 'untamed mythical impulses'.[68]

Both these explanations do, however, run into problems. The attempt to interpret the Serb aggression as religiously motivated does not take account of the fact that the different religions have co-existed in relative harmony in the Balkans for centuries and that multi-religiosity does not always mean clash of religions and certainly does not with any necessity lead to genocide. Furthermore, surveys from the 1980s reveal that the Serbs were in fact the least religious of the Yugoslavs and that the popular interest in religion remained relatively low during the conflict.[69]

However, totally downplaying the strictly Christian elements of the conflict would also seem to be a mistake. Serbian monks and priests were among the first to launch the idea of an alleged campaign of jihad by Albanian fundamentalists to clear Kosovo of Serbian Orthodox Christianity.[70] Moreover, 'political capital' of the Orthodox Church inherited in the 'control of relics'[71] was instrumental in setting the stage for Milošević's reclaim of the Serbian Kosovo-heritage on the 600th anniversary of Lazar's death at the hands of the Turks. The Serbian understanding of the conflict was also in many ways coated in a religious language: the Serbian right to Kosovo was God-given.

A way to balance the two positions is to view Serbian interest as motivated by the national 'civil religion'. Civil religion, a term originally used by Rousseau to designate a 'minimal' religion consisting of the existence of God, the life to come, the reward of virtue and the punishment of vice, and the exclusion of religious intolerance, was first used as a sociological term by the American sociologist Robert Bellah.[72] In 1966, Bellah used the term to designate the existence of a religious dimension to political life, evidenced in particular by references to God in presidential speeches. According to Bellah, civil religion is thus present in many different societal contexts but shows itself most clearly in the words and sayings of the people in the highest offices, who are obliged to try to articulate this religious dimension on behalf of the subjects they represent. An alternative and more direct definition has been forwarded by Hammond, who defines civil religion as 'any set of beliefs and rituals, related to the past, present, and/or future of a people ("nation") which are understood in some transcendental fashion'.[73] Civil religions thus consist of rituals performed on specific days of national remembrance and on myths explaining the specific historical role of the nation.

It seems that the vocabulary of civil religion is indeed useful in relation to an understanding of the importance of Kosovo in Serbian national self-understanding, and the way that this imagery may have triggered acts of genocide. Serbian national self-understanding clearly takes the form of a set of rituals and myths of which the most important are Vidovdan and the story of Prince Lazar's defeat at Kosovo Polje. The idea of Lazar's death as inaugurating the era of 'heavenly Serbia', through a deal with God, the 'Kosovo covenant'[74] is central in this. These elements form the national self-understanding according to which Serbia is a nation of a suffering, but also a chosen people, who will eventually be rewarded for that suffering.

It is central to emphasize that civil religion as a 'cultural resource' is available 'for selective use rather than a fixed institutional entity'.[75] That means that civil religions put forward symbols which can be used for political purposes, but never presents them in a determined pattern. It is thus telling that in the sixteenth and seventeenth century, which were characterized by peaceful Turkish rule, Prince Marko Kraljević, who served the Turks, was more popular among Serbs than Lazar or Miloš Obilić who fought them.[76] Because Marko struggled both for and against the Ottomans he was a much better role model for mediation between Orthodox Christianity and the Ottoman Empire than the uncompromised martyred figures.[77]

It is also relevant here to compare the way Lazar's widow dealt with the death of her husband. She wanted her son, Stefan Lazarvic as the ruler of a greater Serbia, and thus worked persistently to mythologize Lazar. Lazar's status as a saint could be used in authorizing Stefan's reign. Likewise Milošević could claim to be a descendent, to have a holy root and thus exploit the religious connection. The relationship between state and the church have been exceptionally close, which is why one justified speaking of a 'Saint-Savaism'. Saint Sava, the founder of the Orthodox Church, was the youngest son of the founder of the ruling Nemanja dynasty and a brother to the first Serbian king. Of the 59 saints celebrated by the Serbian Orthodox Church 26 were rulers or members of ruling families.[78]

'The fusion of the ecclesiastic and political spheres corrupts both', Anzulovic concludes his short analysis of Saint Savaism – and certainly the cocktail is a potentially dangerous one. The Church may stop being a corrective to the government which imposes moral restraints on it and might instead confer sacral aura on those in power.[79] Though Milošević and his allies can be accused of manipulating 'Kosovo symbols',[80] civil religious symbols in some sense always call for manipulation. Though it would certainly be a mistake to draw a straight line of causation from the Serbian nationalist literature to genocide,[81] any attempt to understand the conflicts will need to include an understanding of the semantic universe in which these take place. Attempts to reconcile the conflicting parties will also need to take this point of departure and will probably also need some to take up manipulating civil religious symbols.

Albanian national myths

Bellah confined his original analysis to American civil religion, but, in a preface to a reprint of the article, states that he is 'convinced that every nation and every people come to some form of religious self-understanding whether the critics like it or not'.[82] Though this statement is contested[83] it may be relevant to ask whether Albanian national self-understanding may not also in some sense be understood in terms of the existence a national myth. However, the existence of a Kosovo-Albanian national myth has only rarely occupied scholars.

Unlike the Serbian claim that the Muslim Albanian presence in Kosovo is the result of intermarriage with the conquering Turks, Albanians themselves claim to be direct descendants of the Illyrians, who are known from Greek and Roman sources. Consequently, Albanians believe that they are the ones who have the longer history in Kosovo, the Serbs only having invaded the country in the sixth century. Yet the Albanian claim for historical support for their version is as weak as the corresponding Serb one.[84]

It could be interesting to note that at the turn of the nineteenth century there were in fact attempts to construct an Albanian national identity on the basis of a joint Muslim religious identity. The Albanian national poet Naim Frashëri thus tried to introduce the Shiite symbols of Kerbala, the traumatic battlefield where Muhammad's grandson Husayn was killed in 680. In the Albanian struggle for independence from the Ottoman Empire, this event has been used in strikingly similar fashion to the way the Battle of Kosovo was enrolled in the Serbian fight for independence.[85] Like Kosovo, Kerbala contains undertones of suffering and defeat by its very name: the hero is decapitated and the troops brutally slaughtered. Husayn, the hero of the story, is in a vision-like dream given a choice between allegiance to caliphYazid which would make him a traitor, or resistance to him which would surely lead to his death. He chooses to resist and becomes a martyr – as Lazar did. Finally, the sacrifice of Husayn will lead to redemption for those who avenge his death – just as Serbs will be redeemed by avenging of Lazar.[86] Being a symbol of the Muslim divide between Sunni-Muslims and Shiites, Kerbala was unable to unite the different Albanian Muslim groups which consist of Sunni-Muslims and Shiites, as well as various Sufi orders. Ultimately, the historical attempt to inject a religious element into Albanian nationalism has therefore not been very successful.

Yet the Serbian insistence in framing Albanian national identity as religious in terms of a Muslim nation or Muslim fundamentalists has pushed the Albanians to take on a minimal national religious identity, which is 'ecumenical' rather than 'Muslim'.[87] The Albanian patriot Pashko Vasa's oft-quoted statement 'The religion of the Albanians is Albaninism' seems then still valid.[88] Language and not religion is the glue of Albanian nationalism. However, in its emphasis on the sufferings of the Albanians and their right to 'first possession' of Kosovo the two myths differ little. It may therefore be suggested that in this way they hold similar potential for conflicts.

This became evident shortly after the withdrawal of Serbian troops from Kosovo. Myth became reality as Serbs were harassed or even murdered. As Serbs had previously destroyed mosques, Serbian monasteries were now under attack. The signs of a Serb presence in Kosovo were to be erased. And in March 2004, ethnic minorities were ferociously attacked in mass riots of at least 50,000 participants. UNMIK and KFOR lost control as Serb, Roma and Ashkali homes as well as schools, post offices and other facilities run by the Serb minority were burned down. In sum, 550 houses and 27 Orthodox churches were burned down, leaving more than 4,000 individuals without a home.[89] Many individuals were beaten with wooden or iron sticks, 19 of whom died.

The March riots were provoked by a series of 'minor' events. First, on 15 March, there was the shooting of an 18-year-old Serb. The bullets were fired from a car and the victim, Jovica Ivić, claimed that the attackers who shouted at him had Albanian accents. Some Serbs responded in blocking the Prisna–Skopje highway, an economic lifeline for Kosovo.[90] On the 16 March, there was a series of demonstrations by 'war associations' – groups representing the KLA and victims of previous Serb attacks. They protested against the detentions of KLA's leaders incited for war crimes and more generally against the 'neo-colonialist' UNMIK. Finally, the situation exploded on the 17 and 18 of March: inflammatory news stated that angry Serbs had chased four Kosovo-Albanian boys into the Ibar River and that three of them had died. Experts and representatives of the ethnic Albanian community were queuing up to condemn the action of the Serb 'bandits'. However, the surviving boy only claimed that Serbs at some distant houses had sworn at them. Furthermore, no Serbs fitting the description given by the boy could be found.[91]

The parallel to previous Serb atrocities against Kosovo-Albanians should be noted: the attacks were informed by the ideology of an Albanian right to Kosovo. Within it, there is a nationalist credo, much like the Serbian version, according to which people are reduced to membership of an ethnic group for whose past, present and future actions they must answer. Finally, in both cases, the stories that have incited genocide are marginal and disputed.

The future of a myth

The centrality of the Lazar myth in the conflicts of the former Yugoslavia in general and over Kosovo in particular, poses the question of whether peaceful coexistence between people who have come to see each other as historical enemies is liable at all. It is a fact that important actors in the conflict, such as the Serbian Orthodox Church, continue to regard the conflict in civil religious terms (the homepage of the Serbian Orthodox Church refers to the March violence as 'pogroms'). Though Vojislav Koštunica, the Serbian President, has seemingly refrained from using the symbols associated with Serbian civil religion[92] it seems that the attempts to 'disarm' the Kosovo myth have not been successful. The civil religion of Serbia is like the Serbian Orthodoxy 'imbued with a strong sense of victimisation and suffering'.[93] As long as the Serbian people continue to regard themselves as victims of suffering, the symbols of Serbian civil religion are likely to remain important. The question of reconciliation and stable peace will therefore by necessity include reference to the continued relevance of the Kosovo symbols.

The case against Milošević is illustrative. In a similar way to Mitterrand's visit to Sarajevo, the symbol of multinationalism, on Vidovdan, 1992 – the surrender of Milošević, also on Vidovdan, could be seen as a step in the creation of a democratic counter-myth. Finally, after hundreds of years of struggle, the Serbs won their freedom. The reason why Milošević was handed over might, however, reflect the prospect of a reward of 1.3 billion rather than a genuine wish for working through the past.[94] It is not just Milošević's Socialist Party and Vojislav Sesejl's radical right-wing party who claim that Serbia is living under a US and EU dictate. Similar views are expressed by Koštunica and other members of the Democratic Opposition (DOS).[95] Koštunica claims the Hague court to be controlled absolutely by the American government.[96]

This attitude towards the court, which is shared by many Serbs, might in fact be an example of how the Kosovo myth continues to shape beliefs and opinions. The work of the ICTY is seen as just another way of punishing the Serbs and as such it does not allow for any working through the tragic policies of the 1980s and 1990s.[97] Milošević has of course used this theme with skill: the revamped Ustasha movement, foreign mujahideen and NATO imperialists are the ones guilty of war crimes committed. The Srebrenica massacre was orchestrated by the work of French intelligence. It was common practice that the Muslim side killed their own people attempting to get the West involved, and so on.[98]

In a May 2002 poll of the Serbs, the National Democratic Institute (NDI) found that only 30 per cent thought the Hague war-crimes tribunal (ICTY) was conducting a fair trial. Fifty-seven per cent thought it was unfair. Another poll showed that only 32 per cent of the Serbs supported cooperating with the tribunal.[99] The year before, in 2001, public polls found that 52.5 per cent of respondents could not name a single war crime committed by Serb forces while half could name at least three crimes committed against Serb civilians by other forces. Furthermore, Radovan Karadižić and Ratko Mladić were considered to be the two 'greatest defenders of the Serb nation'.[100] On the whole, there seems to be a continuous denial of war crimes committed by Serb forces.[101]

On the Kosovo-Albanian side, the picture is equally dismal. The March riots were a major setback. The Albanian leadership had the opportunity to condemn the violence but did so only hesitantly. On the first day of the riot, the Kosovo Parliamentary Assembly (the provincial parliament) issued the following statement: The Parliament 'voices its disagreement with the lack of commitment by UNMIK to provide security for all Kosovar citizens. The tolerance for Serb parallel structures and criminal gangs that murder Kosovar citizens is the wrong policy, and will destabilize Kosovo'.[102] Sitting president Rugova's statement expressed his deepest regret for wounded UNMIK and KFOR personnel but did not mention the Serb victims.[103] There was no audible regret for what was happening. One cannot avoid the suspicion that the Albanian leadership felt that the Serbs got what they deserved. It goes without saying that such a view is a major obstacle towards the creation of multicultural Kosovo and for the cessation of violence.

However, there are some reasons to be hopeful. The Serbian and Albanian religious communities are more willing to talk to each other than other sectors of Kosovo society[104] which of course indicates that religion may also be a resource in working towards a common understanding and lasting peace. In any case, myth might even aid the process of reconciliation. Myths tend to be subject to change: 'myth – the eternal, fixed archetype – turns out to be creative'.[105] In regard to American civil religion, of which he was certainly not uncritical, Bellah emphasized the inclusive nature of this. American civil religion thus did not include confessional references, or even references to Jesus, in order not to exclude people of a wide variety of faiths in the national community.

Finally, like their classical Greek counterparts, modern myths might teach us humility and modesty by reminding us of our fragility. Thus the difference between beneficial and harmful myths might be due to what they convey of human nature. Anzulovic sees the idea of man as by nature good and capable of eradicating evil from the world as the main danger. These ideas are found in Enlightenment myths, which allow for a glorification of particular classes, races or nations and for the denigration and perhaps even eradication of others. Old myths, those originating in Ancient Greece and from the canonical religions, may through the recognition of the concept of original sin teach us that there is a capacity for evil in every human being and thus a recurring need for a critical interrogation of one's actions.[106] This then might be a first step towards a less violent society, a society in which myth is a genuine source of community and sharing.

Notes

1 Ernst Cassirer, *The Myth of the State*, 1946, quoted in Ivan Čolović, *The Politics of Symbol in Serbia* (London: Hurst & Company, 2002), p. 3.
2 William E. Paden, *Religious Worlds. The Comparative Study of Religion* (Boston: Beacon Press, 1994), p. 69.
3 Russell McCutcheon, 'Myth', pp. 190–200 in Willi Braun & Russell McCutcheon (eds), *Guide to the Study of Religion* (London and New York: Cassell, 2000).
4 Ibid., p. 200.
5 Roland Barthes, *Mythologies* (London: Paladin, 1973), pp. 123–4.
6 Ibid., pp. 135, 140, 155–7.
7 Ibid., p. 156.
8 Jean-Luc Nancy, *The Inoperative Community* (Minneapolis: University of Minnesota Press, 1991), p. 53.
9 Philippe Lacoue-Labarthe and Jean-Luc Nancy, 'The Nazi Myth', *Critical Inquiry*, 16, 4 (1990), pp. 291–312.
10 Barthes (n. 5 above), pp. 117–19.
11 Nancy (n. 8 above), p. 50.
12 Ibid., p. 48.
13 Ibid., p. 50.
14 Ibid., p. 50.
15 Ibid., p. 50; Barthes (n. 5 above), p. 117.
16 Nancy (n. 8 above), p. 51.
17 Čolović (n. 1 above), p. 5.
18 Ernst Cassirer, *The Myth of the State* (New Haven: The Yale University Press, 1974), pp. 53–77.

19 Milne Holton and Vasa D. Mihailovich, *Serbian Poetry from the Beginnings to the Present* (Columbus OH: Slavica Publishers, 1988), pp. 95–6.
20 Tim Judah, *Kosovo. War and Revenge* (New Haven and London: Yale University Press, 2000), pp. 4–8; Branimir Anzulovic, *Heavenly Serbia. From Myth to Genocide* (London: Hurst & Company, 1999), pp. 11–17; Michael A. Sells, *The Bridge Betrayed: Religion and Genocide in Bosnia* (Berkeley: University of California Press, 1996), pp. 29–31; Ger Duijzings, *Religion and the Politics of Identity in Kosovo* (London: Hurst & Company, 2000), pp. 176–202.
21 Sells (n. 20 above), p. 31.
22 Thompson quoted in Duijzings (n. 20 above), p. 185.
23 Dvorniković quoted in George V. Thomashevich, 'The Battle of Kosovo and the Serbian Church', pp. 203–26 in Wayne S. Vucunich and Thomas A. Emmert (eds), *Kosovo. Legacy of A Medieval Battle* (Minnesota: University of Minnesota, 1991), p. 209.
24 Judah (n. 20 above), pp. 7–8.
25 Anzulovic (n. 20 above), p. 39.
26 Judah (n. 20 above), p. 5.
27 Duijzings (n. 20 above), p. 182.
28 Ibid., p. 204.
29 Ibid., p. 184.
30 Sells (n. 20 above), p. 31.
31 Duijzings (n. 20 above), p. 188.
32 Paden (n. 2 above), p. 80.
33 Alois Schmaus, 'Einleitung', in Petar P. Njegoš, *Der Bergkranz* (München: Otto Sagner, 1963), p. xxxiii.
34 Ibid., p. xxxiii.
35 Milorad Ekmečić, 'The Emergence of St. Vitus Day as the Principal National Holyday of the Serbs', pp. 331–42 in Wayne S. Vucunich and Thomas A. Emmert (eds), *Kosovo. Legacy of a Medieval Battle* (Minnesota: University of Minnesota, 1991), p. 331.
36 Anzulovic (n. 20 above), pp. 83–5.
37 Ekmečić (n. 35 above), p. 331.
38 Ibid., p. 338.
39 Anzulovic (n. 20 above), p. 84.
40 Čolović (n. 1 above) , p. 12.
41 Duijzings (n. 20 above), p. 198.
42 Judah (n. 20 above), p. 39.
43 Ibid., p. 197.
44 Sells (n. 30 above), p. 45.
45 Slobodan Milošević, 'Kosovo Polje Address' (1999[1989]), http://www.geocities.com/Athens/Trov/3757/Serbia/articles/kosovo_polje.html, p. 1.
46 Ibid., p. 1.
47 Ibid., p. 2.
48 Ibid., p. 4.
49 Wendy Bracewell, 'Rape in Kosovo: masculinity and Serbian nationalism', *Nations and Nationalism*, 6, 4 (2000), pp. 563–90, see p. 563.
50 Julie A. Mertus, *Kosovo. How myths and truths started a war* (Berkeley: University of California Press, 1999), p. 104.
51 Ibid., p. 107.
52 Petition on Djordje Martinović quoted in Bracewell (n. 49 above), p. 571.
53 Mertus (n. 50 above), p. 108.
54 Milošević, quoted in Duijzings (n. 20 above), p. 180.
55 Milošević, quoted in Judah (n. 20 above), p. 29.
56 Quoted in Branka Margaš, *The Destruction of Yugoslavia. Tracking the break-up 1980–92* (London: Verso, 1993), pp. 49–52.
57 Quoted in Mertus (n. 50 above), p. 109.

58 Ibid.
59 Letica quoted in ibid.
60 Bečković quoted in Čolović (n. 1 above), pp. 66, 17.
61 Čolović (n. 1 above), p. 9.
62 Marković quoted in Duijzings (n. 20 above), p. 181.
63 Mitja Velikonja, *'In Hoc Signo Vinces:* Religious Symbolism in the Balkan Wars 1991–95', *International Journal of Politics, Culture and Society*, 17, 1 (2003), pp. 25–40, p. 32.
64 Quoted in Margaš (n. 56 above), pp. 49–52.
65 International Crisis Group (ICG), *Religion in Kosovo,* Priština/ Brussels: IGC Balkan Reports, No.105, 2001, p. 14.
66 Samuel Huntington, *The Clash of Civilizations and the Remaking of World Order* (New York: Simon & Schuster, 1996).
67 Anzulovic (n. 20 above), p. 85.
68 Popovic, quoted in ibid.
69 Anzulovic (n. 20 above), p. 26.
70 Duijzings (n. 20 above), p. 179.
71 Čolović (n. 1 above), p. 167.
72 Robert N. Bellah, 'Civil Religion in America', pp. 168–98 in Robert N. Bellah, *Beyond Belief* (Harper & Row, 1970).
73 Philips Hammond, 'The Sociology of American Civil Religion: A bibliographical essay', *Sociological Analysis,* 37, 2 (1976), pp. 169–82, see p. 171.
74 Anzulovic (n. 20 above), pp. 4–5.
75 Meredith B. McGuire, *Religion. The Social Context* (Belmont CA: Wadsworth, 2002), p. 205.
76 Anzulovic (n. 20 above), p. 56.
77 Sells (n. 20 above), p. 37.
78 Anzulovic (n. 20 above), pp. 23–4.
79 Ibid., p. 29.
80 Sells (n. 20 above), p. xvii.
81 Duijzings (n. 20 above), p. 188.
82 Bellah (n. 72 above), p. 168
83 Alan Aldridge, *Religion in the Contemporary World. A Sociological Introduction* (Cambridge: Polity Press, 2000), p. 157.
84 Judah (n. 20 above), p. 2.
85 Duijzings (n. 20 above), p. 158.
86 Ibid., pp. 171–2.
87 Ibid., p. 164.
88 ICG, (n. 65 above), p. 3.
89 Human Rights Watch, *Failure to Protect: Anti-Minority Violence in Kosovo*, 16, 6 (D) (2004), pp. 1–2.
90 Ibid., p. 16.
91 Ibid., pp. 19–20.
92 Čolović (n. 1 above), pp. 305–8.
93 Duijzings (n. 20 above), p. 178.
94 Slavenka Drakulić, *They Would Never Hurt a Fly. War Criminals on Trial in the Hague*, London: Viking, 2004, p. 122.
95 Ana Devic, 'War Guilt and Responsibility: the Case of Serbia. Diverging Attempts at Facing the Recent Past', *GCS Quarterly*, Spring, http://www.ssrc.org/programs/gsc/gsc_quarterly/newsletter8/content/devic.page, 2003, p. 3.
96 Ibid., p. 93.
97 Ibid., p. 2.
98 Gary J. Bass, 'Milosevic in The Hague', *Foreign Affairs*, 82.3 (May/June 2003), pp. 82–96, see pp. 89–91.

99 Ibid., p. 93.
100 Devic (n. 95 above), p. 2.
101 Ibid., p. 4.
102 Quoted in Human Rights Watch (n. 89 above), p. 58.
103 Ibid., p. 58.
104 ICG (n. 65 above), p. iii.
105 Paden (n. 2 above), p. 91.
106 Anzulovic (n. 20 above), p. 181.

3 The logic of genocide and the prospects of reconciliation

Arne Johan Vetlesen

What peculiar logic is there to genocide? Can such a logic be shown to have been operative in the Serb campaign against Kosovo in 1998–99, thereby demonstrating that the campaign was an instance of genocide? In what sense were the large-scale Serbian atrocities committed against Albanian Kosovars driven by objectives, notions and sentiments of an ideological nature? What background is there for the often-repeated notion that, historically, the Serbs are victims but never aggressors? And finally, depending on how these questions might be answered, what are the prospects for reconciliation in post-war Kosovo?

In this chapter, it will be argued that the Serbian atrocities committed in Kosovo in 1998–99 constitute genocide. In developing this argument, I will focus on the instrumental role played by ideology – that is, by the peculiar ethno-nationalist ideology articulated by powerful politicians and intellectuals rallying behind the Serbian 'cause' in Yugoslavia since the 1930s and arguably much longer. In analysing this ideology, including its history and its message, I focus on the role played by former President Slobodan Milošević. It is thanks to his tremendous strategic skills, combined with a rare gift for timing and a mindset dominated by cynicism that the long-standing ideology in question – hailing the rights of Serbs everywhere as threatened by their alleged oppressors – in a very short time could become truly explosive, producing the gravest humanitarian disaster(s) in Europe since the end of the Second World War. The last section of the chapter is an attempt to explain why reconciliation is an exceedingly precarious and complex endeavour in Kosovo and in any other place where intrastate conflict has caused one group to engage in genocide against another (whether actually completed or not). Examining this connection, a comparison is made between Bosnia and Kosovo.

Genocide: its nature and its logic

The main criterion of genocide, according to the 1948 Convention on the Prevention and Punishment of the Crime of Genocide is that it is directed at people, not in their capacities as individuals but as members of the national, ethnic, racial or religious group to which they belong. By definition, then, genocide signifies one group's attempted destruction of another group. This collective nature of the phenomenon is built into the juridical understanding of genocide.

Concomitant with this, individuals in their singularity (uniqueness qua individuals) do not feature in the group-oriented outlook characteristic of genocidal ideologies. While international law, most prominently in the case of genocide, recognizes that particular groups or collectives are the (ideologically defined) victims, the *protection* international law sets out to offer is to that of the individual, resting as it does on normative assumptions about the inviolability of human individuals.[1]

This conceptual dissimilarity carries over into the opposition between essentialism and optionalism. The message conveyed to the individual by doctrines of a collectivist kind is that '*your group is your destiny*'. There is no escape from the presumption that one is a carrier of certain identity features associated with the group one is seen to belong to. This assumption must be understood as in itself positing the features of identity that truly count as inborn: features that are not a product of choice. The individual has no possibility to modify, negate or otherwise invalidate the identity in question, for example, the identity he or she carries as a Jew or as a Muslim.

It is my contention that this holds for the Serbian ideology behind ethnic cleansing in Bosnia and in Kosovo. However, to point out that notions of agency, identity, and moral standing are conceived of in a collectivist manner hardly suffices to explain the remarkable *mobilizing* power of Serbian nationalism. Like other similar ideologies, Serbian ethno-nationalism does not rest content with *explaining* the relationship between in-group and out-group, friend and foe, the pure and the impure, and so forth. Rather, the ideological construction of the parties is built around the putative life-and-death struggle and preparation for action. The message conveyed to the adherents of the ideology is thus eminently *practical*, not theoretical; rather than merely explaining how things are, or how they historically came about, the principal task is to instigate in people a sense that action needs to be taken, that 'things cannot go on like this', that the present situation is one of imminent danger. In short, action is to be seen as urgently needed, decisive action that requires determined leaders and loyal followers.

There is no doubt that for centuries Kosovo has been a special site of tension between Albanians and Serbs. This tension was constantly exacerbated in the nineteenth and twentieth centuries by patterns of emigration by Serbs and immigration of Albanians, producing a situation by the late 1980s where ethnic Serbs comprised no more than about ten per cent of Kosovo's population. In the twentieth century, obsessive concern with the dangers represented by this demographic trend was a hallmark of Serbian nationalist programmes. It is important to be aware of this historical fact, since it allows us to situate in *long duree* Milošević's determination to exploit ordinary Serbs' preoccupation with 'the issue of Kosovo' as *the* issue of survival; indeed as the existential-collective issue *par excellence*.

For example, in 1937, the prominent Belgrade University professor Vasa Čubrilović gave an address to the Serbian Culture Club in which he sketched an ambitious plan for forced deportation, terrorization, and re-colonization of the Southern lands of Serbia, which included Kosovo.[2] The decisive response to the history of Albanian 'penetration' into these parts of Serbia, urged Čubrilović, was the removal of the Albanian population by the use of force. Claiming that the trend of Albanian encroachment into Serbia could only get worse due to the 'exceptional' fertility of Albanian women relative to Serbian women, Čubrilović went on to advocate the forcible eviction *en masse* of the Albanian population to lands in Albania and Turkey, and repopulation of the ethnically 'cleansed' areas with Serbs.

My point is that there is a remarkable continuity from Čubrilović's policy recommendations in 1937 to the notorious *Memorandum* signed by 200 prominent Belgrade intellectuals some 50 years later. Leaked to the wider public in January 1986, and immediately causing great political upheaval, the *Memorandum* revolves around the assertion that a multifaceted 'genocide' is being carried out: 'The physical, political, legal, and cultural genocide of the Serbian population in Kosovo and Metohija is the worst defeat in the battles for liberation that Serbia waged from 1804 (Orasac) until the revolution in 1941'.[3] Against this dramatic historical background, and seeing the life-form and existence of Serbs as subject to the gravest danger, especially in Kosovo,[4] the *Memorandum* demands the 'right to spiritual identity, to defence of the foundations of Serb national culture and to the physical survival of our nation on its land'. It goes on to say, 'We demand decisive measures, and that the concern and will of all Yugoslavia be mobilized in order to stop the Albanian aggression in Kosovo and Metohija'.[5]

The upshot of the *Memorandum*, later to be exploited to tremendous effect by Milošević, is that Serbian history is tantamount to a history of victimization; it is the history of domination and repression at the hands of enemies of all ideological stripes, continuing to this day, it is claimed, in the gestalt of the nascent movements for autonomy taking hold in other parts of Yugoslavia – that is, the threat posed by 'Islamic fundamentalism' under the lead of Alija Izetbegovic in Bosnia-Herzegovina and the threat posed by Kosovar proponents of a Greater Albania rid of Serbs. In my view, the fate of the Serbs in Kosovo always played a much bigger role for Milošević personally – symbolically, emotionally, and rhetorically – than the fate of the Serbs in Bosnia.

In a decisive manner, Milošević's self-transformation as the leader of 'all Serbs, wherever they might be' helped render the anti-Albanian sentiments a constitutive element of what was to count as the 'proper identity' of Serbs. Milošević's declaration ('You will not be beaten again') seems to have been received precisely the way it was intended: as his promise to his tormented yet proud people that he took it upon himself to revenge past wrongs by aiming at a future where no Serb person – be it as a member of a demographic majority or minority – would ever again have reason to feel insecure and marginalized.[6] With the support of the minds behind the *Memorandum*, in addition to such self-styled ideologues as Radovan Karadižić and Vojislav Seselj, Milošević became extremely adept at articulating the major motifs of Serbian top-down propaganda. This served to legitimate the violent 'ethnic cleansing' that was to follow (roughly) in three waves: the first launched in the summer of 1991 (reaching a peak with the Serb forces' destruction of the Croat city of Vukovar), the second in early April 1992 in Bosnia, targeting the Muslim part of the population as the main enemy, and the third in the Spring of 1998 in Kosovo, targeting the KLA in particular (labelled Tirana-led 'terrorists') and Albanians in general as the main enemy.

The central propaganda message is simple: the Serbs are never, and have never been, aggressors; they are 'liberators' who try – unselfishly and by way of great sacrifices – to help others (other Serbs) in need, yet who are invariably thwarted in this justified mission by the aggression of their neighbours (be they Albanian, Muslim or Croatian) and by the hostility of the outside world, ostensibly fed by centuries of anti-Serbian propaganda. Since Western media typically show no interest in paying attention to atrocities against the Serbs (such as those that took place in the concentration camp Jasenovac, run by Hitler-friendly Croats at the height of the Second World War), the long-standing situation in which Milošević seeks to take decisive measures is claimed to be one of a powerful and ubiquitous conspiracy against Serbs. Hence, so the propaganda goes, what are portrayed as unjust acts of aggression on the part of the Serbs fighting in Bosnia and later in Kosovo, are in fact the opposite: it is the only response left for a people surrounded by enemies wanting to eliminate them by way of 'culticide' and physical genocide. In other words, it's a matter of self-defence and, ultimately, of sheer survival.

It is not that Serb leaders Milošević and Karadižić tried to deny, say, the *de facto* multiple character of a Bosniak's identity, of his or her self-understanding.[7] Rather, they declared that such absence – in their parlance, lack – of homogeneous, ethnically exclusivist identity, represented an 'artificial' or 'degenerate' state of affairs, a cultural development that needed to be halted and eventually reversed, lest the 'natural' or 'genuine' identity of the *Serbs* – presumably at the core an unequivocal, unmixed identity – evaporate. Therefore, when it is said today that the purification of ethnic identity – *either* Serb *or* Croat *or* Muslim – is to be condemned because it threatens a multicultural polity comprised of individuals who see themselves as carriers of multiple identities, Karadižić's point of departure was the very opposite: that a multicultural polity is to be combated because it threatens the homogeneity of identity.

The mobilizing thrust behind Karadižić's rhetoric consists of the assertion that a multicultural polity, to the extent it is admitted to exist, is undesirable and – more importantly – *unworkable*. In Karadižić's words, 'Serbs, Croats, and Muslims can no longer live together'. 'You can't keep a dog and a cat in a box together. Either they would always be quarrelling and fighting or they would have to stop being what they are'.[8] In other words, the prospect of continued cohabitation within the same nation state and the same territory is tantamount to the eventual cessation of ethnic identity in its pure, exclusivist sense.

As to the question immediately encouraged – *why* precisely such an end to alleged purity would be disastrous – no clear answer is provided. My suggestion is that the answer has everything to do with power and little, very little to do with a concern for the well-being of the people. Propagating identity as a matter of purity, of protecting something pristine and natural from degenerating through what is deemed artificial and unviable, is a strategic device employed to provide, for in-group and out-group alike, a rallying point around which to perceive and encounter each other precisely as foes, not as fellow members of the same polity; foes because of this partaking in mutually exclusive identities.

The elevation of identity in this puristic, exclusivist sense to the truly principal issue of politics has the effect that politics become a matter of being prepared to *take action*, to implement the measures necessary to protect what is truly one's own against its being destroyed by what is alien and, as a corollary, hostile. Thus, fear is the feeling evoked in people on all sides of the ethnic divide. Participating in 'decisive action' against the groups said to threaten one's identity, understood non-optionally and essentially as comprising one's innermost being, is the only offered exit from the fear instilled by waves of ethnicity-obsessed propaganda.

As indicated above, the principal role of ideology in connection with the carrying out of genocide is to provide *justification* – internally as well as externally – for the action taken. It is a fact that genocide, being in my understanding the thought-out and accomplished act of a collective (though often ordered top-down), can only be carried out on the condition that a large number of people are willing to do their share of participation. This is particularly true in cases of large-scale atrocities carried out, not in a hi-tech manner, but rather as many instances of hands-on violence up front, physically close to the victim.

The ideological justification for inflicting suffering of the gravest kind upon the chosen target group invariably refers to the deeds of that group, in order to establish the moral legitimacy of what is to pass. Such justification may take several forms, two of which stand out as particularly salient: when focussing attention on the past wrongs caused by the target group, justification for the action now taken assumes the form of *retaliation*; when focussing on the wrongs (allegedly) planned and just about to be performed by the target group, justification takes the form of *preemption*. In both cases, the ideologically produced upshot is that the action taken by one's own group has the character of *self-defence*. In both cases, too, what is being done, or at least urged – in terms of organized killings, rape, expulsions and similar crimes – is precisely what the enemy is alleged to have done or is about to do. In this sense, the enacted genocide has the form of repetition and imitation, but with a role-reversal so that the victims of the past transform themselves into tomorrow's perpetrators.

Self-defence provides a moral justification for acts of aggression; it is invoked as a license to kill precisely those *deserving* to be killed. To my knowledge, all genocidal ideologies – that is ideologies planning, implementing, and justifying collectively undertaken acts of aggression amounting to genocide against a named group – have one mechanism in common: they all contend that what is being done is a matter of re-establishing a balance or equity lost due to offences of the other party. Indeed, psychologically speaking, the ideologies in question would never enjoy the support of masses of people were it not for the fact that the 'license to kill' they formulate resonates deeply with all-too-human – however 'primitive' – notions of moral desert and justice.

The Serbian campaign in Kosovo 1998–99

With this logic of genocide in mind, it is important to take a closer look at the so-called 'Operation Horseshoe' sponsored by Belgrade in the phase prior to NATO's military intervention in Kosovo. The precise nature and status of this operation is (and continues to be) shrouded in mystery, giving rise in the winter of 1999 to a string of rumours that were eagerly seized upon (or *sui generis* invented according to some observers) by Western media. Was the plan a fake on the part of the Milošević-led Serb forces in order to scare the Albanian population into leaving? Was it rather a bluff on the part of Western powers intent on alarming Western audiences, making them ready to accept the legitimacy of the long premeditated military attack on Yugoslavia launched on 24 March 1999? Was the plan invented after the event, that is, after the mass purges had already taken place?

It is beyond the scope of this chapter to try to answer all these questions, but a way of looking at it that I find plausible, is that certain remarks by General Sreten Lukic (the officer who commanded the Racak massacre and a close associate of Milošević) – remarks which were leaked to Western intelligence as early as September 1998 – were of such an alarming nature that grave concern for the fate of the Albanian population in Kosovo was called for following the precautionary principle.[9] According to General Lukic 'Operation Horseshoe' is the name of an operation meticulously planned in Belgrade (much like the Ram-plan developed prior to mass killings of non-Serbs in Bosnia)[10] with the aim of driving over one million people from their homes in Kosovo and out of the country amid organized massacres and the systematic destruction of Albanian property (as part of what has come to be called 'culticide').

Although the existence and realization of this plan are yet to be fully established, I believe that the decision to take leaked information about the plan seriously was well-founded, not least in light of the horrible reality of ethnic cleansing in Bosnia a few years earlier. As for the often raised question of whether NATO's attack on Yugoslavia in fact precipitated rather than prevented mass deportation and killing by Serb army and police forces in Kosovo, there was, once again, a strong historically based case for applying the precautionary principle. Considering the situation in which Milošević's regime found itself in late 1998 and early 1999, one could even say that the Serb determination to carry out an aggressive war of 'ethnic cleansing' in Kosovo was over-determined: first, because Kosovo held pride of place as far as identity-related symbolic significance is concerned, and second because the world knew only too well that in times of rising domestic crisis, Milošević was a leader willing to opt for war as a means to consolidate his power and rally his increasingly poor, disillusioned and atomized people behind him and behind an ostensively 'common' cause – that is, so as to secure their common destiny and their survival as a people.

Did genocide really take place in Kosovo? If not, what does this mean with regard to the legitimacy of going to war against Yugoslavia in March 1999? The evidence available today supports the claim that genocide was the *intention* behind the Milošević-led Serbian campaign in Kosovo, although the objective of genocide was not fully completed – thanks, I would say, to NATO's military intervention. There is no doubt that the inhabitants of Kosovo who were killed, raped, or deported, were subject to this wilful aggression *qua group members*, not qua unique individuals; they were targeted in their quality as representatives of a collective and that is the essence of the formulation in the 1948 Genocide Convention: 'acts committed with intent to destroy, in whole or in part, a national, ethnical, racial or religious group as such'.[11] The question of whether someone has committed genocide crucially turns on the word 'destroy'. Two questions must be asked here: is destruction of the group an intended objective and have the relevant acts of genocide actually been carried out to a significant extent?

Recent developments in international humanitarian law indicate that the first of the two questions asked has gained primacy over the second: intent weighs heavier than extent. Following Pierre Prosper, the African American prosecutor who (successfully) set out to prove that Jean-Paul Akayeshu, the Hutu mayor of Rwanda's Taba commune, attempted to destroy the Tutsi by raping the women, I find it to be truly in the spirit of Raphael Lemkin's original definition of genocide to urge that *'destruction' be equated with attacks on the 'very foundation' of the group*, that is, the 'debiliatation' of a group to such an extent that the remaining members can no longer contribute to society in a meaningful way. Prosper's view, which I support, is that a group could physically exist, or escape wholesale extermination, but be left so marginalized or so irrelevant to society that it was, in effect, destroyed.[12]

Although this position was developed with regard to Rwanda, the focus being, moreover, on rapes, not killings or expulsions, I believe that Prosper's argument applies to Kosovo as well. Milošević and his associates are to be viewed as guilty of genocide in Kosovo no less than in Bosnia, regardless of the fact that the number of killed and raped persons is considerably higher for Bosnia than for Kosovo. But again, quality is more important than quantity. What matters is the *intention* to *destroy a group in whole or in part* in the sense elaborated by Prosper – leaving only secondary importance to the (often eminently contingent) issue of the exact extent to which this intention was actually completed.

For the record, the main figures pertaining to Kosovo are as follows:[13] While some 860,000 persons were reported to have been forcefully deported (in accordance with the objective of ethnic cleansing to rid territories of unwanted persons and groups) from Kosovo during the NATO air campaign, at least one million persons left the province from March 1998 through to the end of the armed conflict. In addition, over 590,000 became internally displaced persons within Kosovo. Taken together, these figures demonstrate that over 90 per cent of the estimated Kosovar Albanian population in 1998 were displaced from their homes. This is a staggeringly high number. As for killings, it is estimated that approximately 10,500 Kosovar Albanians were killed between 20 March and 12 June 1999. As for rapes, Human Rights Watch has confirmed 96 documented cases, but because of the likelihood that the stigma attached to this form of violence in traditional Albanian society led to rather gross under-reporting of rape in Kosovo, the number given here represents only a fraction of the actual incidents.[14]

Whereas Carla del Ponte, the UN Chief Prosecutor in the Hague, decided to charge Milošević and his closest associates with genocide in Bosnia, the UN would 'only' charge him for crimes against humanity in Kosovo. It should be noted, however, that in juridical terms (the statute of the International Criminal Court) the latter indictment comprises murder, torture, rape, deportation, forced disappearance and persecution, when committed 'as part of a widespread or systematic attack directed against any civilian population, with knowledge of the attack'.[15] My impression is that del Ponte's reasons for taking this decision were circumstantial rather than principal, in the sense that the Hague prosecutors have secured stronger evidence to prove genocide in Bosnia than in Kosovo (Srebrenica plays a crucial role in this). For the purposes of this article, however, the important thing to point out is that both types of crimes must be viewed as genuine products of one and the same ideology: the ethno-nationalist one we have seen Milošević embrace at a crucial point and largely for the strategic interests of power-seeking.

Reconciliation I: the third party perspective

Bearing in mind that Kosovo has recently been the scene of acts of genocide and crimes against humanity, and that these crimes have been fuelled and legitimized by reference to ethno-nationalistic myths and ideologies, what are the prospects for reconciliation? Is reconciliation possible at all under such circumstances?

Although reconciliation fundamentally involves two parties – aggressor and victim – it invariably involves some kind of facilitating role for third parties. In an important essay, Michael Ignatieff puts the problem faced by the third party like this:

> it is an illusion to suppose that 'impartial' or 'objective' outsiders would ever succeed in getting their moral and interpretive account of the catastrophe accepted by the parties to the conflict. The very fact of being an outsider discredits rather than reinforces one's legitimacy. For there is always a truth that can be known only by those on the inside. Or if not a truth – since facts are facts – then a moral significance to these facts that only an insider can fully appreciate. The truth, if it is to be believed, must be authored by those who have suffered its consequences. But the truth of war is so painful that those who have fought each other rarely if ever sit down to author it together.[16]

I believe that Ignatieff overstates the problem. In so far as there is something valuable for the affected parties attributed to the role played by a third party, it must lie precisely in the way the latter represents 'those not there', that is to say, the outside world, the general public or quite simply humanity. Though not directly affected, humanity is affected nonetheless – not physically but morally. In fact, and as we shall elaborate below, perpetrators and victims alike, if they are to recover and get on with their lives, need to understand that what passed between them is of such a nature as to engage the outside world.

Ignatieff's statement that 'the very fact of being an outsider discredits rather than reinforces one's legitimacy' is accurate as a way of capturing the narrow-minded narcissism and self-righteousness often encountered in people overwhelmed by the traumas of war, not least 'uncivil wars'. While the readiness of one's adversary to listen and to understand may be ruled out, because viewed as unrealistic, such readiness on the part of bystanders will indeed be expected as well as strongly desired. The view that outsiders don't understand, simply due to their being outsiders, may be prevalent as a psychological point of departure, but it is not a view bound to last forever, or for very long. By the same token, the 'truth' about what happened that Ignatieff speaks about, is one that crucially needs the effort that only a non-party can offer, again precisely because they are non-party. While Ignatieff is right to challenge the idea that truth is wholly disinterested, objective, neutral, and the like, he goes too far in the opposite direction. The implications of this are highlighted in Ignatieff's further observation that 'the problem of a shared truth is also that it does not lie 'in between'. It is not a compromise between two competing versions'.[17] Exactly! Both parties urge that their own version be heard; and since they don't expect it to be heard by the other side to the conflict, the judgment about their presented version put forward by a third party will be all the more important to them.

Of course, and in keeping with Ignatieff's pronunciations, the reaching out to the third party may take the form of more or less outright attempts to *enlist* that party as a subscriber to one's own version of the truth. The third party would not live up to its function if it were ignorant of this and unable to take measures against being recruited, more or less blindly and uncritically, by one of the parties. To say this is not to make an abstract point. It is to point out that what happened in Bosnia has provided material for a continual moral learning process, as highlighted in the shift to interventionism in the case of Kosovo

A number of scholarly books have documented beyond reasonable doubt how top UN and EU envoys to the Balkan conflicts adopted one party's version – namely, the Serbs' – to the detriment of the others (with Kosovo again marking a turning-point, albeit very belatedly).[18] The problem here was not impartiality *per se* but partiality masquerading as impartiality: non-intervention in the guise of neutrality in a situation where deliberately chosen and enduring passivity meant freezing a blatant asymmetry of power between the parties affected, thus permitting the consequences of such asymmetry in terms of the human suffering it inflicted upon the inferior party in particular. Later on in his essay, Ignatieff writes: 'ethnic cleansing eradicates the accusing truth of the past. In its wake, the past may be rewritten so that no record of the victim's presence is allowed to remain. Victory encloses the victor in a forgetting that removes the very possibility of guilt, shame, or remorse, the emotions necessary for any sustained encounter with the truth'.

These are vital insights. What the observations about the plight of the victors and that of their victims combine to show, is that they are both, for obverse reasons as it were, incapable of establishing adequate conditions for reconciliation and justice. These depend on truth, or more precisely, that a truth be established that is acknowledged by both or all parties. If, as Ignatieff says, truth must be authored by those who have suffered its consequences, the chances that such authoring will take place certainly seem meagre, to say the least, unless representatives (individuals as well as institutions) of third parties combine efforts to help the affected parties come together to start such authoring. What Ignatieff has shown is that the process by which such things as truth, justice, and reconciliation may be achieved cannot be left to the parties themselves.

Just as with truth, for justice to be attained the effort of the third party is crucial. The meaning of justice here is well put by Ignatieff: 'the vital function of justice in the dialogue between truth and reconciliation is to disaggregate individual and nation, to disassemble the fiction that nations are accountable like individuals for the crimes committed in their name'.[19] Hence the central task is to individualize guilt, to 'relocate it from the collectivity to the individuals responsible'.[20] Much in the spirit of my introductory remarks, justice requires that the collectivization of human agency advanced by genocidal ideologies be reversed, so to speak, so that the mythically proclaimed one-to-one relationship between individual and collectivity (for example nation or ethnic group) can be dissolved. Only individuals bear responsibility and guilt; only individuals can be reconciled to each other.

Reconciliation II: the reality and pitfalls of collective agency

Philosophically as well as legally, to speak of guilt as 'collective' does not stand up to closer scrutiny. The received wisdom has it that *individuals* act, individuals make choices as to how to act and for what reasons, therefore individuals have to take responsibility for concrete actions, for the choices they made and for the consequences that follow. In rational terms, this is fine as far as it goes. But how far is that?

To begin with, it must be stressed that we need to maintain the insistence that *morally and legally* agency is a property of concrete individuals and not collectives. Disaggregation is a must when it comes to making judgments about responsibility and guilt. However, it does not follow from this that one should reject collectivization of agency as a *phenomenological and mental fact*. Doing something together with someone else, acting in concert as an experimental modality of being-in-the-world, of being-there-with-others, is a daily experience of being unaware of exactly where I began and you came in, of strictly separating and demarcating the 'me' contribution and the 'you' or 'they' contribution.

In extraordinary settings and situations, the we-quality alluded to will take on stronger forms. For example, in the mass rapes in Bosnia, and later in Kosovo, the impact exerted upon the individual participant by peer pressure can hardly be exaggerated. Ideologies suited to mobilize individuals to take part in mass rapes, and to provide them with psychological motives as well as morally legitimizing reasons for doing what they do, are expertly tailored to give perpetrators the impression that they are indeed a 'we' doing this, and similarly doing it against a 'they'. On both sides of the deed, so to speak, on that of the perpetrators no less than that of their victims, *aggregation* in the sense of individuality-robbing and individuality-denying, thus amounting to what I term 'collectiving', makes its strong psychological and emotional impact.

We need to acknowledge the extent to which atrocities such as rape and killing take place in an atmosphere permeated by group-think, the effect being that the distinction between oneself and other(s) tends to be blurred to the point of obliteration. According to the self-understanding typically shared by perpetrators, each is doing what he does not as a unique individual, but solely in his capacity as a member of a particular group; the same is perceived to hold for the victims. Participants in the organized gang rapes in hotels, prisons and camps in Bosnia report that they are unable to recall the faces of the women they raped; all of them are depicted in the same manner: 'tall, dark-haired'.[21] So, even though these assaults took place in conditions of proximity, on a person-to-person basis, what prevails in the minds of the perpetrators is an attitude of indifference.

What we witness here is the experiential correlate to Adorno's depiction of genocide as the effectuation of a 'total reduction of the individuality of the individual to its generic concept': genocide is 'absolute integration', a process whereby 'the last, the poorest possession left to the individual is expropriated'. Since, in Adorno's account, the grounds for identifying the victims are conceived of 'in total independence of the actual person in view, strictly speaking the immediately affected victims of the administrated mass killings were not individuals, but *specimens*, i.e., samples or instances of a class, genus, or whole, where only the universal counts as ground for assessment of worth'.[22]

My claim is that Adorno's observations are acutely apt with respect to ethnic cleansing in Bosnia and in Kosovo, despite the differences between quasi-industrialized large-scale killings and hands-on violence. What truly merits attention is the by now well-documented fact that indifference, loss of individuality, blurring of the self-other distinction, and so forth, are *not* the prerogative of the perpetrators' experiential perception of their victims; rather, the processes in question comprise the perpetrators themselves *as well as* (their perception of) their victims. If genocide is about groups killing groups, the experiential correlate is that the killing is done *by* members *to* members, thereby reducing individuals on both sides to entirely indistinguishable and exchangeable instances of some ideologically defined identity.

Why do I so belabour this one point? I do so because the experiential impact of processes reducing or downright obliterating *a sense of individuality* – be it now on the part of the perpetrator-agent and not exclusively his targeted victim – clearly flies in the face of the notion of human agency as the property of a specific nameable *individual* that is the operative *sine qua non* of law, hence all our established institutions of justice. Such institutions are by principle, intent, and design a rejection of any notion of human agency to the effect that agency is a property of some group or collective. To put it in a nutshell, then, the institutions of law and the experiential processes precipitated by what I have termed genocidal ideologies are at loggerheads with each other.

A spontaneous rejoinder to this would be that the state of affairs – that is, the blatant contradiction – recorded here is thoroughly sound, and should not cause concern. Since, the reasoning would go, law is established in order to prevent and punish transgressions such as those performed in the spirit of ideologies of a collectivistic bent, it is only *to the point* that law at the most fundamental level rejects the collectivization of human agency (hence of notions of responsibility, guilt, and so on) advocated by and engendered in such ideologies. I think that this response, though not very sophisticated, has a lot going for it. Its gist is to make a requirement, stronger still – a virtue – of the recorded mismatch between the assumptions made about the nature of agency in the two cases. Indeed, it is thanks to the mismatch between the two that the one (law) is enabled to act according to its seminal purpose, namely that of marking a *corrective* with respect to the outlook characteristic of the other (genocidal ideologies).

The issue of *reconciliation*, however, highlights the consequences of individualist as against collectivist notions of agency from a different angle than the purely legal one. Among victims no less than perpetrators, the perception is likely to prevail that what happened to one person happened precisely to one as a member of a group and as performed by members of the other group. The 'me' disappears behind the 'we' or 'us', the 'you' behind the 'they'. So who is to seek reconciliation? Who is reconciliation between?

Reconciliation III: who are the appropriate parties?

It is tempting to answer in a directly analogous way to the rejoinder given above. That is to say, the parties between whom reconciliation is to take place need to be disaggregated, so that the parties recognize each other not as members of specific groups but instead in their capacities as distinct individuals – for instance, as *a* Muslim woman (Bosnian or Kosovar) having been raped by *that* particular Serb man. For reconciliation to do the work of healing it is ideally thought to do, it has to assume the form of a mutual recognition between unique individuals wherein each is fully prepared to take responsibility, to concede guilt, to express shame or remorse, and so on.

I have some doubts as to the validity of an analogy between what is required for *legal* processes to operate as they should and what is required for *reconciliation* to take place between the directly involved parties. Legal processes cannot do without formalism. They cannot set aside the primacy accorded to the notion of agency as something individual, not collective. By contrast, reconciliation is less of a formalized procedure than a troubled undertaking involving lots of emotions and lots of psychology, on both sides of the legal divide between sinner and sufferer. The notion of reconciliation derives from religious contexts, where it designates the re-establishing of a broken relationship between man and a deity (God). The dominant rendition is that reconciliation means the re-establishing of this relationship in so far as the human being becomes aware of his/her personal guilt towards the deity, who then forgives his/her. Note the close connection between the admission of guilt on the one part and the offering of forgiveness on the other: the former serves as a necessary condition for the latter.[23]

On a sociological level, it should be pointed out that in Kosovo, as Samantha Power writes,

> there was no original conciliation to *re*do. Albanians and Serbs had cohabitated in the province for generations, but unlike in Bosnia and Rwanda, where an ethnic map once showed intermingled blots and colours reminiscent of a Jackson Pollock painting, the two groups in Kosovo had rarely mixed. Intermarriage was virtually unheard of. This history did not mean that Albanians and Serbs could not live side by side; it just meant that they were unlikely to do so for some time.[24]

Providing further obstacles to the prospect of reconciliation between the ethnic groups in Kosovo is the fact that Serbs have been killed there in considerable numbers, not only (or even primarily) by members of the well-armed KLA, but by ordinary Albanian Kosovars who, upon returning to their land after the Serbs declared defeat in June 1999 and again in the March riots, have turned against their tormentors (or anyone perceived as somehow representing them, taken as a collective rather than as distinct individuals), unleashing waves of summary executions in addition to going out of their way to force the still remaining Serbs to flee.

Some commentators have gone so far as to call this development ethnic cleansing in reverse. In my view, this charge is exaggerated. To insinuate that the Kosovars, threatened with genocide, exploited NATO's victory against their victimizers to effect this kind of simple role-reversal, is not borne out by fact. A distinction must be made between a political regime (that is, a state) which, using all required resources, plans, organizes, and sets out to accomplish genocide against another group qua group; and, on the other hand, individuals or gangs of individuals who, seeking vengeance and taking the law in their own hands, in a spontaneous and erratic manner, attack (and sometimes kill) individuals belonging to the other group.

To be sure, the pitfalls of moral equalizing – allocating blame and responsibility in relatively equal measures to all the parties involved in what is seen as a war, or 'civil war'; asserting that 'all sides are guilty' so as to avoid taking action – are not novel to the last decade's events in the Balkans. The prominent American legal scholar Mark Osiel writes that:

> negotiating reconciliation can prove highly complex, since often each party will have valid grievances against each other. In such circumstances, apology is easiest when it is reciprocated, that is, when X can acknowledge its wrongs against Y as Y acknowledges its' against X. Reciprocity is particularly fitting where the adversaries have become mutually implicated in each other's vices. This is often true of war, as each side escalates its wrongdoing in retaliation for the enemy's wrongs, real or imagined.[25]

Though persuasive on an abstract and general level, Osiel's observations strike me as unsuited to meet the challenges left by the catastrophes of Bosnia and Kosovo. The mechanisms of reciprocity on which Osiel puts so much emphasis in sketching a framework for reconciliation, are conspicuous by their absence as far as Bosnia and Kosovo are concerned. In both cases, the wrongdoing with respect to which reconciliation is subsequently to be achieved is that of genocide, and as in previously recorded cases genocide is not a 'mutual' type of wrongdoing but a one-sided one (again, my point is qualitative, privileging intent).

Short of the condition of reciprocity (escalation as mutually caused), where does the radical asymmetry between the principal parties involved in genocide – aggressor group and victim group leave any prospect of reconciliation? One may wish to moderate the problem somewhat by pointing to the fact that, even in the two examples I refer to, each side to some extent *did* escalate its wrongdoings 'in retaliation for the enemy's wrongs, real or imagined' (to invoke Osiel's formulation). One could cite that both Croats and Muslims committed horrific and unpardonable atrocities against (civilian) Serbs; one could cite the killings of Serbs committed by KLA. Asymmetry, it would seem, is never total or complete after all.

However, this response does not stand up to closer scrutiny. My point is not falsified by the indisputable fact that the victims of genocide sooner or later in the process, to various extents and dependent on the means at hand, become murderers themselves. Now calmly consider the facts of the two cases discussed: when the genocide against the Bosnian Muslims and Croats was put to an end due to the internationally supported air campaign conducted against Serb forces in the summer of 1995, the aggressor's objectives had in fact been largely achieved: a multi-ethnic society had been destroyed. In Kosovo four years later, a somewhat less multi-ethnic society had likewise been largely destroyed, this time to a significant extent as the combined result of mutual escalation, considering how, without doubt, the KLA sought a post-war scenario where Kosovo would be rid of every single representative of the ethnic group which sought to 'cleanse' Kosovo of all Albanians – namely, the Serbs.

The point which, sadly, holds for both cases is that when the unfolding genocide was effectively put to an end, the territory was already ethnically 'clean' (homogeneous), so that the parties between whom reconciliation was to take place were not *cohabitating* any longer. They had parted company, physically (geographically) as well as psychologically and morally, just as the *genocidaires* desired they would. The fact, rarely noted and reflected upon, is that the world has very little direct experience of how to achieve reconciliation, to speak in moral terms, and with how to re-establish a society's multi-ethnic character, to speak in political terms, when what necessitates both tasks is a completed or near-completed genocide of one group against another (in an intra-state context). In this context, we must ask ourselves how many Muslims will return to the Serb parts of Bosnia? Furthermore, recalling the central goal of genocidal ideology, namely the traumatizing of any surviving victims for the rest of their lives, how many surviving Muslims *will want* to return to the places where their unspeakable suffering took place?

Does this imply that genocide and those who deliberately pursue it must be seen as forever gaining the upper hand? To my mind, we haven't understood what genocide is as long as we fail, or neglect, to recognize that *rendering reconciliation impossible in any foreseeable future* is one of the *genocidaires'* chief goals. Is this also a recognition that genocide – also when it is 'only' intended, and, materially speaking, 'only' accomplished *in part* – is such a terrible crime exactly because it cannot be undone or reversed? For a start, I see my judgment on the long-standing effects of (completed or near-completed) genocide(s) as one inspired by realism – no more, no less. The complementary acts of asking forgiveness and being granted it are, let's face it, exceedingly difficult when the parties concerned are split into aggressors and victims of genocide. When the relationships that once existed between the two parties have been damaged beyond repair, when re-cohabitation for all sorts of pragmatic reasons is no viable option (for either of the parties), reconciliation will appear to have more to do with the wishful thinking of well-meaning outsiders than with the realistic outlook of those affected.

I said above that only individuals, not nations, can be reconciled. Yet, as Ignatieff remarks,

> individuals are helped to heal and to reconcile by public rituals of atonement. When President Alwyn of Chile appeared on television to apologize to the victims of Pinochet's crimes of repression, he created the public climate in which a thousand acts of private repentance and apology became possible.[26]

Certainly, the prospect that President Milošević will offer the public act of atonement toward the people of former Yugoslavia that President Alwyn did in Chile, seems meagre, to say the least. Beginning with his very first appearance in the Hague courtroom, Milošević-the-accused's stance has been that of no regrets, ridiculing all evidence brought against him and exploiting every testimony given by his victims to add as much insult to the injury already inflicted upon them as his energy permits. So again, we are a far cry indeed from the public endeavours of reconciliation that take place in a nation such as, for example, South Africa.

The assumption is that it is only in and through 'full disclosure (truth-telling) that justice *as acknowledgement* can be attained and this, in turn, opens up the possibility of reconciliation', in as much as 'public recognition and acknowledgement of injustices constitute the basis for the attainment of justice'.[27] As is well known, in South Africa the Truth and Reconciliation Commission, modelled explicitly on the Chilean example and chaired by Desmond Tutu, encouraged perpetrators of abuses to make full disclosures of their crimes in return for amnesty. Not surprisingly, the Commission has been accused of sacrificing justice for reconciliation, not least by those (many of whom, but not all, are victims or relatives of victims) for whom justice entails prosecution and punishment of perpetrators, leading to their imprisonment if found guilty.

Truth commissions such as those established in Chile and South Africa rest heavily on the assumption that the sheer act of coming forward to tell the truth, to give one's honest version of what happened, and without fear of consequences for doing so, will have a *cathartic* effect on all affected parties. Truth-telling *in itself* serves to heal wounds and to make living together with the other party possible in the future. However, different individuals will respond in different ways. For some of those victimized by ethnic cleansing, the opportunity of candid 'truth-telling' on both sides will be a sufficient means of coming to terms with a traumatic past as it really took place; for some, perhaps a larger portion of the perpetrators, it may have the same effect. But it would be misleading to imply that both sides will be equally content with 'truth-telling'. The nature of the subject of truth-telling is simply too diverse: it is not a case of trauma against trauma, but trauma against pride, perceived unjustified suffering against perceived justified aggression in the name of self-defence (to allude to the impact of ideology). Asked what would be the effect of their actions on the rapists involved in mass-scale rapes, Muradif Kulenović, a professor of psychiatry, replies: 'you mean whether they will have psychological problems in returning to normal family life as good husbands, best fathers, gentle sons! Forget it. They will not have psychological problems'.

If Kulenović is right, it is difficult to see what could possibly be a common ground on which victims and perpetrators might meet in order that the repentence of the latter could be met by the forgiveness of the former, in order to stick to the formula of reconciliation introduced above. What gives the act of rape a special twist in the context of ethnic cleansing, is the fact that it is a particularly direct and visible way of showing that 'your ethnicity is your destiny', in addition to being a particularly cruel way of humiliating the male members (fathers, sons, brothers) of the (Muslim) enemy group insofar as they are forced to witness the utmost degradation of their women's purity with no possibility of protecting them.[28] In this sense, raping a woman here is as much an assault on the dignity and worth of (their) men as on that of the women being raped.

I have dwelled upon the case of rape because I see it as depicting the crime of ethnic cleansing in a nutshell. For one thing, the raped women of Bosnia and Kosovo are not likely to wish to return to the place of their life's worst trauma (cf. above). That is to say, rape is an integral part of the goal of removing people – for good – from their homeland. The other important feature is that rape takes place between distinct individuals; accordingly, the question whether and how reconciliation will be possible allows no universally valid answer, but will depend on the particular individuals involved.

I have not forgotten my earlier remarks to the effect that the rapist perceives his victims in a deindividuated and indifferent manner, so that in the end the victims come to form a grey mass, as it were. For many victims, it will be otherwise. Reading interviews with raped women in Bosnia, one is struck by the frequency with which the women are able to name the men who raped them, often adding that they knew each other from school, and so on.[29] This goes to show that, to the extent that anonymization of the other takes place here, it does so much more commonly among abusers than victims; and even here, anonymization – 'not remembering' or 'not knowing' who one's victims were – is largely a psychological matter, taking place *post festum* so as to take the sting out of having to live with one's victims as so many *faces*, so many unique persons.

Focusing on the case of rape – again, a crucial and by no means contingent feature of ethnic cleansing[30] – puts the prospects of reconciliation in former Yugoslavia in sharp relief, at least when contrasted with the processes well underway in Chile and South Africa. So much stands in the way, not legally, but morally and especially psychologically, of reconciliation here assuming the form of a successful (if always troubled) two-way affair, one exhibiting readiness to reconciliation as a desire shared by both affected parties. Against Ignatieff's relatively optimistic view, one could well argue that the willingness of both parties to agree on the principle of impunity does not by itself resolve the issue – and task – of reconciliation, not to mention the even deeper one of justice.

What I have in mind is the question whether *everybody* – in the greatest sense humanity itself, meaning/implying you and me – can or should accept the belligerent parties' agreement about impunity as the last word. Third parties – outsiders, bystanders of all sorts – could object to the arrangement that justice be done by way of removing punishment of the sinners. I mention this – the question of whether humanity ought to be willing to stomach or, obversely, *ought to be outraged by* (to allude to Grotius) – because I think that, principally if not always practically, third parties (significantly forming a plural, thus allowing for disagreement) *do* have a valid say as to which crimes permit impunity and which do not – regardless of the attitude taken by the affected parties themselves, resting as it does on the idea that justice in a principled way, as opposed to reconciliation in a pragmatic sense, is a matter for third parties also.

David Rohde[31] puts the point well: 'If no accurate history emerges, Srebrenica is doomed to join the myriad of real and imagined atrocities that nationalist leaders can play on in five or fifty years to incite the next round of bloodletting. A young Ratko Mladic may have been born during the fall of Srebrenica. This time, a Muslim will be brought up on tales of atrocities committed against his people'. The events in Kosovo in 1998–9 bring this out with unwanted clarity and cruelty. Having 'lost' parts of what promised to form the territorial borders of 'Greater Serbia' as defined and conquered by the campaign of ethnic cleansing against Bosnian Muslims and Croats between 1992 and 1995, Milošević cast his eyes on Kosovo, citing the endangered position of the Serb minority as a pretext for letting loose another round of ethnic cleansing dressed in ethno-nationalist ideology. My point is that Racak could well become to Albanian Kosovars what Srebrenica may become to future generations of Bosnian Muslims, provided that the real Ratko Mladic and his associates are not brought to trial and held responsible for their actions. In a sense, another Racak, by way of the implied (and notorious) role-reversal, has already happened. I am referring to the fact that most of the Serb minority in Kosovo has been forced to leave their homeland: by intimidation, by murder, by enforced expulsion, and by means of the methods characteristic of ethnic cleansing, only this time with the roles reversed, as was all too evident from the 2004 March riots.

The much-debated military intervention into the conflict by a third party (that is, NATO) has not succeeded in its proclaimed aim of *preventing* developments amounting to the creation of ethnic homogeneity in Kosovo; instead, NATO's intervention can now be seen to have helped *precipitate* this very trend. Setting aside the upbeat ethical rhetoric of a Clinton and a Blair accompanying the newsreels from Yugoslavian cities hit by 'humanitarian' NATO bombs, the question that continues to haunt us even today, in hindsight, is whether *ordinary people* living in Kosovo – irrespective of ethnicity – would have been better off had NATO not intervened the way they did. For what it's worth, I for one still think that more reasons counted (and count) in favour of the intervention than against it.

There are still other tasks that only members or institutions of third-party status can accomplish for reconciliation and justice to take place – or *fail* to accomplish, thus jeopardizing the latter. I must restrict myself to mentioning a single illustration. In December 1999, UN Secretary-General Kofi Annan delivered his *Srebrenica Report* to the General Assembly. The report makes for remarkable reading. The amount and depth of self-criticism on behalf of the UN (and by implication the leading powers in the world) is exceptional. What we read here are the words of the head of a seminal third party to the Yugoslav tragedy. These are words of repentance, demonstrating that repentance is not the prerogative of the perpetrator (although of course never a substitute for the latter). Particularly striking is the fact that the tenor of the report is moral, not legal or *realpolitisch*. Annan takes the organization he heads to task for having subscribed to a philosophy and a practice of *moral equalization*, meaning that the parties to the conflict were seen as equally responsible for and implicated in acts of aggression amounting to genocide. Annan admits that errors of judgment were made – 'errors rooted in a philosophy of impartiality and non-violence wholly unsuited to the conflict in Bosnia'.[32]

I know that many will not be impressed. While one can say that Milošević subjected Kosovo to a new round of ethnic cleansing as his way of seeking revenge for territorial conquests lost to Bosnian Croats and Muslims and sealed by the Dayton agreement, and further that Montenegro is likely, nay bound to be, Milošević's future target to revenge a Kosovo about to be emptied of Serbs by way of ethnic cleansing in reversal, one may also say that Rambouillet was a fake conducted in bad faith and that the use of force over Kosovo was Western powers' (especially Madeleine Albright's) preconceived act of revenge against Milošević for the horror his regime wrought in Bosnia, springing in no small measure from bad conscience on the part of the United States in particular over the passivity so long held on to in the face of the destruction of Yugoslavia. In other words, the 'humanitarian' and 'moral' motives cited by Western leaders may hide an underlying logic of revenge not much ethically superior to that of their current chief adversary.

I am not so naive as to deny the plausibility of such a version. But I don't see it as being the whole picture. A report such as the one submitted by Kofi Annan gives us – critical commentators to events, most of us enjoying the safety of armchair-style criticizing – a chance to take a chief agent at his word, and to judge his actions immanently. *We* must see to it that the language and standards of morality do not become the privileged (play)ground of powers that be, pursuing in actual fact aims of a blatantly *immoral* nature.

That said, the important thing is that as long as atrocities are taking place, third parties are obliged to signal to perpetrator and victim alike that what is unfolding is being seen, is being recorded so as to form the basis for ensuing attempts at achieving justice: namely, doing justice to the nature of the crime, while knowing full well that some crimes explode our capacities of comprehension, of forgiveness, and perhaps even of repentance. However, in real life, it is often not enough to signal that what happens has witnesses besides the parties themselves: witnessing needs to cease to be an act of on-looking, of taking note, and become instead a task of intervening so as to stop what happens from happening.

Notes

1 This is also evident from the definition of the crime of genocide offered in the *Convention on the Prevention and Punishment of the Crime of Genocide*, 1948, although the combined effect of the crimes listed in the definition in Article II amount to a protection of the group as such: '(a) Killing members of the group; (b) Causing serious bodily or mental harm to members of the group; (c) Deliberately inflicting on the group conditions of life calculated to bring about its physical destruction in whole or in part; (d) Imposing measures intended to prevent births within the group; (e) Forcibly transferring children of the group to another group'. Reprinted in Ian Brownlie, *Basic Documents on Human Rights* (Oxford: Clarendon Press, 1992), pp. 31–4.

2 Philip Cohen, *Serbia's Secret War* (College Station: Texas A&M University Press, 1996), pp. 4, 19, 44ff.

3 Borivoj Covic (ed.), *Roots of Serbian Aggression* (Zagreb: AGM, 1993), p. 324.

4 Ibid., p. 326: 'the fate of Kosovo remains a matter of life and death for the Serbian people'.

5 Ibid., p. 335.

6 Thomas Cushman, 'The Reflexivity of Evil', pp. 79–100 in Jennifer L. Geddes (ed.), *Evil after Postmodernism* (London: Routledge, 2000), pp. 87ff.

7 David Campbell, *National Deconstruction. Violence, Identity, and Justice in Bosnia* (Minneapolis: University of Minnesota Press, 1998), p. 108.

8 Quoted in Aspen Institute, *Unfinished Peace* (Washington: Brooking Institute Press, 1996), p. 16.

9 See *The Observer*, 'Milošcvić and Operation Horseshoe', 18 July 1999.

10 Beverly Allen, *Rape Warfare* (Minneapolis: University of Minnesota Press, 1996), pp. 56ff.

11 See Brownlie (n. 1 above).

12 Samantha Power, '*A Problem from Hell'. America and the Age of Genocide* (New York: Basic Books, 2002), pp. 485ff.

13 The Commission on Kosovo, *The Kosovo Report* (Oxford: Oxford University Press, 2000), pp. 307ff (Annex 1: Documentation of Human Rights Violations).

14 Ibid.

15 See the discussion of war crimes, crimes against humanity and genocide in Naomi Roht-Arriaza, 'Institutions of International Justice', *Journal of International Affairs*, 52, 2 (Spring 1999), pp. 473–91, esp. pp. 481–3.

16 Michael Ignatieff, *The Warrior's Honor. Ethnic War and Modern Conscience* (London: Vintage, 1999), p. 175.

17 Ibid.

18 Norman Cigar, *Genocide in Bosnia* (College Station: Texas A&M University Press, 1996); Michael A. Sells, *The Bridge Betrayed. Religion and Genocide in Bosnia*

(Berkeley: University of California Press, 1996); David Rieff, *Slaughterhouse. Bosnia and the Failure of the West* (London: Vintage, 1995); Laura Silber and Alan Little, *The Death of Yugoslavia* (Harmondsworth: Penguin, 1995); Thomas Cushman and Stjepan G. Mestrovic (eds), *This Time We Knew. Western Responses to Genocide in Bosnia* (New York: New York University Press, 1996); Branimir Anzulovic, *Heavenly Serbia. From Myth to Genocide* (London: Hurst, 1999); Allen (note 10 above); Peter Maass, *Love Thy Neighbor. A Story of War* (New York: Random House); Keith Doubt, *Sociology after Bosnia and Kosovo* (Lanham MA: Rowman & Littlefield, 2000).

19 Ignatieff (n. 16 above), p. 178.

20 Ibid.

21 Alexandra Stiglmayer, 'The Rapes in Bosnia-Herzegovina', pp. 82–169 in Alexandra Stiglmayer (ed.), *Mass Rape. The War against Women in Bosnia-Hercegovina* (Lincoln: University of Nebraska Press, 1992).

22 Adorno, quoted in Espen Hammer, 'Adorno and Extreme Evil', *Philosophy and Social Criticism*, 26, 4 (2000), pp. 75–93.

23 See Bård-Anders Andreassen and Elin Skaar (eds), *Forsoning eller rettferdighet?* (Oslo: Cappelen Akademisk Forlag, 1998), p. 23.

24 Power (n. 12 above), p. 465.

25 Mark J. Osiel, *Mass Atrocity, Collective Memory, and the Law* (New Brunswick NJ: Transaction Publishers, 2000), pp. 128ff.

26 Ignatieff (n. 16 above), p. 187.

27 Ibid.

28 See Slavenka Drakulic, *As If I Am Not There* (London: Abacus, 1999).

29 See Seada Vranic, *Breaking the Wall of Silence. The Voices of Raped Bosnia* (Zagreb: Aktant, 1996).

30 Allen (n. 10 above).

31 David Rohde, *Endgame. The Betrayal and Fall of Srebrenica* (New York: Farrar, Straus and Giroux, 1997).

32 Kofi Annan, *Srebrenica Report* (New York: United Nations, 1999), pp. 88, 89.

4 The Kosovo experiment

Peacebuilding through an international trusteeship

Lene Mosegaard Søbjerg

The establishment of an experiment

With the adoption of Security Council resolution 1244 on 10 June 1999, the United Nations took over full administration of Kosovo and the territory became a trusteeship[1] in everything but name.[2] For the first time in recent history, the UN undertook the role of administering an entire territory[3] and the challenges presenting themselves to international society[4] in Kosovo are quite different from previous UN experience. There is thus little prior expertise to assist the UN in its dealings with the administration of Kosovo and the operation is in certain respects an outright experiment. The question is why this type of operation was chosen and whether the operation has been able to achieve the goals set out in resolution 1244.

The conflict in Kosovo did not receive much international attention during the 1990s despite Serbian repressive conduct against the Kosovar–Albanian population. Conflicts in other parts of the former republic of Yugoslavia, especially in Bosnia-Herzegovina and Croatia, occupied international society and the less violent conflict between the ethnic groups of Kosovo was more or less ignored. However, as the other conflicts in the rest of the former Yugoslavia came to an end and the oppression in Kosovo escalated to atrocities and forced expulsion of Albanian populations, international society could no longer watch in silence. Unable to obtain a UN mandate, NATO initiated an attack against Serbia in March 1999. As the air strikes approached the closing stages, it was evident that there was a pressing need to reconstruct Kosovo as a democratic and multi-ethnic community in order to avoid future relapses into war and ethnic cleansing. The need to prevent future conflicts was obvious, but the question was how to ensure the democratic development envisaged and desired by international society. The solution adopted by the Security Council was the establishment of a trusteeship. It is consequently relevant to examine whether this type of operation has been able to achieve the goals desired by international society.

The analysis presented in this chapter suggests that the trusteeship operation has had positive effects on the humanitarian and democratic stability in Kosovo, although certain aspects of the current operation are indeed the causes of continued conflict in the territory. Following this conclusion, it is interesting to consider how the experiment in Kosovo has affected the trusteeship institution as such. It is argued that despite the encouraging results of the Kosovo experiment, a genuine revival of the trusteeship institution does not appear to be immediately forthcoming.

The chapter opens with a presentation of the UN's past experiences with trusteeships in order to clarify the dilemmas and problems connected with this type of operation. At this point, I will draw on the ideas of the English School in order to connect the history of trusteeships and international intervention to relevant theoretical considerations. This leads to a presentation of the possibilities available to international society and the UN vis-à-vis Serbia back in May–June 1999, followed by a detailed analysis of the discussion leading to the Security Council's adoption of resolution 1244 on 10 June 1999. The implementation of the resolution will then be explored, leading to an evaluation of the ongoing experiment in Kosovo and the future prospects for the trusteeship institution.

Historical and theoretical perspectives on trusteeships

The notion of 'trusteeship' represents the idea that advanced states or territories undertake the responsibility of administering less advanced or weak territories. During the colonial era, a normative doctrine indicated that colonial powers had a duty to administer their colonies with due respect for the people in question,[5] but no formal institution supervised the devotion to this doctrine. With the establishment of the League of Nations, the concept of trusteeships was institutionalized in a Mandates System in which weak territories were placed under the authority of a mandatory power, usually equivalent to the former colonial master. With the founding of the United Nations, the Mandates System was succeeded by a Trusteeship System where weak and dependent territories (typically former colonies) were placed under the trust of an advanced state until they were believed to be able to manage their own administration. The trust state was in turn under the supervision by the UN Trusteeship Council in order to ensure that the administration of the trusteeship was conducted properly.[6] Eleven territories were placed under the Trusteeship System, which functioned according to the instructions laid out in the UN Charter until 1960. Although the Charter does permit the UN to be the sole administrator of a trusteeship under the Trusteeship Council, none of the eleven trusteeships were administered directly by the UN.[7]

As a growing number of former colonies gained independence and became members of the UN, the attitude towards trusteeships changed and with the adoption in 1960 of the *Declaration on the Granting of Independence to Colonial Countries and Peoples* (Declaration 1514) by the UN General Assembly the legitimacy of the Trusteeship System was undermined. Declaration 1514 stated that all peoples had the right to self-determination and the idea that former colonies and dependent territories needed to achieve a certain degree of development in order to be accepted as independent states was thus abandoned. Advanced states thereby lost the privilege of determining which territories were to become independent and which were to be placed under the Trusteeship System. All former colonies obtained the right to independence and no territories have been placed under the Trusteeship System since 1960.[8]

From 1960, the UN's activities in connection to less developed and conflict-torn territories and states have been confined to peacekeeping operations and distribution of development aid.[9] Peacekeeping can be defined as 'the stationing of UN military personnel, with the consent of the warring parties, to monitor cease-fires and dissuade violations through interposition between competing armies'.[10] The role of the UN has been to intervene between aggressive parties and support peace processes. A local government has always been in place and the UN has worked with this government in the process of establishing peace. The peacekeeping operations have ended when law and order have been restored, as the right to self-determination presumes that all territories are able to develop and sustain stable institutions by themselves. Peacekeeping is in other words not to be associated with any idea or practice of external governance of dependent territories.

Theoretically, this change in the attitude towards trusteeships can be explained with reference to the modern conception of international society developed by the English School. Within this conception, international society is understood as a society of independent states with equal right to sovereignty and non-intervention.[11] This international society sanctions the existence of a plurality of states with different levels of development and governmental style (giving the name 'pluralists' to theorists of this notion).[12] Since the concept of trusteeships involves a distinction between which states or territories are capable of administering themselves, and which are not, the concept of trusteeships is fundamentally at odds with this understanding of international society as a society of equals.[13] The attitudinal change expressed with the adoption of Declaration 1514 on the granting of independence to colonial countries and peoples can thus be explained as recognition of sovereignty, pluralism and the rights of states as the most important features of international relations.

Contemporary international society can, however, be viewed from a slightly different perspective too. Although states are rightfully the primary actors of international society, individuals and peoples have rights as well. Respect for human rights and the welfare of individuals are equally important in international society and the sovereignty of states is not unconditional. Violations of individual rights are in opposition to the interest of international society just as violations of sovereignty are.[14] Solidarity with individuals plays a vital role in international society and since a temporary transfer of administration of a territory to an outside party can enhance the well-being of individuals, trusteeships can be seen as a valuable instrument in international society. An outright encouragement of the use of trusteeships is not inherent in this solidaristic perspective, since sovereignty and respect for the general order of international society is recognized as being important but the practice is acknowledged as a useful tool in the development of individual rights.[15] The more pluralist theorists see trusteeships as generally illegal[16] although an opening is given in cases where no other possibilities for restoring peace and justice are available.[17]

The focus on individuals and human rights has increased since the end of the Cold War. Traditional peacekeeping operations have been expanded to include the development of democratic and stable institutions. Peacemaking, peace enforcement and peacebuilding are new conceptions, which have been incorporated into the language of the UN.[18] The concept of peacebuilding is especially interesting here, since peacebuilding operates in the space between traditional peacekeeping and trusteeships. Peacebuilding can be defined as 'efforts to identify and support structures which will tend to consolidate peace and advance a sense of confidence and well-being among people.'[19] This signifies an increasing role for the UN in a territory, although a significant element separates peacebuilding from trusteeships.

Both within international law and international relations theory, there is continually a significant difference between peacekeeping and peacebuilding on the one hand and trusteeships on the other in terms of the amount of responsibility and authority placed with the UN. In a peacekeeping operation, the UN works *with* the existing government in a territory or state, while the role of the UN in a trusteeship is *to be* the government. This latter type of operation has been outlawed since 1960, and although a change has occurred and the UN has assumed an increasing number of responsibilities since the end of the Cold War, a complete legalization of the right to intervene in the affairs of other states does not exist. The sentiments promoting state pluralism as were expressed in Declaration 1514 in 1960 have been challenged but since sovereignty and the rights of states are still principal elements of international society, it is relevant to look at the reasons behind the UN Security Council's decision to revive this otherwise abandoned practice with the *de facto* trusteeship in Kosovo.

The possibilities for international society in June 1999

During the 11-week campaign against Serbia, the important issue of the future of Kosovo was not discussed within the primary organ of international intervention, the UN.[20] The legitimacy of the bombing was placed on the Security Council's agenda by Russia, which presented a resolution condemning the attack. This resolution was rejected by the vote by 12–3, which indirectly legitimated NATO's manoeuvre.[21] The question of what was to happen after the bombing was, however, not discussed in the Security Council. In academic and diplomatic circles, the question was less controversial and a noteworthy debate on the possible outcomes of the conflict took place. Different possibilities were presented and discussed, involving different levels of international involvement. The final status of Kosovo was an important issue, but the most urgent question was how to implement and uphold peace in the territory.

Two primary possibilities were discussed regarding the immediate implementation of a peace agreement. One model was synonymous with the Rambouillet Accords.[22] These Accords had been accepted by all parties to the conflict except Serbia and although the actual Accords were no longer an option, the model inherent in them was a possible outcome of the situation. This model, which can be characterized as a 'helping hand',[23] assigned the role of assistant to international society in the rebuilding of Kosovo. The model presumed the presence of an existing government and the executive power over Kosovo was to be divided between the existing local authorities and an appointed Chief of the Implementation Mission (CIM). This model was strikingly similar to the peacekeeping operations traditionally operated by the UN and it thereby had the advantage of building on a well-established institution for post-conflict peacekeeping. In spite of these apparent advantages, the Rambouillet Accord was not generally accepted.

The International Crisis Group (ICG) argued against Rambouillet by pointing to the operation in Bosnia-Herzegovina where the 'helping hand' operation was considered problematic since a lack of power vested in international society and the CIM had produced difficulties in the creation of democratic institutions. As an alternative, they encouraged the establishment of a trusteeship in which the international administrator had the overall executive power of the territory.[24] The establishment of a trusteeship had been proposed as early as 1993[25] and a trusteeship solution was supported by diplomatic notabilities such as the EU's former negotiator in Yugoslavia, Lord David Owen[26] and British Defence Minister George Robertson.[27] However, the trusteeship solution had opponents too, notably Carl Bildt, former Swedish prime minister and the UN's first High Representative in Bosnia 1995–97, who considered a trusteeship in Kosovo a short-sighted solution to the problems facing the Balkans.[28]

Recalling Declaration 1514 from 1960 and Yugoslavia's right to sovereignty, it is furthermore evident that the establishment of a trusteeship in Kosovo was at odds with existing international law. Current international society is based on the equal rights of sovereign states and since the creation of a trusteeship in Kosovo would disregard the rights of Yugoslavia, this solution to the situation in Kosovo was highly controversial. A return to the use of trusteeships might jeopardize the existing order of international society in which non-intervention is a cornerstone[29] and in spite of the support from academic as well as diplomatic circles, the model was disputed. Given the controversial nature of the trusteeship solution, it is worth taking a closer look at the debate leading to the adoption of resolution 1244 in order to determine the underlying arguments behind the decision to establish a *de facto* trusteeship in Kosovo.

The Security Council meeting of 10 June 1999

Intense diplomatic negotiations took place during the last weeks of the air campaign against Serbia in an effort to persuade the Serb president Milosevic to accept a peace plan. The negotiations paid off on 1 June 1999 as Milosevic agreed to the Athisaari–Chernomyrdin plan, which demanded immediate cessation of repression and violence in Kosovo, withdrawal of Yugoslav armed forces, acceptance of an international civil and military presence and the right of return to all refugees.[30] As the Serbian parliament adopted the plan on 3 June 1999 the road was paved for the UN to begin the process of implementing the peace plan. On the agenda of the Security Council meeting on 10 June 1999 was a draft resolution outlining an international presence in Kosovo equivalent to a trusteeship.[31]

The meeting was initiated with a statement by the Yugoslav representative, who reaffirmed the Yugoslav consent to the Athisaari–Chernomyrdin plan and emphasized that all demands in the plan had been accepted by his government.[32] They recognized that a lasting peace in the Balkans was not possible without the involvement of the UN and it was stressed that Yugoslavia was willing to accept the deployment of a UN peacekeeping mission in Kosovo. However, Yugoslavia was not prepared to accept a disregard of its sovereignty and independence and it was explicitly stated that 'the Federal Republic of Yugoslavia cannot accept a mission that would take over the role of government in Kosovo … or any other form of open or hidden protectorate'.[33] The existing draft resolution, which involved a *de facto* trusteeship in Kosovo, would, if adopted contrary to the will of Yugoslavia, be '*one of the darkest pages*' of the history of the Security Council.[34] Not only would the UN disregard the sovereign rights of a member state, it would create a precedent for future unauthorized interventions and legitimate violent rebellion by secessionist groups in weak states around the globe. So, despite Yugoslavia's consent to the principles of the Athisaari–Chernomyrdin plan, the draft resolution was therefore not acceptable to Yugoslavia.[35]

Yugoslavia's emphasis on sovereignty and the right to non-intervention did not generate the desired support from the remaining delegates at the meeting. Human rights and the establishment of a lasting peace were the primary concerns of the Security Council. Several countries stressed the resolution's promise to respect the sovereignty of Yugoslavia, but emphasis was predominantly on peace and the need to restore respect for individuals and human rights in Kosovo. Slovenia explicitly declared that sovereignty was not an acceptable argument for neglecting basic human rights.[36] The Norwegian delegation was closely linked to the recommendations from ICG in stating that the UN should learn from the experiences in Bosnia and go all the way in establishing a significant international presence with comprehensive powers in Kosovo.[37] The majority of states argued in a similar manner and concern for the well-being of the population of Kosovo and a wish to do justice to the oppressed Kosovar–Albanians were the main arguments presented at the meeting.

The only voices supporting Yugoslavia's petition to respect sovereignty came from Cuba and China, who both confirmed the emphasis on sovereignty and rejected the implicit acceptance of the right to intervene in the internal affairs of states. As Cuba had no seat in the Security Council, its objections were inconsequential. China, in contrast, had the possibility of rejecting the resolution. However, due to the Yugoslavian acceptance of the underlying peace plan and an acknowledgement that the joint adoption of the draft resolution would re-establish the unity of the Council, the Chinese delegation abstained from voting.[38] resolution 1244 was subsequently adopted with 14 votes in favour and none against.[39]

The arguments presented prior to the adoption of the resolution show that humanitarian considerations were the primary issues for the Council members.

Concern for the rights of the Kosovar–Albanian people had priority over the sovereignty of Yugoslavia, which indicates that solidaristic values played a significant role in the Council's decision. Although, in its initiating speech, Yugoslavia pointed to the importance of upholding the sovereignty of the state and requested the Council not to sanction the establishment of a trusteeship, the Council members spoke in favour of human rights, peace, and stability in sympathy with the Kosovar–Albanian population. With this line of reasoning the decision to disregard the Yugoslav plea to respect its sovereignty can appropriately be understood as a concern for the population and a fear that entrusting authority of the territory to the Serbs could jeopardize the development of a lasting peace in Kosovo. The majority of the Council decided to opt for a controversial trusteeship solution in order to fulfil the ambitions of advancing humanitarian and peacebuilding objectives in Kosovo. Concern for the individuals in Kosovo was certainly the primary reason for adopting resolution 1244.

However, the value of consent should not be underestimated. The entire Security Council supported the resolution, which was of significant importance. China's decision not to veto the resolution despite the fact that the trusteeship solution was in contrast to China's principles can be seen as a desire to reconstruct the unity of the Security Council. The lack of a UN mandate behind NATO's attack on Serbia and the conflict between the members of the Security Council regarding Kosovo had threatened to destabilize the existing order of international society.[40] The Chinese decision not to block the resolution can consequently be understood as an attempt to restore order in the UN Security Council.

Since China is not a member of the NATO alliance, a veto against the draft resolution, which was supported by all other members for the Council, could additionally have had fatal consequences for China's possibilities of influencing the future outcome of the matter. NATO's decision to attack Serbia without a UN mandate was unlikely to be the only unauthorized action the alliance would engage in. NATO had made it perfectly clear that the Serbian mistreatment of the Kosovar–Albanians was not acceptable and restoring the administration of Kosovo to Serbia was thus an unlikely option after the failure at Rambouillet. Had China or Russia vetoed the draft resolution, they might have forced NATO to engage even further in the Kosovo conflict and compelled the organization to establish a NATO trusteeship in Kosovo. This would have excluded both China and Russia from having any say on matters concerning Kosovo in the future, which would have been an unacceptable outcome to these non-NATO states. The establishment of a UN trusteeship returned the question of Kosovo to the UN Security Council, which meant that China and Russia once again had a voice regarding future decisions on Kosovo. Supporting a UN trusteeship in Kosovo might thus have appeared to be the only option since the consequences of vetoing the trusteeship resolution were worse than accepting the disregard of the principle of sovereignty incorporated in the trusteeship.

The establishment of a trusteeship was thus made possible due to several factors. Human rights and concern for individuals were important issues in international relations at the end of the 1990s, which made the majority of the

Council members favourable towards an experimental trusteeship. Moreover, the alternatives to a UN trusteeship were unacceptable to those influential states, China and Russia, which traditionally value order and the rights of states over the rights of individuals. The experiment of Kosovo was established by a combination of benevolent wishes for the future of Kosovo and an assessment that a UN trusteeship was the better of two bad options. Altogether, the adoption of the resolution implies that international society had a genuine concern for the security and well-being of the Kosovar–Albanian population. The act of the Security Council was primarily based on humanitarian and peacebuilding intentions but considerations of international order and sovereignty played their part in the decision as well.

Resolution 1244

The humanitarian sentiments expressed at the Security Council meeting were put into practice by a two-sided operation containing a civil and a military mission. Resolution 1244 determines that the situation in the region continues to pose a threat to international peace and security. These 'magic' words allow international society to act under Chapter VII of the UN Charter and intervene in the domestic affairs of states, which is the foundation of the UN military presence in Kosovo (KFOR). The principal responsibilities of the military presence involve preventing renewed hostility, demilitarizing the KLA, establishing a secure environment and providing public safety, and ensuring free movement for everyone in Kosovo. These tasks are equivalent to traditional peacekeeping responsibilities as they were defined earlier. The definition of peacekeeping as the monitoring of ceasefires and prevention of renewed violence corresponds with the tasks assigned to the military presence since it is possible to perform these tasks in cooperation with a local administration in Kosovo. As the Yugoslavian government had previously given its consent to a presence of this kind, the first part of the resolution resembles the authorization of an international peacekeeping operation. However, in addition to this traditional military presence the UN decided to:

> establish an international civil presence in Kosovo in order to provide an interim administration for Kosovo under which the people of Kosovo can enjoy substantial autonomy within the Federal Republic of Yugoslavia, and which will provide transitional administration while establishing and overseeing the development of provisional democratic self-governing institutions to ensure conditions for a peaceful and normal life for all inhabitants of Kosovo.[41]

The operation was entitled the United Nations Mission in Kosovo (UNMIK) and the primary responsibilities entrusted to this civil presence were determined to be: promoting the establishment of substantial autonomy and self-government in Kosovo; carrying out basic civilian administration; organizing the establishment of democratic institutions; supporting the reconstruction of infrastructure; supporting provision of humanitarian aid; maintaining law and order; protecting and promoting human rights; and finally assuring the safe return of refugees.

The tasks entrusted to UNMIK incorporate a much wider range of responsibilities than a traditional peacekeeping operation. Supporting the distribution of humanitarian aid and the reconstruction of infrastructure, protecting human rights and maintaining law and order could be identified as borderline tasks, which an extensive peacekeeping mission might cover. Performing civil administration, developing democratic institutions and assuring the return of refugees are however not functions which can rightfully be classified within a peacekeeping operation. These functions require a mandate that goes far beyond working together with an existing government. The operation holds the power to execute full authority over all aspects of civil administration in order for the administration to be efficient and to ensure that the mandated establishment of democratic institutions takes place. In basic terms, the UN civil presence becomes the government of Kosovo. With these wide-ranging and far-reaching responsibilities, the operation in Kosovo is truly a trusteeship in everything but name.

As can be observed from the quote above, the words ‘trusteeship’ or ‘protectorate’ do not appear in the resolution. The omission of these words indicates the controversy behind the establishment of this kind of operation. For one thing, Yugoslavia had clearly stated that it would oppose the establishment of an operation resembling any kind of international trusteeship. Furthermore, since Declaration 1514 of 1960 banned the use of trusteeships as an instrument in the relations between independent states, the term ‘trusteeship’ is highly disputed. The word has bad connotations to most third world countries that oppose the idea of some states being placed under foreign administration – however benevolent the administration might be. Leaving out the word trusteeship is unquestionably a conscious attempt to avoid the situation in Kosovo drowning in a controversy over the use of a word of redundant practice. Another more practical argument for not using the word trusteeship is that the Trusteeship Council of the UN is currently not operative and the supreme authority in Kosovo was not to be the Trusteeship Council as was the practice with the previous type of trusteeships, but the Security Council.

The elements that constitute the *de facto* trusteeship in Kosovo are incorporated in the civil presence. Due to the uncertain security situation in Kosovo, a civil mission would not be able to work effectively without a military presence and the military mission is thus an important aspect of the total trusteeship operation. Without KFOR as the stabilizing force, UNMIK would not have been able to commence operations and the military presence continues to play a vital role since the maintenance of law and order is essential for UNMIK to perform its duties. The civil mission is nevertheless the more experimental and controversial part of the mission and will be the focus of further examination.

UNMIK

Administering an entire territory as is the task of UNMIK in Kosovo is a giant assignment. To facilitate the implementation of the mandate, the operation was divided into four pillars each managed by a different organisation. The four pillars and their organisations are: Civil administration: UNMIK (UN), Humanitarian assistance: UNHCR[42] (UN), Institution-building: OSCE, Economic reconstruction: EU.[43]

A major concern to the UN was to ensure that the tasks performed by the different organisations would be conducted in an integrated manner with a clear chain of command. Accordingly, a Special Representative of the Secretary General (SRSG) with overall authority was appointed as head of mission. To assist the SRSG four Deputy Special Representatives (DSR) were appointed. Each DSR was assigned the responsibility of one pillar and together the five Special Representatives formed the Executive Committee of UNMIK, which ultimately was inaugurated as the government of Kosovo.

The overall strategy of resolution 1244 involved five phases. During the first phase, an interim civil administration controlled by UNMIK was to be established. The interim administration was to be strengthened and a gradual transfer to the population of Kosovo was to begin during the second phase, while preparations for election were initiated. The holding of elections were to constitute the third phase, leading to the establishment of provisional administrative institutions in the fourth. In the fifth phase, when the future of Kosovo had been finally resolved, the provisional institutions and the overall administration of Kosovo were to be transferred to a permanent civil administration directed and controlled by the local population.[44]

The day-to-day work of UNMIK takes place within the four organisations that have full authority to pursue the goals assigned to their pillar. Different management structures and varying policy priorities within the organisations' headquarters have created complications in the implementation. One problem has arisen due to a division between the priorities between long- and short-term policies. The interaction and dependence on developments within different pillars has made it difficult to count on the outcome of a particular policy for the authorizing pillar. One example is a controversy between the UN and the EU on whether short or long-term instruments should be used to establish essential public services.[45] Competition and lack of cooperation between the pillars on the operational level has furthermore created a great deal of conflict.

Conversely, the complex structure gives a large degree of flexibility to the operation. The differences existing between the policies implemented make it possible to pursue various objectives at the same time. After initial uncertainty regarding the division of competences, cooperation between the four DSRs and other senior heads of the four pillars has assured a greater knowledge and understanding of the tasks performed by the various organisations in the operation leading to a smoother implementation of policies.[46]

The fourth phase of UNMIK

At the time of writing, the operation in Kosovo has been running for more than five years. During the years, the administrative structure of UNMIK has been amended several times. The latest amendment was presented in 2001 and represents a move to the fourth phase of the implementation of resolution 1244, the establishment of provisional administrative institutions. These were defined in the Constitutional Framework for Provisional Self-Government,[47] which is the current legal constitution governing Kosovo.

The Constitutional Framework explicitly states which powers and responsibilities are reserved for the SRSG and which are to be pursued by the Provisional Institutions of Self-Government. These institutions are made up of an Assembly, a President, a Government and Courts. The responsibilities entrusted with the institutions of self-government are primarily concerned with economic and financial policy such as budgetary issues, customs activities and trade. Education, culture, health, environmental protection, and tourism are other issues assigned to the institutions along with a number of issues related to local administration.[48] However, the powers continually vested with the SRSG make it very clear that Kosovo is still a trusteeship. The SRSG has 'full authority to ensure that the rights and interests of Communities are fully protected'.[49] This includes the power to dissolve the Assembly and call for new elections, final authority to decide financial and monetary policies and to appoint judges and prosecutors. The SRSG's power can be illustrated by the adoption of six new laws by the Kosovo Assembly in 2003. One of these laws was considered outside the Assembly's jurisdiction with the result that the SRSG plainly annulled the adoption of that particular law.[50] As can be identified by this division of labour, Kosovo continues to be a trusteeship as the SRSG has powers far beyond the necessary means to support the institutions of self-government.

Challenges to the trusteeship operation

Although the operation in Kosovo has made significant progress in terms of infrastructure, public services and the establishment of local institutions, much still remains to be dealt with. A serious challenge to the operation in Kosovo is keeping the two main ethnic groups apart and establishing a safe environment in which all ethnic groups can live peacefully together. The ferocities occurring during the war are still remembered and reconciliation is happening at a very low speed.[51] Freedom of movement is a privilege for the Kosovar–Albanians only, while Serbs continually need the protection of the international presence. Attacks on Serb minorities continue to cause insecurity and frustration among the minority population as well as among international observers. The seriousness of this hostility became evident in March 2004, when rumours that a group of Serbs had caused the deaths of three Kosovar–Albanian boys in the divided city of Mitrovica instigated fighting between the ethnic groups in several parts of Kosovo. Serb houses and villages and UN depots were damaged or burnt, at least 19 civilians died, hundreds were injured and millions of Euros worth of infrastructure was destroyed.[52] Prior to the March incidents, a significant reduction in cases of murder, burglary and robbery had occurred, signifying that progress was under way. The violence was a serious setback to the entire peacebuilding operation as it jeopardized the establishment of a multi-ethnic Kosovo and it was an obvious demonstration of the continued need for an international presence in Kosovo.

The real question is nevertheless whether the solidaristic and humanitarian considerations behind the operation in Kosovo could have been implemented in an alternative and less problematic manner. In other words, has the trusteeship produced better results than a conventional peacekeeping operation could have done? It is obvious that the discrimination faced by the Kosovar–Albanians has ended as a result of the air campaign and the following establishment of the trusteeship. The ethnic oppression of the Kosovar–Albanians was one of the primary reasons behind the establishment of the trusteeship as expressed at the 1999 Security Council meeting. However, an ethnic cleansing on a smaller scale has occurred in reverse as part of the Serb population in Kosovo has been forced to flee the territory and the remaining Serbs live in enclaves where KFOR and UNMIK are incapable of providing 100 per cent safety for the people. Without an international presence of the size of UNMIK and KFOR in Kosovo it is possible that the brutality against the Serbs would have been worse and more people would have been killed or forced to flee. The presence of KFOR, which is equivalent to a traditional peacekeeping operation, plays an indispensable role in the maintenance of peace in Kosovo and with reference to the March 2004 violence KFOR still has an important role to play in the operation. A military mission alone would, however, have been insufficient in generating the improvements that have taken place in Kosovo.

Despite of the existence of the Rambouillet accords and their acceptance of a re-establishment of Serbian rule in Kosovo, the rejection of the accords by the Serbs and the following escalation into war with NATO meant that a return to Serb rule was not an actual option. The Kosovar Albanians rejected a return to Serb rule and fighting was likely to have restarted had the authority of Kosovo been returned to Belgrade. Establishing a peacekeeping operation in a Kosovar–Albanian dominated province without a civil, administrative component would conversely have made it difficult to engage in long-term peacebuilding. All Kosovar–Albanian authority had been suspended since 1989 and a sole military peacekeeping operation would have worked in a power vacuum. Building a state administration takes time and since peacekeepers would have no authority to interfere in the establishment of the administration, a military presence without a civil component would lack a government to work for.

Furthermore, majority rule (meaning Kosovar–Albanian rule) is likely to have meant reverse oppression, placing the Serbs without influence in the new administration. UNMIK has set up structures to ensure representation of all ethnic groups in local and municipal councils. A proportionate equal representation is believed to force the ethnic groups to cooperate and thus inspire a similar cooperation in the population as a whole. However, difficulties connected to the election of a president of the Assembly show that equal representation is no guarantee of easy implementation of institutions, as cleavages are present even within the same ethnic community. Counterproductive measures taken by the Serb government in Belgrade as well as local resistance from Kosovar–Albanians or Serbs, respectively, has continued to delay the reconciliation process.[53]

Compulsory representation of minorities in the Provisional Institutions is a conscious attempt to avoid the ethnic inequality and force the ethnic groups to work together for a common future. This provision of minority representation is unlikely to have been approved, had the establishment of a constitutional framework been left either to the Yugoslavian government or an independent Kosovo dominated by Kosovar–Albanians. The comprehensive civil component, which is the essence of the trusteeship, is vital to the establishment of both short- and long-term stability. Although there are obstacles to a complete implementation of the equality measures presented in the framework, the existence of a SRSG with authoritative powers remains crucial to the development of impartiality and appeasement in Kosovo.

The establishment of a *de facto* trusteeship has been an effective way of advancing the humanitarian and solidaristic goals expressed by the Security Council. The problems encountered by the trusteeship are different from the problems a peacekeeping operation would have encountered, since a peacekeeping operation would not have had administrative responsibilities and associated administrative and democratic problems. The problems are, however, not dissimilar to the problems facing other regions recovering from civil war and the international presence has facilitated the transition to peace in ways a peacekeeping operation could never have done. A peacekeeping operation would have left the population in Kosovo to its own devices and the ongoing rivalry between the ethnic groups indicates that this would have had fatal consequences to the minority groups in Kosovo. The peacebuilding goals incorporated in resolution 1244 are thus advancing at a reasonably fast speed because of the establishment of a trusteeship operation, although one serious problem still needs to be dealt with.

The unresolved future

The largest obstacle to the consolidation of democratic peace in Kosovo is inherent in the structure of the UN operation: the unresolved end-status of the territory. It is clearly stated in resolution 1244 that Kosovo is a legal part of Yugoslavia[54] and Yugoslavia has no intention of allowing Kosovo to leave the federation.[55] The Kosovar–Albanians nevertheless demand an independent state and are not willing to accept a return to the former status of being an integrated province in Serbia. One of the first statements made by the newly elected president of Kosovo, Ibrahim Rugova, was to demand independence and although this was immediately rejected by UNMIK the demand for independence has been repeated on several occasions.[56] International society is, however, still reluctant to bestow independence on Kosovo and the situation in the territory remains unresolved after more than five years of international trusteeship.[57]

The principle behind the Constitutional Framework is a policy of ‘standards before status’.[58] Unofficially it has been stated for years that Kosovo needs to acquire a certain level of ‘political maturity’ before the question of independence versus integration can be resolved.[59] How and when this level would be achieved was however not estimated and the uncertainty of the situation prolonged essential reconciliatory processes leading to peaceful relations between the ethnic groups. The population of Kosovo lived with anxiety and uncertainty about the future, which was not constructive to the reconciliatory processes in the territory since both ethnic groups still hoped that they would 'win'. The Serbs wanted Kosovo to remain a part of Yugoslavia and the Kosovar–Albanians wanted an independent state, and the ongoing struggle for sovereignty between the groups prevented the development of 'political maturity' and democracy keeping Kosovo in a vicious circle where the political situation remained immature and the future uncertain, with no sign that either aspect would improve.

In December 2003, an official set of 'Standards for Kosovo' were finally presented. The standards involve the development of a 'truly multi-ethnic, stable and democratic Kosovo'[60] which is approaching European standards in economics and democratic aspects. In order to determine the exact actions to be undertaken and when the standards are achieved, a Kosovo Standards Implementation Plan was presented in March 2004. The Implementation Plan outlines eight areas of priority.[61] Within each of these areas the standard to be achieved is listed followed by the exact action to be taken. The responsible actor(s) of each action are stated as well as supportive actors and pillars, and a timeline (or deadline) for the action and standards is also defined. The progress of the overall standards situation will be evaluated in mid-2005 leading to further consideration of when and how Kosovo's final status will be determined.

The official presentation of the Standards and the Implementation Plan represents a big improvement of the situation in Kosovo. It is now observable to all actors where the peacebuilding process is headed and the ethnic groups no longer need to guess what the next move from UNMIK might be. Although the Kosovo Standards Implementation Plan signifies a positive development and shows that Kosovo's final status is coming closer, it must however be stressed that this final status is not yet decided and that the trusteeship is not likely to be terminated in the near future.

The uncertainty of when and how the trusteeship will end, are the exact arguments presented by Robert Jackson in his line of reasoning against trusteeships. Jackson argues that while the decision to establish a trusteeship might seem to be the only way forward in a conflict situation, the decision to terminate the operation is much harder because who is to say when a territory has gained a sufficient level of development to become independent and whose opinion counts the most: the neighbouring states who may have been directly involved in the conflict, or more distant 'strangers' who have no immediate interest in the success or failure of the operation? Furthermore, an expression like 'political maturity' brings back recollections of the former Trusteeship System in which advanced states determined which territories were to be placed under the System, and when these territories were ready for independence.[62] A revival of the use of trusteeships points in the direction of an international society which is not inhabited by equals and among the more pluralistic quarters in academic and diplomatic circles this is believed to be a dangerous road to embark upon.[63]

The UN's initial inability to determine what the required level of 'political maturity' was and to present a reasonable set of guidelines concerning the final status of Kosovo could be understood as an indication of the scepticism against trusteeships being justified. However, the lack of a clearly defined end status and end date has had one clear advantage. As long as there is no specific date stating when the operation will be terminated, the UN is demonstrating that it is in Kosovo for the long-term and it will stay until the tasks it has set out to do have been accomplished. Peacebuilding operations have often been criticized for being concerned with short-term achievements only and for ending too soon, leading to renewed fighting and instability in post-conflict territories.[64] Although the UN's reluctance to present a decision regarding the future status of Kosovo has created frustration and delayed reunification, the message is that the UN is determined to stay for as long as it takes in order to develop a stable democratic Kosovo.

The positive outcomes of the trusteeship achieved so far indicate that a trusteeship with peacebuilding objectives, which is inevitably a long-term commitment, can produce significant results in building peaceful democratic institutions. The intentions of the Security Council were to facilitate the promotion of human rights, democracy, peace and stability in Kosovo. The goals have not yet been fully met, but significant progress has been made. The establishment of UNMIK has made it possible to promote the desired democratic goals of the Security Council and although there are difficulties with the implementation of aspects of resolution 1244, establishing a *de facto* trusteeship appears to have been a wise decision. The uncertainty of the future continues to be a considerable and increasing dilemma, but this cannot justify classification of the experiment as a failure. The results to date are positive and although there is still a long way to go, the ambitions of the UN Security Council are on their way to being fulfilled.

Once in a lifetime?

The trusteeship established in Kosovo in June 1999 can be characterized as an experiment in the sense that the United Nations has never performed this kind of operation before. The extensive powers vested with the UN and its SRSG have placed Kosovo in a position outside the standard order of international society built on the sovereignty of equal states. The primary motive behind the experiment was a desire to help the population of Kosovo obtain lasting peace and security. To date the trusteeship has encountered problems of several kinds but a preliminary evaluation of the experiment suggests that the peacebuilding ambitions behind the establishment of the trusteeship are gradually being accomplished.

A few months after the adoption of resolution 1244, the Security Council established another *de facto* trusteeship in East Timor. This trusteeship was terminated in May 2002 when East Timor gained independence and subsequently became a member of the UN. With these two trusteeships established within a short period and the suggestion of establishing trusteeships in connection to conflicts in Afghanistan, the Middle East and Iraq,[65] a revival of the concept of trusteeships seemed to be a possibility. Yet, none of these territories have come under UN governance (and Iraq has become a military trusteeship instead), and it is still too early to conclude that a genuine revival of the trusteeship institution has occurred.

Taking a comparative look at Afghanistan, the Middle East and Iraq where the security situation is unstable and often outright dangerous to both the general population and the peacekeeping troops stationed there, it is obvious that the trusteeship operation has had positive effects on security and democracy in Kosovo. In spite of major set-backs like the March riots of 2004, the combination of a military presence and peacebuilding institutions has altogether produced a significantly calmer and more stable situation in Kosovo than is currently present in other post-conflict territories. This suggests that a revival of trusteeships including an actual institutionalization of this type of operation could benefit both the people in war-torn territories and the stability and order of international society as a whole.

Notes

1 The concepts 'trusteeship' and 'protectorate' are considered to be different expressions for the same kind of foreign involvement in a territory. Ralph Wilde ('From Danzig to East Timor and Beyond: The Role of International territorial Administration', *The American Journal of International Law*, 95, 3 (2001), pp. 583–606) argues that the two concepts are dissimilar because protectorates are not formally institutionalized (as opposed to trusteeships which are an integrated part of the UN Charter). The operation discussed in this chapter is not based on the Trusteeship System of the UN Charter but since a distinction between the two concepts is unnecessary for the argumentation in this chapter, the term 'trusteeship', which is generally associated with the UN will be used consistently without further discussion.

2 Robert Jackson, *The Global Covenant – Human Conduct in a World of States* (Oxford: Oxford University Press, 2000), p. 306; William Bain, *Between Anarchy and Society. Trusteeship and the obligations of power* (Oxford: Oxford University Press, 2003), p. 154.

3 The UN has performed a variety of operations and has been prepared to assume administrative functions within states in operations such as Congo (1960–64). Despite of the willingness to perform extensive administrative functions, these operations have not been as wide-ranging as the current operation in Kosovo. However, in October 1999, four months after the deployment of UNMIK, another trusteeship was established in East Timor. This operation was terminated in May 2002.

4 International society is often used to represent a group of states who agree to the same norms and values (Hedley Bull, *The Anarchical Society* (New York: Colombia University Press, 1995), p. 13).

5 Edmund Burke, 'Speech on Mr. Fox's East India Bill, 1 December 1783' in *The Works of the Right and Honourable Edmund Burke* (Boston: Little, Brown and Company, 1899), p. 60; Jackson (n. 2 above), p. 301.

6 For further information on the League of Nations' Mandate System or the UN Trusteeship System, see Charmain E. Toussaint, *The Trusteeship System of the United Nations* (Westport: Greenwood Press Publishers, 1975).

7 Ibid., p. 208.

8 The Trusteeship System is still a part of the UN Charter, but with the independence of the last trust territory, Palau in 1994, the UN Trusteeship Council suspended its operations.

9 Since 1960, there has been one exception to this rule in the case of the former Dutch territory of West New Guinea (West Irian), which was administered by the UN for the duration of seven months in 1962–63. This operation, composed of a civil UN component supported by a military UN security presence was considered a peacekeeping operation despite the fact that full authority of the territory was vested with the UN (see Sally Morphet, 'Organizing Civil Administration in Peace-Maintenance', pp. 51–60 in Jarat Chopra, *The Politics of Peace-Maintenance* (Boulder: Lynne Rienner Publishers, 1998), p. 45, and Paul W. van der Veur, 'The United Nations in West Irian: A Critique', *International Organization*, 18, 1 (1964), pp. 53–73.
10 Steven R. Ratner, *The New UN Peacekeeping* (London: Macmillan, 1995), p. 10.
11 Bull (n. 4 above), p. 8.
12 Bull, 'The Grotian Conception of International Society', pp. 51–73 in Herbert Butterfield and Martin Wight (eds), *Diplomatic Investigations. Essays in the Theory of International Politics* (London: George Allen and Unwin Ltd, 1966), p. 52.
13 Jackson (n. 2 above), p. 314.
14 Tonny Brems Knudsen, *Humanitarian Intervention and International Society: Contemporary Manifestations of an Explosive Doctrine*, PhD Thesis (University of Aarhus: Department of Political Science, 1999), p. 52.
15 Peter Lyon, 'The Rise and Fall and Possible Revival of International Trusteeship', *The Journal of Commonwealth and Comparative Studies*, 31, 1 (1993), pp. 96–110, p. 107.
16 Jackson (n. 2 above), p. 314.
17 William Bain, 'The Political Theory of Trusteeship and the Twilight of International Equality', *International Relations*, 17, 1 (2003), pp. 59–77, p. 75.
18 Boutros Boutros-Ghali, *An Agenda for Peace. Second Edition with the New Supplement and Related Un Documents* (New York: UN Department of Public Information, 1995), pp. 51–62.
19 Ibid., p. 61.
20 Adam Roberts, 'NATO's Humanitarian War over Kosovo', *Survival*, 41, 3 (1999), pp. 102–23, p. 105.
21 Although the rejection of Russia's resolution against NATO's attack on Serbia is understood as an indirect authorization of NATO's actions by several political scientists, the rejection of the resolution cannot be understood as a legitimization of the attack in official legal terms. For further information on this draft resolution see Knudsen (n. 14 above), p. 44; Roberts (n. 20 above), p. 105.
22 The Rambouillet Accords, www.kosovo.mod.uk/rambouillet_text.htm (1999).
23 International Crisis Group (ICG), *Kosovo: Let's learn from Bosnia. Models and Methods of International Administration*, www.icg.org: ICG Balkans Report No. 66, 17 May 1999, pp. 2–3.
24 Ibid., p. 23.
25 Independent International Commission on Kosovo (The Kosovo Commission), *The Kosovo Report* (New York: Oxford University Press, 2000), p. 48.
26 Pamela Taylor, 'Kosovo: Partition or Protectorate?', *Voice of America*, 13 May 1999, act 2.
27 *The Economist*, 'Europe: Land ahoy', 24 April 1999, p. 1.
28 Carl Bildt, *Beyond Protectorates. Possibilities for Peace in South-Eastern Europe*, speech held at the United States Institute of Peace, 16 March 1999, www.usip.org/events/pre2002/bildt_cib.html.
29 Jackson (n. 2 above), pp. 314–15; Bain (n. 17 above), pp. 74–5.
30 The Kosovo Commission (n. 25 above), pp. 95–6.
31 The draft resolution was sponsored by Canada, France, Gabon, Germany, Italy, Japan, the Netherlands, the Russian Federation, Slovenia, Ukraine, the United Kingdom of Great Britain and Northern Ireland, the United States of America and Bahrain (S/PV.4011:3).

32 With Serbia being a member of the Yugoslavian Federation, the Serbian Parliament's acceptance of the Athisaari–Chernomyrdin plan indicated that the Yugoslavian state had accepted the plan.
33 S/PV.4011, *Security Council Meeting on Kosovo – Provisional*, 10 June 1999, p. 5.
34 Ibid., p. 6.
35 Ibid.
36 Ibid., p. 10.
37 S/PV.4011 (1), *Security Council Meeting on Kosovo – Resumption*, 10 June 1999, p. 4.
38 S/PV.4011 (n. 33 above), p. 9.
39 S/RES/1244, *Resolution on the establishment of UNMIK and KFOR*, 10 June 1999.
40 Jackson (n. 2 above), pp. 281–7; Peter Viggo Jakobsen, 'Kontaktgruppen i Kosovo: Koncert trods mislyde', *Politica*, 32, 2 (2000), pp. 157–85, p. 160.
41 S/RES/1244 (n. 39 above).
42 The second pillar was originally concerned with the return of refugees and managed by UNHCR. This pillar was phased out in May 2001 as the majority of refugees had returned and it was replaced by a police and justice pillar managed directly by the UN (www.unmikonline.org).
43 S/1999/972, *The Structure of UNMIK*, 12 June 1999.
44 Hans Hækkerup, *Kosovos mange ansigter* (København: Lindhardt & Ringhof, 2002), pp. 79–80.
45 Alexandros Yannis, 'Kosovo Under International Administration', *Survival*, 43, 2 (2001), pp. 31–48, p. 32.
46 Ibid., p. 33.
47 UNMIK, *On a Constitutional Framework for Provisional Self-Government in Kosovo*, UNMIK/REG/2001/9, 2001.
48 Ibid., ch. 5 & 8.
49 Ibid., ch. 8 (1a).
50 SC/7785, *Press release at 4770th Security Council Meeting*, 10 June 2003, p. 2.
51 Simon Chesterman, *No Strategy Without an Exit? Elections and Exit Strategies in East Timor, Kosovo and Beyond*, Paper delivered at International IDEA, Cambridge, UK, 22 October 2001, p. 7.
52 UNMIK, News Letter, March 19 2004, www.unmikonline.org/archives/news03_04full.htm#1903 (2004)
53 Hækkerup (n. 44 above), pp. 224–53.
54 The Federal Republic of Yugoslavia changed its name to Serbia and Montenegro on 4 February 2003. All privileges formerly belonging to Yugoslavia now belong to Serbia and Montenegro, but for reasons of simplicity the former name of 'Yugoslavia' will be used throughout this chapter.
55 The Kosovo Commission (n. 25 above), p. 275.
56 Simon Chesterman, *Kosovo in Limbo: State-Building and 'Substantial Democracy'*, http://www.ipacademy.org/.
57 For a detailed discussion of the possibilities of determining the final status of Kosovo, see Knudsen's chapter in this book. See also the chaper by Rasmussen.
58 SC/7785, p. 1.
59 Chesterman (n. 51 above), p. 6.
60 UNMIK, *Kosovo Standards Implementation Plan*, www.unmikonline.org/pub/misc/ksip_eng.pdf (2004) p. 2.
61 The areas of priority in the Kosovo Standards Implementation Plan are 1) Functioning democratic institutions, 2) Rule of law, 3) Freedom of movement, 4) Sustainable returns and the rights of communities and their members, 5) Economy, 6) Property Rights, 7) Dialogue and 8) The Kosovo protection corps.
62 Jackson (n. 2 above), pp. 300–1.
63 Bain (n. 2 above), p. 160.

64 Roland Paris, 'Peace-building and the Limits of Liberal Internationalism', *International Security*, 22, 2 (1997), pp. 54–89, p. 88.

65 Jarat Chopra et al., *Planning Considerations for International Involvement in Post-Taleban Afghanistan*, Report from informal meeting on Afghanistan hosted by US Army Academy, Carlisle, PA, 14 November 2001; Jarat Chopra, 'World Help Needed in Palestinian Rebuilding', *The Boston Globe*, 5 May 2002; P. Kennedy, 'UN Trusteeship Council Could Finally Find a Role in Postwar Iraq', *Daily Yomiuri*, 9 May 2003.

5 Local governance in Kosovo

A link to democratic development?

Mark Baskin

Introduction

In two days of riots throughout Kosovo's municipalities in March 2004, 19 people were killed, 954 wounded, and 4,100 displaced. On top of that, 730 houses were damaged and 36 Orthodox Churches, monasteries and other religious sites were burned, looted or damaged. More than 50,000 Albanians took part in these disturbances. Neither the lightly armed UN International Police nor the lightly armed Kosovo Police Service had the capacity to stem the tide of violence. The heavily armed Kosovo Force (KFOR) did not offer much of a deterrent to the rioters. This disorder took place just two days after the UN Undersecretary General for Peacekeeping had concluded a visit to Kosovo by remarking on the UN's visible progress in providing security.[1] It may well be that effective and democratic local government would have provided mechanisms to reduce or eliminate the scope and consequences of this violence.

This confidence in good local government emerges from a growing sense that the development of sustainable democracy at the end of wars begins in local communities – a point increasingly made by the World Bank, the UN, the Organization for Security and Cooperation in Europe (OSCE), the Council of Europe (CoE), and the US Agency for International Development (USAID), among others.[2] The International Institute for Democracy and Electoral Assistance (IDEA) recently described local governance as 'the tier of public authority that citizens first look to, to solve their immediate social problems' and 'the level of democracy in which the citizen has the most effective opportunity to actively and directly participate in decisions made for all of society'.[3] In practice, democratic local governance involves municipal administration that can accommodate needs of diverse populations. It nurtures a community's economic development; it is embedded in networks of independent citizens' groups, but beholden to no single one of them; and it is comprised of sufficiently legitimate institutions that can manage social and political conflicts peacefully.

However, the development of sustainable, democratic local governance at the end of wars presents a series of challenges, since it involves the integration of inclusive political and administrative organizations into a country-wide network of autonomous institutions that function according to basic, agreed-upon political values and principles. It is therefore useful to deepen the discussion of what 'makes local democracy work' at the end of violent conflict and what does not.[4] This chapter examines efforts to develop local democracy with a view towards exploring how international agencies can enhance efforts to support democratic local governance.

The experience in Kosovo since 1999 provides an excellent place to begin such a discussion. In the absence of a broader political resolution to Kosovo's status, UNMIK has focused intensively on enhancing the quality of local governance. The intervention in 1999, which ended a decade in which local government was an instrument of a minority-controlled state apparatus over the overwhelming majority of people in Kosovo, promised to usher in an era of democratic governance. UN Security Council Resolution 1244 of 10 June 1999 mandated UNMIK with 'organizing and overseeing the development of provisional institutions for democratic and autonomous self government'.[5] The UN International officials were supposed to establish democratic local administrations in 30 municipalities,[6] to build the capacity of local institutions, promote reconciliation among groups emerging from violent conflict, and provide a context in which these communities' governments would be democratic for the first time in their history. These activities have enjoyed substantial political and material support from multilateral organizations and national governments.

The discussion below analyses these efforts and the challenges involved from my own experience in Kosovo as Deputy Regional Administrator and Municipal Administrator in Prizren, from subsequent visits to Kosovo, and from the excellent work completed by the International Crisis Group, the European Stability Initiative, the World Bank, OSCE, the Council of Europe, USAID, and the International Institute for Democracy and Electoral Assistance. After addressing the broader context affecting the democratization of local governance, the analysis will explore efforts at local economic reform, the relationships between local government and civil society, and local government as a vehicle for institutionalized conflict resolution. It is argued that the mixed record of local governance in Kosovo since 1999 is, among other things, a function of the majority perception of the threat posed by minority ethnic groups in various parts of the country. Consequently, the improvement of local security and a solution to the question of Kosovo's future status are essential conditions for further progress towards effective local governance supported by domestic as well as international actors.

Towards sustainable local governance in Kosovo: challenges and dilemmas

The effort to establish democratic local government began in the confusion surrounding the end of fighting in June 1999 and has reflected the broader challenges and dilemmas facing Kosovo's postwar development.[7]

As the old regime and its supporters were fleeing, groups associated with the Kosovo Liberation Army (KLA) and the 'Provisional Government' under Hashim Thaqi immediately began organizing local administrations throughout Kosovo.

Others in Kosovo, notably associated with the Democratic League of Kosovo (LDK), rejected these efforts to usurp legitimate authority under Security Council Resolution (SCR) 1244 and remained outside of this assertive political compact. The UN, KFOR, and a host of international NGOs began addressing the immediate humanitarian and administrative needs of people remaining in and returning to Kosovo. Fleeing Serb officials took with them a good many public *cadastre* records, judicial records and political prisoners, all of whose absence would come to impede a relatively smooth transition to democratic local governance in Kosovo.[8]

The confusion marking the early implementation of the Dayton Accords in Bosnia had suggested to UNMIK's planners the necessity to create mechanisms that would facilitate good cooperation and coordination among the implementing agencies from the very beginning.[9] The Special Representative of the UN Secretary General (SRSG) in Kosovo was to coordinate the activities of four agencies within the UN Mission in Kosovo or UNMIK. Each agency was responsible for significant components of the mission. In Pillar I, the United Nations High Commissioner for Refugees (UNHCR) was in charge of humanitarian relief. The humanitarian pillar ceased to exist by the end of 2000, and by mid-2001, in a new Pillar I, the United Nations was in charge of security and justice. In Pillar II, the United Nations was in charge of governance and administration. In Pillar III, the OSCE was in charge of institutions, elections and human rights; and in Pillar IV, the EU was in charge of reconstruction and economic recovery.

In local administration, the UN immediately established five regional administrations that were coterminous with KFOR's multinational brigade areas. However, the UN's early decision to reject the Federal Republic of Yugoslavia's legacy of district (*okrug*) level government from the 1990s meant that there would be an international level of authority in five regions throughout Kosovo with no corresponding domestic counterpart. It was not until January 2000 that the bare minimum of UN staff had been deployed for municipal administrations throughout Kosovo, although a good many posts remained unfilled even then.[10] For the first year or so, international efforts to establish local administration were encumbered by slow deployments of Pillar II officials into the municipalities; by their frequent inexperience in local government; by the absence of clear central direction on the structures and processes of desirable municipal governance; by disagreements between regional leaderships in the UN's Pillar II Administration, the OSCE's Pillar III Institution Building and KFOR in the early phases of operation; and by difficulties in cooperating with emerging local administrations.

The operation opened with six months of open competition for control of municipal government between the UN administration that claimed legitimacy under SCR 1244 and the 'Provisional Government' that was busy establishing local administration throughout Kosovo according to provisions of the never-adopted Rambouillet Accords.[11] This period ended with the 15 December 1999 agreement establishing the Kosovo-UNMIK Joint Interim Administrative Structure and Interim Administrative Council that was signed by three Albanian leaders and witnessed by the SRSG.[12] In consultation with local authorities, international Municipal Administrators began to establish interim local governments throughout Kosovo in which the UN maintained full executive authority pending local elections.

UNMIK passed Regulation 2000/45 on Self Government of Municipalities in Kosovo in August 2000 following a lengthy period of drafting and internal consultation among international agencies and some discussion with central, consultative bodies of Kosovars.[13] This regulation continues to provide the basic institutional framework for local governance in Kosovo. Also of relevance are UNMIK's Regulation 2001/36 on Kosovo Civil Service and Administrative Direction 2003/02 on administering 2001/36. Three distinct reform plans have been developed since 2003 – from the Council of Europe, the Government of Serbia, and an UNMIK Working Group on Local Government.

Municipal elections were held in October 2000 and November 2002. The turnout dropped from 79 per cent in 2000 to 53.9 per cent in 2002.[14] Both elections delivered victories to the LDK under President Ibrahim Rugova's central leadership, but its margin of victory in popular votes and assembly seats dropped considerably between the two elections.[15] The Democratic Party of Kosovo (PDK) under Hashim Thaqi improved its vote total between the two elections. The LDK won majorities in 19 municipalities, while the PDK won in seven municipalities and the Alliance for the Future of Kosovo (AAK) under the national leadership of Ramush Haradinaj won one municipality. Serbs did not participate in the 2000 elections and, in 2002, only 20 per cent of Serbs participated – predominantly in municipalities where they constituted a majority.[16]

The 30 municipalities vary greatly in size, population, and level of economic and institutional development. A number of municipalities (the northern part of Mitrovica, Zvecan, Zubin Potok Leposavic and Strpce) have Serb majorities. The smaller minorities – Bosniacs, Turks, Gorani, and RAE (Roma, Ashkallia and Egyptians) are unevenly distributed throughout Kosovo.

Under the current arrangements, the locally elected president of the Municipal Assembly has executive authority, but can be overruled by international officials. Authority is slowly being wholly transferred to local officials. International Municipal Administrators are now called 'Municipal Representatives' and their tasks are to coordinate activities, to advise local officials, and to monitor their performance.

As we shall see below, the challenges and dilemmas of local governance in Kosovo are currently complicated by Kosovo's uncertain political future and continuing insecurity, which exacerbate efforts to develop local economies, to further local democratic practice and to employ local institutions as instruments to mitigate violent conflict.

Context: security, status, standards

Three related issues provide the background to the development of local government in Kosovo: efforts to establish security and rule of law, the open question concerning the status of Kosovo and the politics surrounding 'standards' of performance of the Provisional Institutions of Self-Government. These specific parameters distinguish Kosovo's efforts to develop local government and administration from those elsewhere.

Democratic local governance requires sufficient security to enable officials and citizens to pursue their livelihoods in physical safety.[17] It also relies upon freedom of movement and freedom of political expression, assembly and participation. Such security is meant to emerge from the systems of policing and judiciary that have been established since 1999. It certainly appears that the Kosovo Police Service has made genuine progress in support of democratic local governance.[18] It is commonly held that the service has been reasonably effective at recruiting a force that is ethnically and gender balanced, at classroom training that introduces new police officers to elements of technical and democratic policing, and at subsequent field training as the officers are deployed on the job.[19] Further, a USAID study found that the service responds professionally to incidents in minority communities. Minorities are well represented in the service and the officers seemed prepared to work in multi-ethnic patrols and willing to speak a non-native language in appropriate situations.[20]

The open questions facing the service became more urgent following the violence of March 2004. It remains for the service to succeed in implementing the community policing approach that is essential to democratic local governance. Community policing involves law enforcement where police officers are integrated into local communities to reduce crime and build good relations between the police and the community.[21] However, there are a number of challenges that remain. For instance, it is not certain that the service will be deployed as a multi-ethnic institution in northern Serb municipalities, nor that it will obtain the substantial additional investment in forensic equipment necessary to improve investigative capacity. Furthermore, it is not clear that the training centre in Vushtrii/Vucitrn will sustain its current high quality when its funding is shifted from international sources to the Kosovo budget in the very near future, or that service salaries will be sufficiently increased so as to enable individual officers to more easily resist corruption. Finally, the service may not in the near future acquire the capacity to take on the sensitive tasks currently part of the SRSG's reserve powers in the Justice Pillar.

These shortcomings may present a significant hurdle, as executive authority for policing is beginning to be handed over from the UN International Police to the Kosovo Police Service, and police operations are becoming significantly more ambitious in scope. They will include efforts to eradicate vital international networks of organized crime, politically malevolent violence against minorities, attacks on international and local police officers, explosive inter-ethnic and anti-international violence that attends the spontaneous political demonstrations and international and Kosovar white collar crime and corruption. This will necessitate close cooperation with international police and KFOR who will remain in Kosovo for the foreseeable future, although it is not clear whether the Kosovo Police Service will win the confidence of KFOR.[22]

The complexity of these tasks is exacerbated by obstacles in establishing an authoritative domestic judiciary, as well as by organizational stovepipes in coordinating the work of Pillar I justice officials with that of Pillar II local administrators. Municipal officials have no control and little say in the work of the police in their municipalities.[23] Finally, it remains for Kosovo's provisional institutions to develop their capacity to investigate economic crime, organized crime and public corruption, which are significant in local government, for example, in health care, education, local administration and decisions about land use and development. In a sense, the most difficult work in establishing security and rule of law lies ahead, in part because it is directly linked to broader uncertainty associated with Kosovo's political future and institutional effectiveness.

The most central *political* issue affecting the development of democratic local governance remains the uncertainty over Kosovo's future status, which colours all aspects of social, economic and political development in Kosovo. Ethnic Albanian leaders place the attainment of independence and sovereignty into the centre of all public activity just as ethnic Serb leaders consider the retention of links between Belgrade and Kosovo a central political goal. Although Kosovo's status has not been formally on the agenda in the period since the adoption of SCR 1244 in June 1999, it has provided a backdrop to almost all political and administrative developments at the local level in Kosovo: in controversies over which flag (UN or Albanian) should fly in public buildings; in the summer 1999 decision to rebuild the house in which the League of Prizren was founded (the house was destroyed by Serbs during the 1999 NATO campaign); or in the 15 May 2003 Resolution of the Kosovo Assembly that the 1998–99 conflict in Kosovo was a 'liberation war of the people of Kosova for freedom and independence' during which Serb representatives walked out of the Assembly.[24]

The status of Kosovo has been directly reflected in the ongoing discussion concerning benchmarks and standards. With the convening of the National Assembly in early 2002, UNMIK formulated a series of benchmarks under its policy of 'standards before status' in which Kosovo's governing institutions prepare for the resolution of the province's political status through concrete achievements in eight areas – functioning democratic institutions, rule of law, freedom of movement, returns and reintegration, economy, property rights, the Kosovo Protection Corps, and dialogue with Belgrade.[25] The UN's frequent public invocation of the 'standards before status' policy in 2002–3 did not appear to be part of a strategic plan that would conclude in a negotiation of status between Belgrade and Pristina. UNMIK's policy succeeded in slowing down the transfer of administrative authority and competencies from international to domestic institutions, although some benchmarks by which domestic institutions were to be assessed remained within the 'reserve powers of the SRSG' as specified in Kosovo's constitutional framework.[26] In December 2003, UNMIK officially adopted a set of 'Standards for Kosovo' with which to evaluate the achievement of benchmarks – after several months of discussion and coalition-building.[27] Before the violence of March 2004, a formal international assessment of efforts to meet these standards was scheduled to take place in mid-2005.

As long as the benchmarks and the standards were taken as an impediment to addressing Kosovo's political status, Serb politicians in Belgrade and in Kosovo appeared to give the exercise considerable support. They frequently called for the literal implementation of standards associated with the return of non-Albanian Internally Displaced Persons and refugees and the 'full implementation' of SCR 1244, among other things. However, as a plan was developed to implement the standards that might serve as a stepping stone to Kosovo's independence, Serb leaders from mainstream and radical parties have come to reject the entire process associated with implementing the standards. In the run-up to Serbia's 28 December 2003 parliamentary elections in which the nationalist Serb Radical Party enjoyed success, Belgrade's moderate Serb Government and Serb representatives to the Provisional Institutions of Self-Government rejected UNMIK's standards as 'unacceptable as a framework for resolving the autonomy crisis' in Kosovo.[28] Serb officials still complain that Kosovo remains an integral part of Serbia and that their suggestions were ignored by Albanian and international leaders. Consequently, Serb officials have refused to participate in the working groups that are developing the next steps in measuring standards, and encouraging Serbs in Kosovo not to vote in elections. Serbs point to failures of the Albanian-led administration to achieve benchmarks and Belgrade focuses on establishing trust between 'Serbs in Kosmet and the Belgrade government,' as one official put it.[29]

Over the past two years, Albanian leaders have been making public efforts to hasten the transfer of authority to Kosovo's provisional institutions, and to ensure their formal independence from Serbia-Montenegro. They prefer that Kosovo gain sovereignty within its current borders, that is, without partition of the Serb-majority areas north of the Ibar River in Mitrovice/a. They argue that partition of the northern borders would necessitate opening negotiations over the Presevo Valley in Serbia and the Western part of Macedonia, both of which are majority Albanian areas. From their belief that the resolution of status is essential to stable institutional development, they have welcomed the adoption of standards as a step towards the independence of Kosovo. However, the current Albanian political leadership continues to act mainly to enhance Kosovo's sovereignty – for example in the Assembly's patriotic declarations or in commissions to reform the constitutional framework – at the expense of careful attention to build capacity in administration and local governance that would serve as a basis on which to lay a technical claim to independence.

The UN's adoption of the standards is hardly the end of the story. Few have actually argued that it has been part of a serious strategy for addressing Kosovo's political crisis. It remains to specify measurements for achieving standards. For example, how will it be known that 'the civil service is professional, impartial and accountable, representative of all communities in Kosovo,' that 'all communities have fair access to employment in public institutions,' or that 'there is a clear understanding among the vast majority of public sector employees of ethnical conduct requirements' to take a few examples from UNMIK's 'Kosovo Standards Implementation Plan' of 31 March 2004?[30] At a minimum, such ambiguities in the standards weaken the trust and predictability essential to democratic local governance, which could pose a genuine political obstacle to the achievement of goals of improving administrative and governing techniques.

The failure to resolve these outstanding issues will strengthen the informal, parallel system of local authority that UNMIK's provisional institutions were meant to replace, although such parallel institutions are not conducive to the development of democratic local governance in Kosovo.[31] The UN has officially reported that parallel Serb structures, which 'exist in virtually all municipalities in Kosovo', not only provide services to Serbs in Kosovo but also 'hamper' legitimate institutions.[32] Two different 'Associations of Serb Municipalities' have been established – one based in northern Mitrovice/a and the second in eastern Kosovo. The Serbian Government in Belgrade has continued to support Serbs in Kosovo with salaries, health and social insurance, pensions, child support, ID cards, drivers' licenses, passports, license plates and other documents. Serbs in Kosovo are thereby encouraged to increase their integration into Serbian institutions and diminish their relationships with Kosovo's provisional institutions.[33] It is doubtful whether Belgrade's creation of such 'facts on the ground' serves the interests of Serbs who choose to live in Kosovo or of those who have moved to Serbia. It certainly does not serve to strengthen the development of Kosovo's democratic local governance.

Among the broader elements that impede democratic local governance in Kosovo are efforts to build on the Kosovo Police Service's fragile progress in enhancing public security, the mainly symbolic participation of Serb leaders in Kosovo's provisional institutions, the extremely low Serb turnout in Kosovo elections, the Provisional Institutions of Self-Government's complex path to achieving standards of performance, and the continued functioning of parallel structures in Kosovo's local administration. It is no surprise that recent reports have noted that Serbs in enclaves complain that they received no concrete benefits from participating in Kosovo's provisional institutions. Economic growth will be necessary for Provisional Institutions to win the loyalty of Serbs in Kosovo.

Economic reform: the development engine of governance

Economic development is an essential component in the democratization of local governance: a well-functioning local economy provides employment for citizens and a tax base for local administration and services. The peace dividend of a UN–EU mediated transition from tyranny to democracy in the economy was meant to provide goods and services for local consumers.[34] A growing economy can serve as a municipality's calling card for cooperation with business in other regions and other countries. And just as economic development can provide an environment conducive for the development of democratic local institutions, an effective and inclusive local government can help to spur the development of local business.

Optimism does not come easy, however.[35] Kosovo's absence of self-sustaining economic growth impedes the development of democratic local governance. The economy has thrived largely on remittances and official transfers, and a significant portion of the labour force works for NGOs and international organizations.

In 2001–2, Kosovo's economy was able to cover only one fifth of its imports with exports, the trade balance deficit accounts for approximately half of the Gross Domestic Product, and foreign direct investment remains quite low.[36] These trends do not improve Kosovo's investment climate.

Neither international nor Kosovar institutions have been able to address these issues authoritatively. The unemployment rate of the majority population is above 50 per cent and that of minorities is even higher. Assessments of Kosovo's development are rich in disappointment in the economic climate: failure to privatize business more quickly; failure to ensure regular supplies of electricity and water; failure to provide a coherent legal framework for the development of private business; and failure to develop the means to expedite exports to Europe. Moreover, high customs and tariff provisions for raw materials and semi-finished goods (26 per cent) penalize Kosovar producers against competitors from abroad and apparently symbolism-driven moves, such as those of the Kosovo Trust Agency to northern Mitrovica, impede the economy's capacity for efficiency.[37] It appears as if Kosovo's economy is not yet on a sound enough footing to develop manufacturing and services essential to a modern, productive economy that can serve as the basis of democratic local government for all citizens of Kosovo, and as its passport to Europe. One finds little optimism concerning the short- to mid-term prospect for growth.

Nor does the apparent absence of coordination leave much latitude in which local government can facilitate economic development. Significant assets in local economic development remain controlled by central authorities in Pristina: public utilities, management of forests, chambers of commerce, and relationships with international business and donors. It may also seem that Pristina's international and Kosovar leaders are so fearful of the supposed incompetence and corruption of municipal-level private and public officials that they continue to monopolize essential activities, such as the Kosovo Trust Agency, public utilities, and socially owned enterprises. The Council of Europe reports that 'many municipalities have failed to establish a proper working relationship with public service providers' in many services falling under local competence, such as water supply, sewerage, road maintenance and local transport.[38] In areas such as health, education and forests, the division of competencies between local and central authorities creates confusion and inefficiencies in management of assets.

Management improvement will not come easily. International officials commonly report that municipal officials are badly prepared for modern administration and that the Institute of Public Administration, organized by OSCE, did not begin to function effectively until almost five years after the initial formation of local administration. It is less common to hear of ways of integrating the university in Pristina with other parts of the education system to provide future experts for administration and economic development. Annual reports for 2003–4 from the UNDP, the Council of Europe and USAID have highlighted popular perceptions of corruption by both international and domestic leaders, as well as ample confusion over who actually controls the operations of a whole host of local public services.[39] Finally, in a system in which perceptions may be more significant than reality, it is common to hear that local tenders are routinely won by friends of the party in power.

These difficulties underline the problems many citizens of Kosovo have in gaining access to municipal services and infrastructure, especially in areas outside the urban core. For example, the villages dotting the Zhupa Valley in the Prizren municipality (an area with Bosniac, Gorani and Serb inhabitants) remain without telephone coverage and many of them require substantial projects in water, rubbish disposal, sewage systems, and electricity to become fully functional communities within the municipality.[40] There are similar stories about infrastructural development throughout Kosovo. It is also not clear whether the many proposed infrastructural development projects outside the urban core have made it to the front of any queue for funding priorities – especially in minority areas where such projects could benefit majority and minority communities and could encourage inter-ethnic and public-private dialogue through the planning process.

A healthy fiscal situation could enable municipal governments to address these problems more effectively. But Kosovo's municipalities are doubly burdened in this matter. First, the Council of Europe reports that Kosovo municipalities only provide 11 per cent of the revenues in their budget, quite low in comparison with other former socialist countries in transition.[41] The control of local officials over priorities is further diminished by their inability to transfer resources from centrally earmarked grants between sectors for healthcare and education, for example.[42] Second, the capacity of local municipalities to collect their own revenues has not been well developed. The Council of Europe reports municipal officials' dissatisfaction with the central control over the types of fees, local taxes and duties that can be collected locally. In addition, the cautious introduction of property taxes in several municipalities in 2003 has not met with much success or approval, a result in part of the shallow process of consultation with local officials and local communities.[43]

The general consensus among the international and Kosovar development communities is that local governments find it difficult to meet their financial needs; they are threatened by high unemployment, the absence of investment and an ill-defined environment for institutional development; and find themselves mired in an unfavourable environment for local economic development. These problems are not transitory and will require more than a simple effort to provide a seamless 'European' framework that efficiently divides competencies among different levels of administration and between the private and public sectors on paper. It will require a significant commitment – both in investment in infrastructure and in transferring a good deal of 'ownership' of strategies of local economic development away from central political leaders to the communities themselves.

These problems should send a signal to international officials to address the deadlocks that have hampered economic development since 1999; to approach consultation with local colleagues so as to engender in them an authentic sense of ownership in local administration and governance; and to consider medium- and long-term requirements for the training of local officials that emerge from the evolving education system.[44] This new thinking would benefit from efforts to democratize local authority, to make it transparent and subject to influence from the community outside the closed doors of international officials, municipal executives and assembly presidents.

Democracy and the role of civil society in Kosovo municipal structures

Local governance is democratic when it is responsive to a community's citizens during policy making. This would involve developing a technically competent and fair local administration, political institutions that are open to input from the full range of interests in a community, and a decision-making process that is sufficiently transparent to provide all citizens in a community with a sense of 'ownership' and loyalty.

These qualities of competence, inclusiveness and transparency are even more significant when viewed against Kosovo's proportional system of local election in which voters select from closed, party lists – a system in which municipal developments are entirely dependent upon central political leaderships. This diminishes political accountability associated with constituency-based politics, strengthens the one-party character of individual local governments, and renders inter-party compromise more difficult. This is particularly significant at the end of wars when political leaders remain mired in wartime's zero-sum conflicts, as between the Serb and Albanian forces and among Albanian political parties. It is no surprise that OSCE reported that it took over five months to break the political deadlock in the one-third of Kosovo's municipalities that were without a clear victor in the elections of October 2002.[45] The Council of Europe reported that members of the opposition often boycott the work of assemblies, which deprives many citizens of any representation in the business of local government.[46] These boycotts are consistent with the general perception that administrative directors are chosen less for their expertise than for their political allegiance, which enables the party in power to dominate all aspects of policy making.[47] Consequently, the current electoral arrangements that ensure majority dominance of government may actually leave the majority of local voters without any effective representation in municipal governance – especially when viewed against the rapidly decreasing voter turnout from one election to the next.

These political deadlocks may exacerbate the absence of professionalism among municipal administrators and councillors. The assessments by the Council of Europe and USAID point to inexperience in drafting regulations and to the absence of transparency in the process of adopting regulations. They highlight the underdeveloped concept of public service and a susceptibility to corruption in Kosovo. They report that municipal governments do not focus on providing services, or that assemblies do not establish committees to examine important matters of policy. One Assembly President did not even convene any such assembly meeting for well over five months in the first part of 2003.

The unhappy constants in Kosovo public life since 1999 are accusations of corruption, nepotism and favouritism; conflict among factions and parties over all manners of policy and institutional design; and dysfunctional inter-institutional relationships in municipalities, between domestic and international institutions, and between central and local administration. These dysfunctional practices – that resemble those of the authoritarian administration of the Yugoslav 'old regime' – only feed perceptions that important decisions are corruptly made behind closed doors.

These difficulties underline the need to ensure transparency in municipal policy as one step in creating a climate in which politicized rumour and innuendo cease to dominate municipal public life. Unfortunately, a relatively well-developed mass media, which includes correspondents of the national press and a host of local radio stations, has only occasionally engaged in critical, investigative reporting of local developments. Such reporting is absent from sophisticated papers such as *Zeri* and *Koha Ditore*. In the past the public watchdog function was ably provided by the ICG and the European Stability Initiative. Local NGOs, such as the Kosovo Institute for Policy Research and Development and the Kosovar Research and Documentation Institute are only just beginning to take on this function that is essential in holding Kosovo's authorities publicly accountable before the court of public opinion – and have only just turned to local government, as well.[48]

It is clear that muckraking journalists and local civic activists will be working against a highly politicized system in which the public, civic institutions initiated by UNMIK remain formal shells that do not command a deeper sense of local loyalty, a problem exacerbated by a deeper faith in one's own political party or social network from one's village of origin. This claim is consistent with the World Bank's report from 2000 that the greatest degree of trust was found in places with the least developed formal institutions. This 'lack of trust among people beyond the extended family system … is one of the key impediments to the growth of inclusive local institutions' and development of civil society.[49] It seems wise to address these political and civic issues as a prelude to significant efforts in supporting the nascent Institute of Public Administration.

Against the background of Kosovo's fragilely evolving local democracy, it seems worthwhile to complement the traditional approaches to supporting the development of local-level civil society with efforts to decentralize local governance further through the development of more genuinely local units of administration and representation in 'local communities' (*bashkesija lokales or mesne zajednice*). The UN's central authorities in administration decided in 1999–2000 not to support the revival of this most local level of government – when the international administration in Prizren sought to work locally with community groups to establish security and development in the ethnically mixed local area called Tusus in Prizren, as well as in the Zhupa valley directly east of Prizren. In effect, UNMIK chose not to support these quiet and initially successful efforts to bring together community leaders from the Albanian and Slavic Muslim communities to address common problems in everyday life.[50] On the other hand, the

World Bank and the Office for Transitional Initiatives of USAID focussed precisely at this local level to work with groups of citizens in villages and local communities in order to identify, develop and implement reconstruction and development projects during that period.[51]

But there has been no shortage of reform efforts. In late 2002, UNMIK invited the Council of Europe to develop a proposal for decentralization of local governance 'in line with local practice.'[52] A team of international officials drafted a far-reaching and complex proposal that is supposed to bring representation and administration closer to people of all ethnicities. Following an incisive critique of the actual functioning of municipal administration, the Council of Europe mission drafted a complex proposal for sharing competencies and decision-making powers between municipal and sub-municipal levels of government, in democratically elected councils of local self-government within municipalities. It was meant to be an administrative reform that did not touch on sensitive issues of status.[53] However, these plans were not the product of a genuine partnership between international and domestic (Kosovar) officials and have encountered a good deal of local resistance.[54] For example, the Council of Europe proposal would transform the lightly inhabited municipalities of Novo Brdo/Novoberde and Zvecan into sub-municipal units of neighbouring municipalities. However, in its current mandate, the Novo Brdo administration is the most ethnically integrated municipal administration in Kosovo in a setting where such decentralization will be judged on its capacity to contribute to the peaceful resolution of potentially violent conflicts and not just on its seamless efficiency of design in the planning stage.

The comprehensive efforts to reform local government in Kosovo that began following the March 2004 violence have given political considerations a central place. It is a 'long term effort' that will be 'based on a firm commitment by all parties to a multi-ethnic Kosovo' in 'an important contribution to set up and consolidate functioning democratic institutions in Kosovo'.[55] A working group that included the UN, the OSCE, USAID, the Council of Europe, the Provisional Institutions of Self-Government, and the Association of Kosovo Municipalities prepared a document intended to provide a broad framework that would amend existing legislation and regulations to achieve three broad goals related to the achievement of governing standards: strengthen the administrative capacity of local administration, ensure that all communities within municipalities have equal access to municipal goods and services, and guarantee that all people of ethnic communities will be able to participate in local government. Among the specific changes put on the agenda by the working group in the summer of 2004 are: new legislation on local self-government and on local finance, consideration of a 'territorial element' in municipal elections, and 'an institutional framework facilitating support to and cooperation with the Kosovo Police Service.'[56]

These efforts have won wide formal support among international and Kosovo institutions. Municipal restructuring is to be tested in a limited number of pilot projects that would demonstrate the benefits of reform at the same time that legislation is under consideration by the Provisional Institutions of Self-Government and UNMIK. What sets it off from the pre-March 2004 efforts at reform is the great effort to challenge the recalcitrant Serb parties to join the discussion of local government as one way of integrating them into life in Kosovo.

Local democracy and conflict prevention

One measure of local government effectiveness is its capacity to prevent local conflicts of interest from escalating into violence or from becoming national issues – and to ensure that conflicts beginning elsewhere will not resonate locally. This matter is especially significant in an area that has long served as a venue for competition between Serb and Albanian political movements. Indeed, the violence of March 2004 demonstrated that almost five years after the adoption of the foundational SCR 1244, the potential explosiveness of this competition has not diminished. UNMIK has addressed this conflict by supporting the creation of multi-ethnic municipal administration that would deliver adequate services and be open to participation by all citizens. Minority employment is meant to broadly reflect its population distribution in the municipality. Municipal budget expenditures are meant to address the needs of minority populations. Minority 'communities' are given a special place in Kosovo's international administration.

However, these efforts have had mixed results. The UN reports that minority employment remains well below the targeted 18 per cent – and Serbs constitute 12 per cent and other minorities 3.3 per cent of municipal employees – but this figure is likely to include employees from Serb-majority municipalities.[57] It is rarely the case that municipalities distribute their assets fairly among majority and minority communities. Under provisions for 'fair-share financing', municipalities are supposed to allocate a percentage of their budget and own-source revenue to minority communities in a manner that reflects their population in the community. By October 2003, only six municipalities have achieved 'fair-share financing' on three budget lines – municipal administration, health and education. Four municipalities achieved two of the three targets; 12 municipalities have achieved minimum targets on one budget line; but five have not achieved the minimum targeted allocation in even one budget line.[58]

These disappointments in achieving a policy conducive to the development of multi-ethnic communities may reflect the modest representation of minorities in local government. Only the small municipality of Novoberde/Novo Brdo appears to enjoy a relatively balanced inter-ethnic representation in the Municipal Assembly – although the initial bargaining over the composition of the government there took a great deal of time. This is also the case with the important Policy and Finance Committee, which is responsible for preparing the budget and formulating each local government's strategic direction. UNMIK itself has reported that only four municipalities have achieved a 'representative range' of appropriate minority employment based on results from censuses in 1981 and 1991. All reports point out that neither the Communities Committee, which is supposed to promote minority interests, nor the Mediation Committees, which are supposed to make recommendations on claims concerning discrimination, function effectively. By mid-2004, Serbs boycotted the committees in seven municipalities; the Mediation Committees were active only in three municipalities; and local authorities generally failed to implement the recommendations of the few Community Committees that met.[59] In addition, official public reports underline that 'the civil service shows a general lack of professionalism in implementing transparent, non-politicized and ethnically balanced procedures in areas such as procurement and recruitment. Furthermore, municipal regulations, once adopted, are often not implemented'.[60]

As one instrument in addressing the minorities' more difficult circumstances, UNMIK began establishing 'local community offices' in each municipality's minority areas in 2000. They are now staffed by international and Kosovar (mainly Serb and Bosniac–Gorani) officials who appear conscientious, well-informed about developments in the community, and diligent in representing the interests of minorities to the majority administration. The Kosovar local community officers are particularly effective in conveying a welcoming environment to minorities in local administration. Serb officers in Gracanica reported that the Albanian-dominated administration in Pristina was pragmatic and fair, and that they travelled each day to the municipal administration to address particular administrative issues.[61] International officials throughout Kosovo (in the municipalities of Gjilan, Leposavic, Orahovac, Pristina, Prizren, Strpce) reported on effective steps in building trust on non-political matters between parties from different ethnic groups.[62]

The local community offices appear to be more effective when one of two political conditions exist. First, Albanian local leaders are less likely to feel threatened by smaller minorities that lack a nearby state sponsor with contending claims in Kosovo. To take one example, municipal authorities in Prizren found it a relatively simple matter to integrate populations of RAE, Turks, Bosniacs and Gorani into local governing and administrative arrangements – almost since the end of the NATO campaign in 1999. To be sure, some post-war local political leaderships have occasionally moved to dismiss 'disloyal' minorities hired following the anti-Albanian purges in the 1990s – especially those who do not speak Albanian – and have based these decisions on the relatively low, centrally determined quotas for minority employment to justify eliminating 'surplus' minority administrative employees. Nonetheless, official tolerance towards non-Serb minorities in Prizren emerges from the common understanding that individuals from these groups pose no political threat to the Albanian leadership throughout Kosovo in municipal and provincial bodies.[63]

Similarly, in areas not contiguous with contentious northern, Serb-majority municipalities, such as Orahovac, Albanian leaders are more likely to take the necessary steps to meet the needs of Serb minorities. At first glance, Orahovac would not seem the type of place to find inclusive initiatives because of the unresolved wartime trauma and very high tensions during the initial period of the UNMIK administration. During a July 1998 Serbian counter-offensive in Orahovac, an authoritative, moderate and tolerant Albanian religious sect leader was brutally murdered.[64] Following the initial deployments in the summer of 1999, KFOR arrested 11 Serbs remaining in Orahovac for suspected war crimes.[65]

A further element of tension was provided by the Albanian blockade established after 20 August 1999 upon the announcement that Russian KFOR troops would be deployed in Orahovac: Albanian residents alleged that Russian mercenaries had fought on the Serbian side of the conflict.[66] Given this background, it is remarkable that by 2003, the Albanian leadership in Orahovac had taken a number of initiatives to integrate Serbs into local government and administration and to address contentious issues concerning education and municipal services. This inclusive approach reflects both the deftness of the local UN Municipal Representative and the genuine will of the Albanian leadership in Orahovac to work in accordance with the international mandate.

In general, where a minority ethnic group presents no political threat, it seems possible to create power-sharing arrangements in which political differences are unlikely to escalate into violence. In such places, domestic 'local community officers' with international support can help minority and majority politicians adapt to changing circumstances in a manner that will allow them to bargain more effectively and make policy that benefits constituents in all ethnic communities.

Local community offices are less likely to be effective in areas with genuine conflicts of ethnic interests, especially in the divided municipality of Mitrovice/a. As long as the status of Kosovo defies resolution, neither side has a genuine interest in attempting to implement technical plans designed to reintegrate north and south Mitrovica as a single unit. Each side is attempting to establish 'facts on the ground' for the coming rounds of bargaining over the municipality's political future. Consequently, neither side will make genuine concessions to each other, nor to UNMIK's cosmopolitan plans to develop multi-ethnic democratic governance. Instead, the leaderships on each side continue to hold out for victory. The decision to integrate the two sides of Mitrovice/a is deeply political, contentious and at the heart of the question of Kosovo's future status. Because partial solutions that attempt to split the difference of interest in the absence of an enduring political solution to Kosovo's status are not likely to succeed, it may be wisest to invest in a political process that will directly lead to a solution to the central issue of contention: the future of Kosovo.

Conclusion: prospects for effective local institutions

Democratic local governance can become sustainable and self-regulating when local institutions function effectively and authoritatively, are valued by Kosovar citizens, and can adapt to changing needs in the community. By these standards, it appears that administration in Kosovo is hampered by multiple legacies of authoritarian governance and ethnic competition; a stagnant economy with few prospects for near-term improvement; uncertain security and occasional violence against minorities and against its own police; awkward coordination between local and central government; and difficulties in settling Kosovo's political status. Against this background, local governance remains genuinely fragile and deeply dependent on international missions that sometimes advance a perverse type of arrested stability at the expense of, and in the name of, democratization. The growth of democratic governance in Kosovo remains hampered by the continued politicization of public life, growing apathy among ordinary citizens, and the increasing impunity of 'spoilers' with no stake in a stable, democratic system. And just as Kosovo's local democracy is not yet self-sustaining, neither have international officials been very effective in using their overwhelming political and economic assets to work constructively with the different groups in building a common, democratic future.

It appears that the solution to these dilemmas would depend on a broader political settlement that successfully addresses legitimate Albanian concerns for popular self-government and legitimate Serbian concerns over security, freedom of movement, preservation of cultural monuments, and the return of refugees and internally displaced persons. Such a settlement might provide a political context in which administrators can become technically competent and begin to acquire some common civic values that underlie narrower political interests. A broader political settlement between the government of Serbia and Kosovo's Provisional Institutions of Self Government will provide the predictability and sense of closure that could guarantee all citizens of Kosovo a common future in peace, dignity and democracy. Such a settlement can also provide a basis on which important Albanian stakeholders can find agreement on the basic values and principles of an enduring political compact.

Such trends would be strengthened were officials in Kosovo to take smaller steps to strengthen local democracy and administration by enlarging the degree of economic, social and political autonomy at the most basic level of governance. Here international officials from the UN, EU, OSCE, KFOR and individual governments continue to command the most authoritative set of assets in the current round of bargaining. It may well be that the current efforts at reforming local government will lead to sustainable improvements in economic management, electoral legislation, and legislative and administrative practice – and that the 'reform process' will generate effective programmes that address the needs of all groups of citizens in Kosovo. However, it will continue to be necessary for international officials to learn how to share 'political ownership' with domestic colleagues from Kosovo and how to devolve increasing formal control over the process of local democratization. This may represent the greatest challenge facing international institutions in Kosovo.

Acknowledgement

This article was completed in the spring of 2005. An early version of it was presented on 16 November 2003 in Oslo, Norway to a working group on local government on Kosovo sponsored by the International Institute for Democracy and Electoral Assistance (IDEA). The author is grateful for the permission of IDEA to publish this work, and for comments from participants in the working group, as well as from Tonny Brems Knudsen, Carsten Bagge Laustsen, Chris Freeman and Paula Pickering.

Notes

1 See UNMIK Press Briefing, 14 March 2004 (http://www.unmikonline.org/press/2004/trans/tr140304.pdf) and Report of the Secretary General, S/2004/348, paragraph 3 (http://ods-dds-ny.un.org/doc/UNDOC/GEN/N04/331/80/IMG/N0433180.pdf?OpenElement).

2 For an intelligent review of the arguments involved here, see Susan L. Woodward, 'Local Governance Approach to Social Reintegration and Economic Recovery in Post-Conflict Countries: the Political Context for Programs of UNDP/UNCDF Assistance', discussion paper for the workshop 'A Local Governance Approach to Post-Conflict Recovery', 8 October 2002 (http://www.theipa.org/publications/woodward.pdf). A review of broader issues is contained in Charles T. Call and Susan E. Cook, 'On Democratization and Peacebuilding', *Global Governance*, 9 (2003), pp. 233–46.

3 See the description of IDEA's project on local governance at http://www.idea.int/publications/democracy_at_local_level/dll_overview.htm. More generally, see Timothy Sisk *et al.*, *Democracy at the Local Level: The International IDEA Handbook on Participation Representation, Conflict Management and Governance* (Stockholm: International IDEA, 2001), and Emilia Kandeva, *Stabilization of Local Governments* (Budapest: LGI Books, 2001).

4 The reference is to Robert Putnam's seminal *Making Democracy Work: Civic Traditions in Modern Italy* (Princeton: Princeton University Press, 1993).

5 UN Security Council Resolution (SCR) 1244 of 10 June 1999, see paragraph 11a.

6 There were 29 municipalities in June 1999. A decision was taken a few months hence to re-establish the municipality of Malisheve/Malishevo, which had been eliminated in the Serbian administrative reforms in the early 1990s.

7 This brief sketch of developments neither accounts for socialist Yugoslavia's multiple administrative legacies, nor for the multiple nuances of developing of local government throughout Kosovo following the war.

8 See Report of the Secretary-General on the United Nations Interim Administration Mission in Kosovo, S/1999/779, 12 July 1999, paragraphs 27, 72, 74, 76 and 78 (http://www.un.org/Docs/sc/reports/1999/sgrep99.htm).

9 See Report of the Secretary-General on the United Nations Interim Administration in Kosovo, S/1999/672, 12 June 1999, paragraph 5, as well as the Secretary-General's Report of 12 July 1999, S/1999/779, paragraphs 53–109, for a detailed description of the mission's structure.

10 S/1999/1250, paragraph 34 (http://www.un.org/Docs/sc/reports/1999/sgrep99.htm)

11 Ibid., paragraphs 34 and 35; and S/1999/987, paragraph 16.

12 Ibid., paragraphs 5 and 6.

13 See http://www.unmikonline.org/regulations/2000/reg45–00.htm.

14 See information provided by the Statistical Office for Kosovo: http://www.sok-kosovo.org/statistics/elections.htm. For 2002, see http://www.osce.org/kosovo/elections/archive/2002/detailed_certified_results_2002_11_02.pdf. For 2000, see http://www.osce.org/kosovo/elections/archive/2000/files/party_standings1.pdf.

15 Rugova became president following the fall 2001 elections to the central Kosovo Assembly.

16 S/2003/113, paragraph 18.

17 See Charles Call, 'Protecting the People: Public Security Choices after Civil Wars', *Global Governance*, 7, 2 (2001), pp. 151–72, and John G. Cockell, 'Civil-Military Responses to Security Challenges in Peace Operations: Ten Lessons from Kosovo', *Global Governance*, 8, 4 (2002), pp. 483–502.

18 See Gordon Peake's assessment of policing in Kosovo, *Policing the Peace: Police Reform Experiences in Kosovo, Southern Serbia and Macedonia* (London: Saferworld, 2004).

19 Ibid., pp. 19–20.

20 See the USAID report: *I was Born in that Village: Prospects for Minority Returns and Sustainable Integrated Communities in Kosovo*, pp. 25–6. (http://www.usaid.gov/missions/kosovo/pdf/returns_report_kosovo.pdf).

21 For an extensive summary of the literature in lessons on democratizing police abroad, see David Bayley, 'Democratizing the Police Abroad: What to Do and How to Do it' (http://www.ncjrs.org/pdffiles1/nij/188742.pdf). On one community policing project in Kosovo, see http://www.balkansjustice.org/Kosovo2.htm.

22 See 'Failure to Protect: Anti-Minority Violence in Kosovo, March 2004', *Human Rights Watch*, 16, 6 (July 2004), pp. 14–5. (http://www.hrw.org/english/docs/2004/07/27/serbia9136.htm).

23 'Limited Scope Assessment of Local Governance in Kosovo, Recommendations for USAID/Kosovo's 2004–2008 Strategy', p. 11 (http://www.usaid.gov/missions/kosovo/pdf/local_government_report.pdf). On the judiciary in Kosovo, see Mark Baskin, *Lessons Learned on UNMIK's Judicary*, Clementsport (Nova Scotia: Peacekeeping Press, 2002).

24 Radio Free Europe, Southeastern Europe Report, 16 May 2003 (http://www.rferl.org/newsline/2003/05/4-SEE/see-160503.asp).

25 The benchmarks were introduced in the first part of 2002 and were mentioned in each subsequent report of the Secretary General. See for example S/2002/779, paragraph 61, or S/2002/1126, paragraph 2. Moreover, the Constitutional Framework assigns the SRSG reserved power to 'ensure that the rights and interests of the Communities are fully protected'. See UNMIK Regulation 2001/09, Chapter 8.1a.

26 This was the case with rule of law and property rights.

27 UNMIK Press Release (UNMIK/PR/1078), 10 December 2003, 'Standards for Kosovo' (http://www.unmikonline.org/press/2003/pressr/pr1078.pdf).

28 *Beta News Agency*, 8 December 2003.

29 Interview with Branko Radujko in *Politika* (Belgrade), 14 April 2003. The term 'Kosmet' refers to Kosovo and Metohija and is Belgrade's preferred term. A 'metohija' is an Orthodox Church landholding.

30 UNMIK, 'Kosovo Standards Implementation Plan', 31 March 2003, pp. 16, 18, 43. (http://www.unmikonline.org/pub/misc/ksip_eng.pdf).

31 See, for example, Report of the Secretary General, 15 October 2003, S/2003/996, paragraph 12, or S/2003/421, paragraph 9.

32 For a detailed description of the system, see OSCE Mission in Kosovo Department of Human Rights and Rule of Law, 'Parallel Structures in Kosovo,' October 2003.

33 Ibid.

34 The European Union heads Pillar IV, Reconstruction and Economic Development

35 See the UNDP Early Warning Reports at http://www.kosovo.undp.org/Projects/EWS/ews.htm; as well as Mario Holzner, 'Kosovo: A Protectorate's Economy', *The Vienna Institute Monthly Report*, No.1, January 2003.

36 Holzner (n. 35 above).

37 'I was Born in that Village' (n. 20 above), p. 24.

38 Council of Europe Decentralization mission in Kosovo, Interim Report, 27 June 2003, p. 7.

39 'Corruption in Kosovo: Observations and Implications for USAID,' 10 July 2003 (http://www.usaid.gov/missions/kosovo/pdf/kosovo_corruption.pdf).

40 'I was Born in that Village' (n. 20 above), p. 26.

41 Council of Europe Decentralization mission in Kosovo, Interim Report, 27 June 2003, p. 13.

42 Ibid., p. 14.

43 Ibid., p. 15.

44 A more positive assessment is in OSCE, *The Municipal Assembly Starter Kit*, November 2002–June 2003.

45 See the OSCE Mission in Kosovo, 'Boycott at the Municipal Level', 15 May 2003 (http://www.osce.org/documents/mik/2003/05/711_en.pdf). A more positive assessment can be found in OSCE, *The Municipal Assembly Starter Kit*, November 2002–June 2003.
46 Council of Europe Decentralization mission in Kosovo, Interim Report, 27 June 2003, p. 9.
47 See the UN Secretary-General's Report, S/2003/421, 14 April 2003, paragraphs 6–7.
48 See for example 'Kosovar Assembly: For the People or for the Party?', KODI Report n.3, Prishtine, 2003; Robert Muharremi, Lulzim Pecii, Leon Malazogu, Verena Knaus and Teuta Murati, *Administration and Governance in Kosovo: Lessons Learned and Lessons to be Learned* (Pristina: KIPRED, 2003), and *Local Government and Administration in Kosovo*, Pristina, KIPRED, 2004.
49 Gloria La Cava, Raffaella Nanetti, Stephanie Schwandner Sievers, Arjan Gjonca, Taies Nezam and Barbara Balaj, *Conflict and Change in Kosovo: Impact on Institutions and Society*, World Bank, 2000, p. 38.
50 The term 'Slavic Muslims' refers to Bosniacs and Gorani.
51 These matters are covered in detail in Mark Baskin, *Between Exit and Engagement: the Balkans in the Age of the International Community*, manuscript in progress.
52 See Secretary-General Information, SGINF(2003)40, 14 November 2003, 'Reform of Local Self Government and Public Administration in Kosovo. Final Recommendation', http://www.coe.int/t/e/SG/Secretary-General/Information/Documents/Other-reports/SGINF(2003)40E.asp#TopOfPage.
53 Ibid., paragraph 1.
54 See Mark Baskin, 'Between Exit and Engagement: on the Division of Authority in Transitional Administrations', *Global Governance*, 10, 1 (2004), pp. 119–37.
55 Working Group on Local Government, 'Framework for the Reform of Local Self-Government in Kosovo,' 19 July 2004, p. 1.
56 Ibid., pp. 2, 8, 17.
57 S/2003/996, paragraph 13.
58 Ibid., paragraph 9.
59 S/2004/613, paragraph 39.
60 Ibid., paragraph 8.
61 Interview with the Author in May 2003.
62 Interviews with the Author in May 2003.
63 Many social and administrative problems remain, but current arrangements provide a framework to dispel the unease and insecurity among Gorani, Bosniacs and Turks in Prizren.
64 For descriptions of the wartime violence in Rahovec/Orahovac, see the OSCE report, *As Seen, As Told*, Vol.I, October 1998 – June 1999, pp. 476–96 (http://www.osce.org/documents/mik/1999/11/1620_en.pdf).
65 See *As Seen, As Told*, Vol.II, 14 June – 31 October 1999, p. 116.
66 Ibid., p. 114.

6 Foundations and fractures of Kosovo's educational system

Towards conflict or peace?

Wayne Nelles

This chapter examines education as a problematic foundation for post-war reconstruction and peacebuilding in Kosovo. It discusses some historical and contemporary problems; issues and initiatives surrounding the reconstruction of Kosovo's educational system; and major problems or obstacles to progress. It argues that in Kosovo education has been a core issue around which many socioeconomic and ethnic problems have arisen, continue to fester, and upon which a more promising future depends. Indeed, I propose that without sufficient and better attention to education now, Kosovo's long-term prosperity and stability is jeopardized.

Little research so far has critically examined recent education developments in Kosovo or broader regional conflict prevention, peace and security implications.[1] But I suggest that the Kosovo situation is particularly vexing because many academics and policy-makers consider education as a nation-building tool while there is no such internationally recognized nation-state of either 'Kosovo' or 'Kosova'.[2] Even if eventually proclaimed, it is likely to remain contested with potential for more violence. This chapter closes offering some suggestions for new education policy dialogue, programme innovation, development cooperation and research.

Conceptual-historic foundations to education, conflict and peace in Kosovo

In their publisher's proposal, this book's editors argued that 'ethnic cleansing must to some extent be seen as a product of the attempt by ethnic groupings to stereotype and devaluate groups they see as their enemies'. They suggested that to bring reconciliation we must reverse 'xenophobic images and the habit of identity formation by means of exclusion'. I wholeheartedly concur, suggesting, in this chapter, insights into education issues, learning processes and necessary reforms can help.

Before moving to Kosovo specifics some broader historical, philosophical conceptual and theoretical foundations are noteworthy. Education's role in personal, national, political, economic and social development has been debated for centuries. In the Western intellectual tradition, scholars since Plato have mused on education complementing citizenship and state formation. Modern researchers and teacher-training institutions have continued discussing related issues.[3]

International development theory and agencies still promote education as an 'investment' in 'human capital' with knowledge and training helping fight poverty. More recently, post-Cold War academic and policy research began examining education's role in violent conflict, terrorism, warfare, and security provision.[4] Some analysts have discussed Europe and the Balkans.[5] Other work focussed on emergencies, conflict zones and post-war peacebuilding generally.[6]

To assess Kosovo's situation, understanding the broader socioeconomic, political, military and educational heritage in the Balkans is essential, but challenging. Here, various nations or ethnic groups have long remembered and taught different histories reflected in diverse education systems, textbooks, homes, religious institutions and communities. Despite eras of relative calm, peace or political stability, violence has periodically flared due to religious, ethnic, nationalist and imperial conflict since at least the 1389 'battle of Kosovo'. Different historical perceptions of Kosovo among Christian Serbs and Muslim Ottomans sometimes justified attacks while interference by outside powers exacerbated problems. After the First World War the Great Powers' decision of 1919 created territorial and legal legitimacy for a Yugoslavia including Kosovo, sowing the seeds for recent crises. Serb migration into Kosovo after 1919 countered Ottoman colonization over previous centuries[7] establishing a broader Yugoslav polity.

Tito era Yugoslavia reflected socialist unity and relative economic prosperity transcending ethnic differences while Yugoslavia was both bridge and buffer between East and West. Education policies helped unify the country. The University of Pristina opened in 1969–70, beginning a progressive era as Albanians were allowed Albanian language instruction and sciences improved. Open ties with Albania brought new books and cultural linkages building Kosovar–Albanian confidence, but raised political expectations. Serb authorities had sometimes arrested demonstrators for nationalist or secessionist activities and vandalism against Serb churches and graves. Still, Belgrade made many concessions, granting Kosovo Autonomy under a new 1974 Constitution and providing representation in Yugoslavia's Federal Presidency. But political advances masked deeper problems, many related to illiteracy, poverty, unemployment and demographics. Regional economic disparities fuelled internal problems and local tensions among Serbs and Albanians.

Intellectual, academic and linguistic ties to Albania (that both Belgrade and Tirana supported out of mutual interest for stability) strengthened Kosovars' identity either in an independent republic or within a greater Albania. Recourse to violence was understandable in the light of Serb repression or neglect, with counter-responses predictable. Education-related socioeconomic development concerns partly explain the riots and resistance that grew in the 1980s. As Woodward emphasized 'the student rebellion in Kosovo in 1981 began not as a secessionist movement, but as a demonstration against the lack of jobs for university graduates …'.[8] The Serbs, fearing more unrest, arrested hundreds of agitators then curbed Kosovo-Albanian rights and cooperation including teacher exchanges while prohibiting Albanian textbooks at Pristina University. Serb scholars in Belgrade criticized the substantial economic aid Belgrade provided to Kosovo amidst growing Albanian power and what some observers argued was Albanian intimidation, physical threats to, and 'ethnic cleansing' of, Serbs throughout the 1980s.[9] Thousands of Serbs felt forced to migrate, further entrenching local Albanian identity and power. This was the backdrop for the Serb Academy of Sciences and Art Commission's infamous 1986 *Memorandum* fuelling Slobodan Milosevic's repressive policies while forcing Albanians to an underground parallel education system of the 1990s.

Education became a central means by which Albanians vied for independence or offered a unique ethnic and nationalist vision through peaceful resistance to Serb oppression.[10] The international community – governments and NGOs – helped negotiate and implement a 1996 Education Accord between Belgrade and Pristina bringing confidence to some that differences could be resolved.[11] Albanians and Serbs would share University of Pristina facilities and a Commission was to supervise the agreement's implementation. But little follow-up came while both Albanian KLA inspired and Serb violence undermined the initiative without needed international technical assistance. Initially 'The Contact Group' of Major Powers supported the Education Accord publicly.[12] Meanwhile, the Organization for Security and Cooperation in Europe (OSCE) was working to contain conflict, de-escalate violence, monitor human rights violations and promote democratization. Some OSCE field officials even argued that the American-led NATO war of 1999 could have been averted had they been allowed to work properly. But the American-led Contact Group soon undermined the OSCE and sided with the militant Kosovo Liberation Army (KLA), choosing military intervention over diplomacy.[13]

There is little doubt that Serbs were responsible for numerous atrocities toward Albanians during the 1990s. But the NATO war simplified a complex set of issues by demonizing Milosevic alone, making heroes out of KLA 'terrorists' (identified by American diplomats in early public statements) and avoiding Western culpability. One way to understand many contentious issues underpinning current reconstruction efforts is the notion of a 'domination pendulum' over Kosovo. Since Yugoslavia's founding the political and demographic character of the region's education helped consolidate power for elites of all kinds. Some argue that shifts after the Second World War came in the following phases: from 1945–66 Serbs had more control; from 1966 to the 1980s Albanians gained greater political power and numbers; from the end of the 1980s to 1999 Serbs again ruled politically, but in each period migrations in and out reflected a repulsion or attraction with respect to the dominant group.[14] Building on this thesis, I argue that the international community's neglect of the importance of education contributed to a full-blown crisis in the late 1990s. The pendulum swung again in 1999 with the NATO intervention. Thousands of Serbs fled, this time from Albanian retaliation, and Albanian domination has characterized Kosovo since. Post 1999 education reforms are now reinforcing Albanian domination and Serb resistance, despite international community pledges to create a pluralist, multi-ethnic society.

International education dialogue, aid and reconstruction projects after 1999

In the wake of the 1999 Kosovo crisis a plethora of education policy debates, conferences, institution-building, aid projects and reforms followed with scores of local or international agencies involved. The NATO war resulted in some 45 per cent of schools damaged or destroyed, while just getting to school posed serious dangers for children and teachers with outbreaks of violence common.[15] The June 1999 South East European 'Stability Pact' outlined principles, priorities and actors for facilitating Kosovo's reconstruction in the region.[16] The Pact affirmed that settling the Kosovo conflict was critical to prevent a resurgence of war. Some 40 countries or organizations signed on including nations prosecuting the NATO war, countries from the region impacted, and donor agencies. The Stability Pact-affiliated 'Taskforce on Education and Youth' that pre-dated the NATO war was given new life, part of a long-term systemic approach within the Education Reform Initiative of South Eastern Europe and existing networks.[17]

Various international agencies, academics and NGOs have been involved. The United Nations Educational, Scientific and Cultural Organization (UNESCO) with the Council of Europe led a 'disarming history' project reflecting on problematic historical perceptions and memory in Southeast European wars to evaluate and improve teaching. Sweden hosted an 'International Conference on Combatting Stereotypes and Prejudice in History Textbooks of South-East Europe'. Recommendations followed to those responsible for education policy, aiming to remove material from textbooks that might incite violence toward other ethnic groups or countries.[18] Independently academics and NGOs began dialogue processes and collaborative research to reconcile competing visions of Southeast European history. A Purdue University project involves an international community of scholars in joint research and conferences to 'resolve the Yugoslav controversies' including theme groups interpreting Kosovo's problematic history. One examines Kosovo's Serb Minority (1974–90), asking to what extent Kosovo's Serbs were subject to discrimination and intimidation by a dominant Albanian majority, realities versus perceptions, and effects on Serb emigration. The other group on Milosevic's Kosovo (1990–9), asks to what extent Belgrade's crackdown in Kosovo was justified, examining Albanian reactions and the role of the KLA.[19]

Scores of other conferences or dialogue efforts have also sought to strengthen regional cooperation or stability through education.[20] Such academic debate has important implications for quality and effectiveness of Kosovo's education reforms, potentially affecting teaching, research, prescribed textbooks or teacher-training programs in subjects such as history or sociology. But most activities require more systematic evaluation to measure impacts and outcomes. One benchmark of a regional approach is how Kosovo furthers European values of the June 1999 'Bologna Declaration' which, after the NATO war, stressed 'the importance of education and educational cooperation in the development and strengthening of stable, peaceful and democratic societies ...'.[21] The Declaration views European education standards as benchmarks for university reforms, new teaching methods and programmes to advance comparable institutions, degrees, credit systems and courses. Implicitly education is also integral to conflict prevention while new political, social or economic reforms help avoid future wars. That is the theory. In practice the politics of Serb–Albanian relations and internal Albanian debates, as well as post-war aid collaboration and international reconstruction efforts, make the challenge exceedingly complex with necessary reforms difficult to implement.

Problematically, and moreover, much regional reconstruction through education after 1999, evident in policy dialogues and projects has been specific to other countries' needs with little direct attention to, funding for, or impact on, Kosovo. Various academics or NGOs from the region or abroad initiated most projects with only a few of Kosovo's post 1999 educational reconstruction efforts financed directly through Stability Pact-approved or coordinated projects. Principal educational reconstruction efforts came through a lead agency system creating a division of labour and donor coordination with bilateral or multilateral flagship initiatives. The Canadian International Development Agency took on teacher training, establishing the Kosovo Education Development Program through a Cdn$8 million initial contract (1999–2002) extended through 2002–5. UNICEF helped finance and facilitate a dialogue and reform process about a primary curriculum for a pluralist, multicultural society.[22] UNICEF's work was financed through a US$ 16,160,000 Japanese grant via the United Nations Human Security Trust Fund. The European Commission's Kosovo Task Force, with the European Agency for Reconstruction, prioritized education and training sector challenges in response to labour market reform needs.[23] And the EU through The German Technical Cooperation organization helped finance vocational and technical training, while the Finnish government supported Special Education.

Other donors or agencies supported complementary efforts. UNDP facilitated rebuilding scores of destroyed or heavily damaged school buildings. UNDP's Schools Rehabilitation in Kosovo project ran with US$ 2.6 million in support, again from the Japanese government.[24] UNDP has also promoted safer learning environments, including training on environmental health and landmine awareness collaborating with the Department of Education, UNICEF, and the Mine Action Centre in Pristina. UNMIK contracted with the Council of Europe for a two-year, $500,000 project in Pristina University to help it meet European standards in legislation, management systems, and upgrading professional qualifications in medicine and law. UNESCO and the International Bureau of Education organized curriculum development and training in Geneva.[25] The World Bank in 2003 approved a $4.6 million project grant to improve student participation, education system management, and school decentralization.[26]

Outside formal education institutions, the OSCE offered police training and democratization programs. Non-governmental organizations and foreign universities began scores of projects from international exchanges, to model United Nations events, to civic education. The United States is funding two 'Balkan Educational Partnerships' projects through the University of Pittsburgh – one a 'Kosova Civic Education Project'[27] and the other 'Street Law Kosovo: Practical

Legal Education in an Emerging Democracy'. A Pristina University based, Kosova Education Center (an Albanian led organization) working with aid agencies is analysing issues, documenting trends and facilitating international cooperation.[28] A private university – The American University in Kosovo – opened in 2003, financed mostly by Albanians offering a full spectrum of courses but focussed on business. The Rochester Institute of Technology, New York manages the curriculum, issuing American degrees.[29]

A comprehensive survey is not possible here, but although some projects have supported Serbs, most have not been integrated with Albanian efforts (even though UNMIK Regulation No. 2000/11 mandated this). Poverty, illiteracy and personal security are still pressing, especially income-related inequalities in rural areas, among girls (there is a a problematic gender gap) and for minority groups.[30] In Pristina University alleged buying of exams and grades, and misuse of donations, perpetuated politics and corruption.[31] Ethnic hatred between the Albanian majority and the Serb minority[32] still poses a security threat while war-related safety and crime concerns remain.[33] The international community goal of multi-ethnic cooperation and schooling is poorly implemented, in part due to lack of physical security for minorities.[34] In addition, various other destabilizing factors remain.

At first many efforts were coordinated through UNMIK–DoES (Department of Education and Science). Local and international NGOs complemented official or non-formal learning activities through everything from helping to build local schools to supplying textbooks, teachers or resource materials. Some are strictly traditional aid groups, while others are religious groups carrying other agendas. Kosovo's education leaders also participate in dozens of international conferences, training sessions and exchanges each year. Some included efforts to help define Kosovo's new curriculum.[35] But two years after the NATO war, and even when an important meeting with 70 internationals and Kosovars was held in Geneva to discuss a new curriculum framework, Serbs were excluded. This event was part of a broader international technical assistance effort that has effectively reinforced Albanian control over Kosovo's education policy. The organizers could only say obliquely that 'very unfortunately, Kosovar Serbs could not attend for security reasons'.[36]

Education in a tenuous security environment: contexts and persistent threats

Poorly addressed security issues have far reaching implications, whether it concerns Serbs and Albanians rarely participating in the same international meetings or their lack of collaboration on home soil. While Albanians in Kosovo once managed its underground education system as Serbs took over Pristina University, many Serbs say they now attend poorer schools arguing that Albanians receive the lion's share of donor funding. My first visit in February 2002 when I met education officials, visited school projects and witnessed an incident at Mitrovica underscored for me deeper problems. For a private citizen crossing the bridge over the river Ibar (separated by French peacekeepers) from the Albanian South to the Serb North was quite simply dangerous. Personal security for Albanians or those considered sympathetic was not guaranteed, while on the Albanian side the same was true for Serbs.[37] The establishment of UNMIK authority in Mitrovica in mid-2002, including a new education office, was helpful but will not permanently solve many broader security and development problems.

The international community goal of multi-ethnic cooperation and schooling is still poorly implemented, partly due to lack of physical security. Either from fear or contempt, Serbs do not attend schools or universities with Albanians, even though UNMIK initially attempted to arrange shift schemes or shared facilities. Up to 200,000 of the Serb minority, which fled mostly after 1999 under an Albanian 'ethnic cleansing' counter response, have yet to return to Kosovo.[38] A United Nations Commission for Refugees report stressed that Serb, Roma and other minorities still need international protection facing problems 'from acute discrimination, marginalization and restricted freedom of movement, to destruction of property and physical harassment, including grenade attacks, landmines, booby-traps, drive-by shootings and arson'.[39] The vast majority of Kosovo Albanians now do not face similar concerns. In a region where religious and educational symbols are an important extension of politics Albanian power has subtly or even overtly been 'cleansing' Serb ethnicity. The new Kosovo Ministry of Education even requested to destroy a Serb orthodox church on Pristina University lands.[40]

Political violence ('terrorism') and organized crime continues through popularly supported former KLA members, as well as within the Serb community, as ethnic divisions hamper reconstruction and regional stability.[41] Broader development and security issues cut across the education sector or school environments. Small-arms proliferation in Kosovo fuels violence and insecurity affecting youthful perceptions and experiences. An International Rescue Committee and UNDP survey highlighted that up to 50 per cent of students said they could get a gun within 24 hours, and that 20 per cent carried guns to school. While school violence was more typically the fisticuffs or intimidation variety, widespread gun presence is a serious problem.[42] Western news reports have been scarce with world attention focused on Iraq and other American-led 'war on terrorism' crises. However, through 2003 there were reports of nasty incidents, including shootings of unarmed Serb youth, and some wider analyses indicate persistent problems.[43] The more extensive Albanian riots of 17–18 March 2004 resulted in at least 19 deaths and 900 injured while over 700 Serb, Ashkali and Roma homes, ten public buildings, 30 Serbian churches and two monasteries were damaged or completely destroyed with some 4,500 people displaced.

An ICG report after the events of March 2004 suggested they were mostly spontaneous, although some were clearly premeditated by Albanian extremists and criminals. Some violence was even foreshadowed among KLA members and militants from the University of Pristina Students Union[44] underscoring educational contexts. Harsher critics, including Jean-Marie Guéhenno, Kosovo's United Nations Under-Secretary-General for Peacekeeping Operations, and some news reports, suggest riots were exploited or well planned. They may well have been part of a strategic initiative that a large Albanian public supported, to intimidate and ethnically cleanse most remaining Serbs from Kosovo. Thousands of Albanians were even brought to various locations by buses to conduct property burnings and a killing pogrom against Serbs.[45] Meanwhile, in the wake of this fiasco, a more damning report underscored that the UN and NATO have (despite their mandate to do so) seriously failed to protect Kosovo's minorities.[46]

Aside from these causes of organized violence broader contexts also bred foment. Socioeconomic factors including poor literacy and unemployment create weak foundations for personal and political security. Useful UNDP analytical work helps to expose this while modelling similar initiatives elsewhere in the Balkans. Its quarterly *Kosovo Early Warning Report (KEWR)* sometimes mentions education or training with links to unemployment. For the youth, from 16 to 24, the rate is a staggering 71.6 per cent amidst 49 per cent for the general population. Regarding education levels, 58.5 per cent are unemployed with only a secondary education, but it drops to just 7 per cent for those with higher education. Underlying policy problems also hamper development and mask unresolved conflicts. One *KEWR* noted that SRSG had not signed a new Higher Education law, causing tensions[47] but raising concerns about implementation of human rights standards and European values to create Albanian–Serb equality.

Another significant, and often ignored, reconstruction challenge is stress caused by low teacher salaries or other education-related problems (such as unemployed or poorly trained youth), as a potential trigger for future violence or civil conflict.[48] The first UNDP *Human Development Report* for Kosovo in 2002 highlighted that informal and formal education issues were beginning to be addressed.[49] UNDP's approach is holistic, emphasizing improved knowledge and skills. UNDP, highlighting education, stressed that this sector comprises some 25 per cent of Kosovo's total budget, with nearly 80 per cent of this spent on teacher's salaries. Yet they are typically low, requiring most teachers to find other income sources to survive, more easily encouraging crime or corruption to supplement meagre salaries. The UNDP report noted interrelated issues such as healthcare promotion and environmental protection requiring more education and public awareness to improve conditions. The capacity for university-level scientific research that focuses on environmental problems adversely affecting health and development is another cross-cutting issue needing serious attention in Kosovo to help relevant Ministries or aid agencies.

To better facilitate democratization, UNDP recommended a larger 'civic education' programme to explain democratic principles and processes with various interventions to promote tolerance and respect. It recommended youth training for active participation in government. Concerning formal education, UNDP raised concerns about the highly centralized system and recommended training local managers. More generally, UNDP stressed 'investing in education' and that youth was 'important to the future of Kosovo'. More attention was needed on: shortages of professional teacher training and the need for adequate salaries; the need for more education specialists transferring duties to Kosovars; the problem of integrating all segments of society (especially minority Serbs and Roma) into the education system; market studies to re-evaluate vocational curricula; understanding interlinked issues such as literacy rates; unemployment exacerbated by poor economic conditions, poverty or inadequate teacher training; public awareness programmes to advance gender issues; and capacity-building for cultural institutions.

Education dilemmas and reconstruction politics under UNMIK, PISG and MEST

In 1999, Kosovo became a *de facto* United Nations protectorate under Security Council Resolution 1244 authorizing an international civil presence to oversee peace and reconstruction efforts. Resolution 1244 affirmed a new complex power sharing challenge amid a broader set of political dilemmas implicating education policy, administration, curriculum development and programming imperatives. Resolution 1244 reinforced the sovereignty and territorial integrity of the then Federal Republic of Yugoslavia (FYR) and previous calls for 'substantial autonomy and meaningful self-administration' for Kosovo. Responsibility for education reforms after June 1999 has passed through three phases so far. Phase one meant emergency efforts until March 2000. Phase two began with the United Nations Interim Administration in Kosovo (UNMIK) and its establishment of the Department of Education and Science (DoES) under UNMIK Regulation No. 2000/11. Phase three began in 2001–2 with initial attempts to transfer power to a provisional government that included a Ministry responsible for Education.

To understand current challenges and imperatives, it is important to outline some key initiatives and policy frameworks. UNMIK in 2000 established its DoES as a temporary measure to help determine domestic reform needs and international aid, technical assistance or cooperation programs. The DoES was created with two 'Coheads' (an international expert civil servant and local Albanian leader) while UNMIK continued to manage planning or donor coordination. Importantly, this new DoES authority stressed that one of its functions was:

> the promotion of a single unified, non-discriminatory and inclusive education system so that each person's right to education is respected and quality learning opportunities are available to all, irrespective of their ethnic or social origin, race or gender, disability, religion, or political opinion.[50]

Under DoES structure, UNMIK began articulating a strategic plan – the Developing an Education System for Kosovo (DESK) initiative. DESK was a small DoES advisory body (22 internationals and 25 Kosovars) and planning process. Three working groups preschool/primary, secondary, and higher education/research focussed activities with special attention to curricula and teacher training. The first DESK draft came 17 October 1999 with March 2000 revisions. DoES International Co-head, Michael Daxner, stressed that DESK attempted to be inclusive of minorities while its main objectives were: 1) to ensure rapid resumption and continued learning during a transition to a democratically elected and accountable government, and 2) to support longer-term reconstruction and transformation of the education system to reflect a modern European society.[51]

By 2001, UNMIK facilitated a Constitutional Framework followed by the establishment of Provisional Institutions of Self-Government (PISG). New UNMIK head, Michael Steiner, began implementing DESK goals and a Transitional Department of Education, Science and Technology. In September 2001 (before November elections) UNMIK Regulation No. 2001/19 created a new provisional (that is, operational but not fully independent) government with five Ministries still under UNMIK's authority. The Ministry of Education, Science and Technology (MEST) mandate allowed it to establish policies and legislation to promote non-discriminatory, relevant, and quality lifelong learning.[52] Despite this new regulation and administrative direction to implement UNMIK Regulation No. 2000/11 under DESK, serious problems remain. The emerging system has mostly responded to the dominant Albanian leadership's demands with little direct contact or effective programme cooperation among Serbs and Albanians.

Despite UNMIK's attempt to support a multi-ethnic Kosovo/Kosova, the Albanian dominated provisional government is essentially building ethnically pure educational institutions. As the first Ministry of Education, Science and Technology annual report stresses, the 'MEST operating strategy is based and planned in accord with the new structure of the education system in Kosova'. The report claims that 'Kosova strives (to) establish a completely new reality, a new vision, in full accord with the principle goal of Kosovar society for integration in international structures and mechanisms.' Its stated credo was 'promotion and implementation of the idea for better education to all in Kosova, always based on the needs of Kosovan society and its individuals'.[53] This idealistic proclamation, however, masks underlying conflicts. By emphasizing 'Kosova' throughout its report (not 'Kosovo' mandated by Resolution 1244 and UNMIK) MEST undermined international law and scuttled Serb collaboration in constructing or delivering Kosovo's new education system. With UNMIK authorization, MEST has operated as a *de facto* Albanian institution. The MEST report simply noted in closing among 'obstacles' that not signing the Higher Education Law resulted in 'unpredictable consequences'. The report pointed opaquely to a state of 'lawlessness' and hindered communication, as well as a lack of sufficient regulations, education experts or sufficient budgets to carry out its work.

Higher education reforms: challenges for Kosovo or Kosova?

The new PISG (and MEST in particular), with its lack of willingness to implement a new Higher Education Law, is a powerful and symbolic statement. With respect to Pristina University in particular Michael Daxner stressed early on that it was at 'the very core of the political conflict' but now it must align with the schools system as a whole, to facilitate 'the disarmament and modernization of the school system' toward a new civil society.[54] But five years after Kosovo became an international protectorate reforms have yet to sufficiently address many underlying ideological, nationalist and security challenges. Regional reconstruction through education, policy dialogues and projects have often been specific to other countries' national interests or initiatives of outside academics and NGOs with little direct attention to, funding for, or impact on, Kosovo. Underlying ethnic or political conflicts (including their educational foundations), that led to the NATO war are far from resolved, and the education system (more correctly now two competing education systems) within Kosovo, are still playing a divisive role.

After 1999, the parallel education system that characterized much of the 1990s continued in reverse. NATO went to war ostensibly to protect Albanian human rights, but created conditions for *de facto* 'ethnic cleansing' of many Serbs from areas once shared with Albanians. Albanians now control Pristina University in the capital, and despite token participation in a new government, Serbs remain marginalized from education reform and rebuilding processes that would contribute to Kosovo as one unified province or multi-ethnic state. The Serbs, for reasons of personal security and politics, with the financial backing of the Serbian Ministry of Education and Sports (SMES), have reinforced their own education system in northern areas. The majority in Serb enclaves use the SMES curriculum and textbooks. This includes another Serb-controlled Higher Education institution initially called 'Pristina University' in Mitrovica, operating outside of UNMIK's authority until Belgrade agreed to cooperate better in 2002.

With the transition to Kosovo's new MEST in 2001, Steiner and UNMIK hoped to empower the new provisional authority while supporting minority rights. An important issue was ensuring equality of Slavic access to higher education, which UNMIK attempted through a February 2002 regulation establishing North Kosovo University, renamed the University of Mitrovica on 6 December 2002 by Executive Decision 2002/15.[55] This effectively offered formal recognition of and support for Mitrovica's previous Serb-controlled Pristina University. This was a milestone in improving Serb–UNMIK relations and in establishing pragmatic foundations for Kosovo's reconstruction. Mitrovica was long a dividing line symbolically, and in reality, separating Albanians and Serbs. With a new UNMIK education office there, there seemed greater promise, but the March 2004 riots also suggested more uncertainty. Even earlier, the Albanian dominated PISG had been obstructionist in not aiding Mitrovica or building a multi-ethnic state to include Serbs on an egalitarian basis, protecting minority interests. Instead the PISG (contrary to UNMIK's wishes) adopted a Higher Education Law on 26 September 2002 that would not incorporate Serb needs within a unified Kosovo.

In light of new challenges, with funding from the World Bank, and at the request of UNMIK's Education Department and co-head, Michael Daxner, the European University Association (EUA) led a mission to evaluate the university situation in Mitrovica. The EUA was commissioned to explore how it could better contribute to the regeneration of higher education in Kosovo.[56] The EUA's work built on Daxner's efforts to support a university in Mitrovica as an important higher education provider rather than a source of further political confrontation. Among EUA's observations were some Serb views on their university as a stepping stone for return to original premises (currently occupied by Albanians) in Pristina. The EUA called this a 'futile and unproductive vision', while its Rector and others recognized it was important to simply settle and properly develop the institution for Northern Mitrovica, closely linked to advances in the rest of Serbia. But so far Mitrovica's university has lacked basic educational resources from books to laboratory equipment, easy internet access and email for professors, and adequate library facilities, sports centres or gathering places to support students or cultural development.

Beyond the obvious there are few mechanisms to support broader reform efforts, much less transparency to enable the examination of funding processes or needs. Moreover, there are poor links with foreign universities that might help integration with European or international standards for teaching and research. Mitrovica is essentially isolated and again breeding insular attitudes. This sad state of affairs points to critical dilemmas for, and contradictory statements concerning, international community views or policies. Despite early criticism over parallel institutions, Mitrovica's university, as the EUA report stressed, serves an important societal need for Serb-language higher education in Kosovo not provided elsewhere. Mitrovica's university is also an important foundation for future economic regeneration in Kosovo as a whole. By taking over, or bypassing PISG authority for Serb higher education in Mitrovica, UNMIK has essentially (and problematically) legitimated a *de facto* parallel system which the international community (recalling the former Albanian institutions which operated prior to 1999) shunned.

To date there have been no serious studies on Kosovo's new education system or long-term implications for socioeconomic reconstruction or a sustainable peace. But parallel Serb institutions, in education, health or police services, remain a serious challenge to Kosovo's governance and important to solving its future. Despite objections by the international community, the Serbs clearly have good reasons for sustaining these institutions. Belgrade and minority Serbs have legitimately not trusted UNMIK (notwithstanding concessions including accepting UNMIK's new presence in Mitrovica). They also do not trust the PISG or MEST to protect their interests, much less provide needed funding or programmes. The ICG pointed out that Serb parallel institutions provide some 75 million Euro from Belgrade to finance vital jobs in an area where minority unemployment is upwards of 90 per cent. Belgrade also continues a pension system offering some security, which is jeopardized if Serbs sign contracts as UNMIK or PISG civil servants. Moreover, Serbs continue to face discrimination by Albanians in social or municipal services while, on the ground, security challenges lead the ICG among others to question whether the stated policy of multi-ethnic integration is realistic at this stage.[57]

The international community, however, gradually began to acknowledge the problem and offer solutions. A recent UNHCR/OSCE report called on UNMIK and MEST to cooperate with KFOR, UNMIK Police and others to develop and fund a comprehensive plan to improve security and access for minority students. It suggests that UNMIK and MEST must place a priority on integrating the education system in consultation with FRY's Ministry of Education.[58] In an April 2003 UN Security Council debate, many delegates criticized the Albanian dominated PISG for not adopting a new law on Higher Education to support the Serb minority.[59] Michael Steiner, before stepping down as UNMIK head, adopted a new regulation on Higher Education in Kosovo that 'adequately covers the rights of all Communities'[60] with an overview of how public and private higher education institutions should be governed, financed and evaluated with European standards and performance assessed by a Kosovo Accreditation Agency. But this still did not deal with the University of Mitrovica. An OSCE report 'Parallel Structures in Kosovo', implied that UNMIK was remiss in not better serving Serbs calling for a thorough assessment of the parallel school system. It recommended MEST and SMES negotiate mutual recognition of diplomas and certificates standardizing requirements.[61]

The Albanian-dominated MEST and the university it controls in Pristina, and the new UNMIK support for a separate Serb university in Mitrovica, reinforces this parallel system. Nonetheless, it still appears to be a necessary stage in helping facilitate socioeconomic development for all Kosovo peoples. Except for pockets of useful collaboration in some communities, widespread Serb–Albanian educational integration throughout the whole system is a pipe dream for now. However, through building the intellectual and institutional capacity for governance through improved social sciences, including exchanges or collaborative projects among Serb, Albanian and international partners, Kosovo's universities are essential for educating and training the next generation's leadership to live in peaceful democratic coexistence. So even though Pristina's Albanian university will likely continue, the UNMIK supported Mitrovica experiment with better external aid may also be a good start toward helping heal old wounds and may ultimately resolve the final status issue in a peaceful manner.

Conclusions: post-war education, research and development dilemmas

It may be time to seriously rethink the entire Kosovo rebuilding project, especially with respect to education. Reconstruction challenges run deep, due to the 1999 NATO war waged ostensibly to solve human rights abuses. Over five years later, new, more complex and difficult to untangle problems are entrenched. On the one hand there appears to be progress, including a new Education Ministry replacing UNMIK–DoES. But this has not resolved the underlying political questions. In fact it may increase divisions, creating an untenable situation requiring an international community presence for decades.

Nonetheless, there is room for modest hope. Michael Steiner stressed (rightly I suggest) that Albanians must facilitate appropriate institutions, laws and intentions for a multi-ethnic and democratic Kosovo before resolving Kosovo's final status. Steiner's 'Standards before Status' policy set targets in eight key areas:

functioning of the democratic institutions, the rule of law, freedom of movement, the return of refugees and internally displaced persons, the economy, property rights, dialogue with Belgrade, and the Kosovo Protection Corps. It is still unclear how new education reforms are overcoming (or exacerbating) discrimination against minorities, destruction of Serb identity in Kosovo, or a chronic 'culture of violence' and criminality that continues among some groups. More research is needed to monitor and evaluate trends. However, the international community and the Albanian majority finally agreed on the need for better mechanisms to resolve the status issue.

The new UNMIK Chief, and the Secretary-General's Special Representative Harri Holkeri (since resigned) with Prime Minister Bajram Rexhepi, leader of the Provisional Institutions of Self-Government in Kosovo, launched a new 'Standards for Kosovo' document on 10 December 2003, International Human Rights Day. This is meant as a clear mandate with defining principles or measurable benchmarks to prepare Kosovo for a decision on final status. Among the important elements impacting education that it calls for are for European standards to prevail in Kosovo. It proposes that parallel structures should be dismantled while continuing to ensure sustainable returns and equal rights for all, and in particular it stresses the need for a curriculum which 'encourages tolerance and respect of the contributions of all communities to the history of Kosovo' and that is accessible to all returnees. It also calls for public education (that is, communications through media, and so on) to support the returnee process led by PISG's example. A Steering Group including provisional government and UN officials will lead smaller Working Groups to implement standards.[62]

In principle all this sounds promising. It marks some maturity of the new provisional government in finally accepting that governance and human rights standards are essential. It was also a more pragmatic move on UNMIK's part. But in practice the outcomes are likely to be a long way off. After the March 2004 riots they seem even more distant, even though the UN Security Council reconfirmed that the Standards Plan was critical.[63] To support a just and effective governance system in Kosovo new initiatives to facilitate civic and human rights education among other useful reforms are especially needed with sustained monitoring and evaluation to measure effectiveness and impacts. Even if the final status issue is resolved the security climate will remain tenuous whether the international community ultimately creates one or two quite separate ethnic states and education systems. If two full systems emerge (this appears to be the direction things are heading) the move would be hypocritical. NATO leaders claimed they went to war to protect minorities yet the United Nations is now supporting *de facto* ethnic cleansing of Serbs and a parallel system which the international community said it would not tolerate. The American-led NATO war has effectively fostered deeper ethnic exceptionalism, new nationalism and exacerbated discrimination while the international community, by not insuring Serb security in a unified state, has enforced a pseudo multi-ethnic model favouring Albanian decision-making.

An ICG report (just before the March 2004 riots) called upon Kosovo's elected PISG, especially in areas of education and health, to take more seriously their authority and responsibilities.[64] It called for an apolitical civil service. Education clearly remains highly political (whether more formally among student organizations and professors' groups or through teachings and curricula). It is also still central to disputes between Albanians and Serbs over Kosovo's future. Nonetheless, a healthy vision for a parallel education sector could still complement (not compete with) 'standards before status' principles and benchmarks. The international community's challenge will be a long-term commitment to help build local education-sector capacity (especially in universities) to support collaborative self-governance. This will not be a quick fix. It can only work if the international community ignores both Albanian and Serb cries to immediately resolve the status question. Instead it should work with international, Serb and Albanian academics to develop a more cooperative, strategic vision and action plan for Kosovo's future. This means no fast pull out or handover to the Albanian-dominated PISG in transition to full governance, but a gradual transition most likely requiring at least another decade of strong international presence in Kosovo. More careful, strategic education investments supporting this will be crucial.

The politics of educational reconstruction in Kosovo deserve separate treatment, and could generate several useful topics for graduate student researchers. We need to know more about the functioning of the new Albanian-controlled Education Ministry, and what is actually being learned or taught in Albanian or Serb schools in Kosovo. We also need to better understand what roles the university sector (whether in Pristina or Mitrovica) play in regional stability with implications of dialogue (or lack of it) between Ministry officials in Belgrade and Pristina. There is little academic research yet being done on these issues, and aid agencies have not commissioned evaluations publicly shared or available for scrutiny by scholars. The OSCE has recommended that 'UNMIK/PISG should make a thorough assessment of the implications that the parallel school system has in Kosovo'.[65] I support this suggestion, but that it be done as part of a more comprehensive independent study of Kosovo's entire education system while long-term technical assistance, monitoring and evaluation projects are carried out with interested scholars and practitioners. Collaboration among international, Serb, Albanian and other education researchers and security scholars working with aid agencies, foundations and provisional government officials would also be extremely valuable.

Acknowledgement

For some of the research reported here I am grateful for a 2002 Canadian Department of Foreign Affairs and International Trade (DFAIT) Fellowship sponsored by the Canadian Consortium on Human Security (CCHS) at the University of Victoria's Centre for Global Studies. I am also thankful for a Canadian Department of National Defence (DND) travel grant for Kosovo field research. My argument does not represent the views or policies of the Canadian government.

Notes

1 With some exceptions this chapter draws from and builds on: Wayne Nelles, 'Education, Underdevelopment, Unnecessary War and Human Security in Kosovo/Kosova', *International Journal of Educational Development*, 25.1, pp. 69–84.

2 Without prejudging any political outcome of its future status in this paper, I mainly use the term 'Kosovo' as the international community norm unless specifically referenced (for example, in Albanian documents or quotes as 'Kosova').

3 For an overview of international education and state-building issues see: Ingemar Fagerland and Lawrence Saha, *Education and National Development: A Comparative Perspective, Second Edition* (Oxford: Pergamon Press, 1989).

4 David Hamburg, 'Preventing Contemporary Intergroup Violence, Education for Conflict Resolution', New York: Carnegie Commission on Preventing Deadly Conflict, December 1999, http://www.ccpdc.org/pubs/ham/hamfr.htm; Mohammed Bedjaoui, 'Preventive Diplomacy: Development, Education and Human Rights', pp. 35–60 in Kevin M. Cahill, (ed.), *Preventive Diplomacy: Stopping Wars Before They Start* (New York: Basic Books, 1996); Kevin M. Cahill, 'Political Violence and Education', *Current Issues in Comparative Education,* Special Issue, 15 November 2000, http://www.tc.columbia.edu/cice/content2.htm; Wayne Nelles (ed.), *Comparative Education, Terrorism and Human Security: From Critical Pedagogy to Peacebuilding* (New York: Palgrave-MacMillan Press, 2003).

5 David Coulby and Crispin Jones, *Education and Warfare in Europe* (Basingstoke: Ashgate, 2001); Nelles (n4 above).

6 Sobhi Tawil (ed.), *Final Report and Case Studies of the Workshop Educational Destruction and Reconstruction in Disrupted Societies* (Geneva: International Bureau of Education, 1997); CIDA, *Education and Peacebuilding: A Preliminary Operational Framework* (Ottawa/Hull: Canadian International Development Agency, 1999), www.acdi-cida.gc.ca/peace; UNESCO, Emergency Educational Assistance Unit (ED/EFA/AEU), *Education in Situations of Emergency and Crisis* (Paris: UNESCO, October 1999).

7 Lenard Cohen, 'Ethnopolitical Conflict in Yugoslavia: Elites in Kosovo, 1912–82', pp. 237–91 in Ronald H. Linden and Bert A. Rockman (eds), *Elite Studies and Communist Politics: Essays in Memory of Carl Beck* (Pittsburgh, University Center for International Studies, University of Pittsburgh, 1984).

8 Susan Woodward, 'Should We Think Before We Leap? A Rejoinder', *Security Dialogue*, 30, 3 (1999), pp. 279–81.

9 For illustration note that Albanian Communist party chief, Becir Hoti, acknowledged that he wanted 'to establish an ethnically clean Albanian republic', quoted in M. Howe, 'Exodus of Serbians Stirs Province in Yugoslavia', *The New York Times*, 12 July 1982, p. 8.

10 Denisa Kostovicova, 'Albanian Schooling in Kosovo 1992–8: "Liberty Imprisoned"', pp. 11–19 in Michael Waller, Kyril Drezov and Bulent Gokay (eds), *Kosovo: The Politics of Delusion* (London/Portland: Frank Cass, 2001); Julie A. Mertus, *Kosovo: How Myths and Truths Started a War* (Berkeley: University of California Press, 1999); Howard Clark, *Civil Resistance in Kosovo* (London: Pluto Press, 2000).

11 Miranda Vickers, *Between Serb and Albanian: A History of Kosovo* (London: Hurst & Co., 1998), pp. 305–6. Also see Stefan Troebst, *Conflict in Kosovo: Failure of Prevention? An Analytical Documentation, 1992–8* (Flensburg, Germany: European Centre for Minority Issues, May 1998), p. 77 for a copy of the Education Accord.

12 See Contact Group Statements 1997–8, http://www.ohr.int/docu.

13 Wayne Nelles, 'Canada's Human Security Agenda in Kosovo and Beyond: Military Intervention versus Conflict Prevention', *International Journal* (of the Canadian Institute for International Affairs), 57, 3 (2002), pp. 459–79 with relevant document

references. For one useful report see: Gordon Gibson, 'Should NATO – and Canada –have gone to war in Kosovo?', *Globe and Mail*, 20 July 1999, p. A11.

14 Chronology to 1999 borrowed from pp. 222–3; 231–3 of Marina Blagojevic, 'The Migration of Serbs from Kosovo during the 1970s and 1980s: Trauma and/or Catharsis', pp. 212–43 in Nebojša Popov (ed.), *The Road to War in Serbia: Trauma and Catharsis* (Budapest: Central European University Press, 2000).

15 UNESCO, 'Central and Eastern Europe, Synthesis Report, Final Version'. Prepared for World Education Forum, Dakar, January 2000, http://www2.unesco.org/wef.

16 The initial agreement: 'Stability Pact for South Eastern Europe', Cologne, 10 June 1999, http://www.stabilitypact.org, was meant to benefit reconstruction and stabilization of the region as a whole, not just Kosovo.

17 See background documents including 'Presidency Conference of Southeast Europe: European Educational Cooperation for Peace, Stability and Democracy', 14–16 November 1998, Graz: Karl-Franzens-Universität, http://www.see-educoop. net.

18 UNESCO, 'Disarming History, International Conference on Combatting Stereotypes and Predjudice in History Textbooks of South-East Europe', Visby, 23–24 September 1999, http://www.unesco.org/opi2/disarminghistory.

19 'The Scholars' Initiative: Resolving the Yugoslav Controversies 2001–2004', http://www.sla.purdue.edu/si/scholarsprospectus.htm.

20 Wayne Nelles, 'Toward Better Communications Cooperation in Central and Southeast Europe: Trends and Prospects', *Higher Education in Europe*, 26, 2 (2001), pp. 227–39.

21 The European Higher Education Area, *Joint Declaration of the European Ministers of Education*, Convened in Bologna on the 19 June 1999.

22 UNICEF Kosovo and DoES-UNMIK, 'The New Kosovo Curriculum Framework: preschool, primary and secondary education – Discussion White Paper', Pristina, September 2001, http://www.see-educoop. net/education_in/pdf/curr_framework-yug-kos-enl-t06.pdf.

23 European Commission Task Force Kosovo, *Education and Training in Kosovo: Post-conflict analysis and support perspectives with the European Agency for Reconstruction*, Pristina, 5 February 2000.

24 UNDP Kosovo, 'Technical Assistance and cooperation in Education: Kosovo project in higher education Schools Rehabilitation in Kosovo (SRK)' covering the March 2001 to May 2002 period, http://www.kosovo.undp. org/Projects/SRK/srk.htm.

25 http://www.ibe.unesco.org/National/Kosovo/kos02000.htm.

26 World Bank, 'Kosovo – Education Participation Improvement Project – Project Information Document PID11486', 2003.

27 I was External Evaluator to this project. Funding comes from the United States Secretary of State, Department of Education and Culture.

28 Dukagjin Pupovici, Halim Hyseni and Januz Salihaj, *Education in Kosova 2000/01* (Pristina: Kosova Education Center, December 2001).

29 http://www.aukf.org.

30 World Bank, *Kosovo Poverty Assessment, Volume I. Main Report Poverty Reduction and Economic Management Unit Europe and Central Asia Region, Report No. 23390-KOS*, 20 December, Washington, 2001, pp. 35–44; World Bank, *Kosovo Poverty Assessment, Volume II. Poverty Reduction and Economic Management Unit Europe and Central Asia Region, Report No. 23390-KOS*, 20 December, Washington, 2001, p. 7; UNMIK, 'UN mission spotlights Kosovo's gender gap in employment and education', 8 June 2004, *UNMIK News*, http://www.unmikonline.org/news.htm.

31 Organization for Economic Cooperation and Development, *Thematic Review of National Polices for Education – Kosovo – Stability Pact for South Eastern Europe, Table 1: Task Force on Education*, Paris: Organization for Economic Cooperation and Development, 22 June 2001, pp. 35, 41.

32 Dukagjin Pupovici, 'Stocktaking Research on Policies for Education for Democratic Citizenship and Management of Diversity in Southeast Europe: Country Report

Kosovo', Task Force Education and Youth of the Enhanced Graz Process Stability Pact, Working Table 1, Democratisation and Human Rights, DGIV/EDU/CIT, 2001, 45, 28 November, Council of Europe, Strasbourg. Pupovoci, 28 November 2001, p. 3.

33 Alissa J. Rubin, 'Police Have Hands Full in Kosovo: Organized crime threatens stability of province, leading U.N. to bolster its operation', *Los Angeles Times*, 13 August 2002, http://www.latimes.com; A. Mustafa, 'Fury at UN Final Status Conditions: Tough pre-conditions dash Kosovo's hopes of early discussion on independence', *The Institute for War and Peace Reporting, Balkan Crisis Report, Kosovo Special*, No. 405, 10 February 2003.

34 C. Chatelot, 'Hate and fear stalk Kosovo's dwindling Serbs', *Guardian Weekly*, 13–19 July 2000, p. 28; Wayne Nelles, *Kosovo Mission Report to Canada's Department of National Defence (DND)*, March 2002, http://www.globalcentres.org/html/defait.html; UNMIK, 'Minorities in Kosovo still face acute discrimination', UN reports. *UNMIK News*, 31 January 2003, http://www.unmikonline.org/news.htm#3101.

35 'Curriculum development in Kosovo – Intensive training workshop: Final Report', Geneva, 1–10 December 2000, http://www.ibe.unesco.org/National/Kosovo/kos02000.htm.

36 *Case studies in curriculum development: contributions to the Kosovo education reform* Pristina, 2–5 May 2001, http://www.ibe.unesco.org/National/Kosovo/pristine.htm.

37 Nelles (n. 34 above).

38 Jan Briza and Zoran Culafic, 'Djindjic Launches Battle for Kosovo', *The Institute for War and Peace Reporting, Balkan Crisis Report, Kosovo Special,* No. 405, 10 February 2003; Mustafa, n33 above; United Nations Security Council, 'Security Council, in Presidential Statement, Reaffirms Commitment to Multi-ethnic, Democratic Kosovo', Press Release, SC/7659, 2 February 2003.

39 UNMIK, 'Minorities in Kosovo still face acute discrimination, UN reports', *UNMIK News*, 31 January 2003, http://www.unmikonline.org/news.htm#3101.

40 Orthodox Diocese of Raska–Prizren and Kosovo–Metohija, 'SCANDALOUS: Kosovo's Ministry of Education requests destruction of a church, ERP', *Serbian Orthodox Church. Information service*, 22 January 2003, http://news.serbianunity.net/bydate/2003/January_22/6.html.

41 Independent International Commission on Kosovo, *The Kosovo Report: Conflict, International Response, Lessons Learned* (Oxford: Oxford University Press, 2000), p. 125; Reuters, 'Car bomb rocks Kosovo capital', *SwissInfo*. 14 December 2002, http://www.swissinfo.org/sen/Swissinfo.html?siteSect=143&sid=1517282; A.J. Rubin, 'Police Have Hands Full in Kosovo: Organized crime threatens stability of province, leading U.N. to bolster its operation', *Los Angeles Times*, 13 August 2002, http://www.latimes.com.

42 Anna Khakee and Nicolas Florquin, *Kosovo and the Gun: A Baseline Assessment of Small Arms and Light Weapons in Kosovo. Special Report* (Geneva: UNDP/Small Arms Survey, June 2003) pp. 39–40.

43 Arie Farnam, 'Deep divide over Kosovo's future', *The Christian Science Monitor*, 14 October 2003, p. 6; Arie Farnam, 'For refugees from Kosovo a long way back home', *The Christian Science Monitor*, 5 November 2003.

44 International Crisis Group, *Collapse in Kosovo Europe Report N0.155, 22 April 2004* (Pristina/Belgrade/Brussels: International Crisis Group, 2004), http://www.crisisweb.org/library/documents/europe/balkans/155_collapse_in_kosovo.pdf.

45 United Nations, 'March Violence in Kosovo "Huge Setback" to Stabilization, Reconciliation, Under-Secretary-General for Peacekeeping tells Security Council', *United Nations, Press Release, SC/8056*, 13 April 2004, http://www.un.org/News/Press/docs/2004/sc8056.doc.htm; Lawrence A. Uzzell, 'Kosovo's religious tables turned', *Christian Science Monitor*, 20 May 2004, http://www.csmonitor.com/2004/0520/p09s02-coop. html.

46 Human Rights Watch, 'Kosovo: Failure of NATO, U.N. to Protect Minorities. Reform of Security Structures Needed as New U.N. Administrator Takes Office', Human Rights Watch, Press Release, Brussels, 26 July 2004, http://www.hrw.org/english/docs/2004/07/27/serbia9136.htm.

47 *Kosovo Early Warning Report, 3 April–May 2003*, pp. 4–6, http://www.kosovo.undp.org/Projects/EWS/ewrn3_eng.pdf.

48 *Kosovo Early Warning Report, 4 May–August 2003*, p. 14, http://www.kosovo.undp.org/publications/ews4/EWS_4_Eng.

49 UNDP, *UNDP Human Development Report, Kosovo 2002*, http://www.kosovo.undp.org/HDR/hdr.htm.

50 UNMIK Regulation N0.2000/11, *On the Establishment of the Administrative Department of Education and Science*, Article 2.1 (b), 3 March 2000.

51 Michael Daxner, *Education in Kosovo: From Crisis to Recovery and Transformation*, paper prepared for Graz Stability Pact meeting, 9–12 March, United Nations Interim Administration in Kosovo (UNMIK) (Pristina: Department of Education and Science, 2000). Also see attached UNMIK, *Developing an Education System for Kosovo (DESK), Executive Summary, Annex 1.*

52 UNMIK Regulation N0.2001/19, *On the Executive Branch of Provisional Institutions of Self-Government in Kosovo*, Annex IV, 13 September 2001. Imposed by the UNSG Special Representative under authority of Security Council Resolution 1244.

53 UNMIK Provisional Institutions of Self-Government, Ministry of Education, Science and Technology, *MEST Annual Report 2002–2003*, Pristina, 10 April 2003, pp. 4–5, 46, http://www.see-educoop. net/education_in/pdf/mest_annual_report_2002–2003-yug-kos-enl-t05.pdf.

54 Michael Daxner, *Education policy statement 2001*, Unpublished (UNMIK), Department of Education and Science, Pristina, 1 July 2001, pp. 9–10.

55 Administrative Direction No. 2002/2, *Implementing UNMIK Regulation No. 2000/11 on the Establishment of the Administrative Department of Education and Science*, 14 February 2002.

56 European University Association, *University of Mitrovica: Report of EUA site visit, 10–13 December 2002*, http://www.unige.ch/eua/En/Activities/South_East_Europe/Mitrovica-EUAreport.pdf; Georg Woeber, *Status Report on the University of Mitrovica, Kosovo: Current Structure Development Perspectives* (Vienna: Woeber Management Consulting, February 2003).

57 International Crisis Group, *Kosovo's Ethnic Dilemma: The Need for a Civic Contract*, ICG Balkans Report 143 (Pristina/Brussels: The International Crisis Group, May 2003), pp. 4–5, 13.

58 UNHCR/OSCE, *Ninth Assessment of the Situation of Ethnic Minorities in Kosovo (Period covering September 2001 – April 2002)*, http://www.osce.org/kosovo/documents/reports/minorities/min_rep_09_eng.pdf.

59 United Nations Security Council, 'Kosovo has 'Some way to go' in Establishing Representative, Functioning Institutions, Security Council Told: Provisional Institutions of Self-government Hampered by Political Struggles, Assistant Secretary-general Annabi says', Press Release SC/7737, 23 April 2003.

60 UNMIK Regulation No. 2003/14, *On the Promulgation of a Law Adopted by the Assembly of Higher Education in Kosovo*, signed by Michael Steiner, 12 May 2003.

61 Organization for Security and Cooperation in Europe, Mission in Kosovo, Department of Human Rights and Rule of Law, *Parallel Structures in Kosovo* (Organization for Security and Cooperation in Europe, Mission in Kosovo, October 2003, http://www.osce.org/documents/mik/2003/10/698_en.pdf).

62 United Nations Interim Administration in Kosovo (UNMIK), 'Standards for Kosovo'. Press Release, PR/1078, Pristina, 10 December 2003, http://www.unmikonline.org/press/2003/pressr/pr1078.pdf.

63 United Nations, 'Security Council Reiterates that Kosovo Standards Plan should be Basis for Assessing Provisional Institutions of Self-Government', *United Nations, Press Release, SC/8082*, 30 April 2004, http://www.un.org/News/Press/docs/2004/sc8082.doc.htm.

64 International Crisis Group, *Two to Tango: An Agenda for the New Kosovo SRSG,* Pristina/Brussels: International Crisis Group, 3 September 2003, http://www.crisisweb.org/home/index.cfm?id=1618&l=1.

65 OSCE (n. 61 above), p. 8.

7 Crime and capitalism in Kosovo's transformation

Michael Pugh

Introduction

In the context of a fragile political and security situation, an ambiguous legal constitutional status and an imprecise and contested balance of power between international 'protection' and local ownership, academic and practitioner strategies in Kosovo have emphasized human protection, military security and public law and order. However, Kosovo is also a site of contention between economic norms. On the one hand, the external agencies have attempted to impose a neo-liberal economic model, rooted in the 1989 Washington consensus on developmentalism. On the other hand, Kosovars have clung to clientism, shadow economic activities and resistance to centrally audited exchange.

This chapter contends that these interactions led to accommodation by the external and domestic actors, but also to friction and contest. To some extent the protectors have cushioned the population from the rigours of neo-liberalism by investing in public services; to some extent Kosovar Albanians have accepted the conditionalities of the peacebuilders as a means to secure independence. By the end of 2002, the population of 1.8 million had benefited from donor reconstruction aid worth \$2 billion. Indeed, economic growth officially increased dramatically in the first two years after the war thanks to donor support, diaspora remittances and UNMIK spending on goods and services. The budget had considerable cash balances reflecting donor contributions, revenue gains from excise duties, the phasing in of income tax and strict monetarist rules on spending. In the absence of reliable official statistics, surveys indicated that per capita gross domestic product (GDP) had climbed significantly above the pre-war level by 2003. However, these calculations certainly underestimated the size of the pre-conflict GDP because the service sector was excluded from the Yugoslav accounting system.[1] Furthermore, the Banking and Payments Authority estimated that in 2002 only about 20 per cent of post-conflict GDP was domestically generated, the rest comprising foreign aid (50 per cent) and remittances (30 per cent).[2] In spite of the internationally financed reconstruction boom, the economy remained one of the weakest in Europe and growth had slowed down from 11.1 per cent in 2001 to 7.0 per cent in 2002.[3] In effect capital expenditure has floated on aid; the domestic authorities are left to fund institutional growth and recurrent disbursements. The weak economic recovery has reflected a long-standing neglect of agricultural and industrial investment, disruption and migration caused by the war, and the uncertainty about Kosovo's future constitutional status, which inhibits post-war investment.

The purpose of this chapter is to interrogate three critical aspects of Kosovo's post-war political economy: 'criminality'; unaccountable external economic governance; and neo-liberal development policy. It argues that Kosovo's post-conflict transformation policies and practices contain contradictions that risk frustrating the goals of economic growth and European integration, and which do little to alleviate the pressing issues of poverty and unemployment. But first it is essential to sketch the antecedents of Kosovo's political economy that confronted the external actors in 1999.

Lineages of resistance and dislocation

Throughout south-east Europe the heads of clans traditionally offered social stability through the distribution of land, revenues and welfare. Ottoman and subsequent Hapsburg efforts to establish property rights in law failed to eradicate the robust clientist and patrimonial systems.[4] Moreover, shadow economies of barter and black markets thrived in the Tito period and permitted the avoidance of socially discriminating and time-consuming bureaucratic obstacles to exchange. Shadow economies, local predation, and reversion to clientist and patrimonial protection of the exposed populations accompanied the economic fragmentation of Yugoslavia.[5]

Paralysis of the Yugoslav command economy was, however, significantly worsened by structural adjustment and austerity in the 1980s, introduced at the behest of the International Monetary Fund (IMF). Purchasing power fell by 30 per cent between 1983 and 1985. By 1990, unemployment had reached about 20 per cent, and perhaps as much as 60 per cent of the Yugoslav population was living at, or below, the poverty line.[6]

In Kosovo, formal GDP subsequently contracted by an estimated 50 per cent in the period 1989 to 1994.[7] Secession, war and sanctions further encouraged predatory war entrepreneurs to demand a cut from smuggling, and invigorated shadow trading as an international business that benefited crime syndicates and corrupt officials.[8] In turn, the conflicts were fuelled by wealth derived from transit trafficking in drugs, weapons, migrants, refugees and women forced into the sex industry.

Oddly enough, Kosovo remained relatively quiescent during the wars further west, though Kosovo Polje was the stage that Slobodan Milošević had used to rally Serb nationalism in 1987 and plunge the federal state into political crisis. In spite of rising unemployment, a precipitous deterioration of the formal economy and political and cultural repression by the Serb authorities, the Kosovar Albanians failed to seize the opportunity of the war in Croatia and Bosnia-Herzegovina to overthrow Serb control. To a large degree this level of neutrality depended on Ibrahim Rugova's strategy of forging democratic change through the creation of parallel social, economic and political structures. However, a kind of *pax mafiosa* also emerged. Sanctions spurred the trade in Turkish heroin and other goods across borders, boosting incomes in the area. Much of it was arranged by three gangsters with connections to state security: Zeljko Ražnatović (Arkan) in Serbia; Momcilo Mandić, a member of the Karadižić government in Republika Šrpska; and Enver Hajin of the Albania Secret Police. The Serbs connived at protecting the route through Bulgaria, Serbia, Budapest and Bratislava, much of it around Plovdiv controlled by a Kosovar, Nazim Delegu.[9] In essence, the *pax* produced a reciprocal relationship of intimidation and subsistence that enabled people to cope and survive which seems to have contributed to keeping Kosovo relatively peaceful. In spite of power struggles with the Croatian and Italian mafiosi over trafficking, the Albanian Kosovars, in collaboration with the Italian *'Ndrangheta'* asserted control of the heroin traffic, laundering the revenues in Switzerland, and financing their own insurrection.[10]

The militarization of the Kosovar Albanian struggle, the contest over trafficking and the failure of the 1995 Dayton Accord to address Albanian political ambitions combined to wreck Rugova's strategy. The peace crumbled in 1997 when a cascade of arms looted from military and police depots in Albania worked its way northwards. The KLA centred on the Jashari clan was the main beneficiary of the Albanian weapons liberation of 1997 and continued to profit from trafficking. Under the leadership of Hashim Thaçi, the KLA became not only a guerrilla force, but an economic structure for controlling the labour market and providing black market civilian goods.[11] By early 1998, the KLA's shadow economy began to co-exist with, and often within, Rugova's parallel economy. This embedding of trafficking corporations in the regional economies proved to be an enduring legacy of the Yugoslav wars.

Meanings of criminality

It is a commonplace perception, both within and beyond Kosovo, that the territory remains a major hub of organized crime. Indeed, south-east Europe's political economies seem to have been archived as 'criminalized'.[12] Regional traffickers and corrupt political leaders have been held responsible by external peacebuilding agencies for resistance to economic modernization and integration with the world economy.[13] As a legal concept, the term 'criminal' signifies behaviour contrary to legislative controls and beyond the rule of law. Economically, it connotes the avoidance of audited revenue payments that would otherwise be available for local authority and government distribution. Politically, it is portrayed as a threat to transparency and accountability, and thus a threat to sustainable democracy. As a social concept, 'crime' indicates moral debasement. But such discussions of 'crime' tend to lack a nuanced understanding of its variations, its relationship to legitimate activities and the inadvertent role of external policies in its perpetuation. Indeed, there is a deeper issue of morality, particularly where people are directly harmed, such as in the trafficking in women and children. From an ethical perspective, any strategy of human protection should undertake to eliminate rights abuses of this kind, and external intervenors merit plaudits for their action to protect the abused. The negative perceptions and representations serve to distance the supposedly virtuous, law-abiding cores of capitalist democracy from phenomena that are categorized as threats to their social well-being. These same cores, and the international financial institutions, are thereby exonerated from complicity in sustaining the demand for shadow activity.

Economic 'crime' in Kosovo can be deconstructed into at least three varieties of 'shadow economy': organized mafia rackets and trafficking; corruption, fraud and nepotism in business and public life; and the coping or survival shadow economies of the population at large. To some degree these varieties overlap (a university professor may take bribes to cope with a newly impoverished status, for example). They probably all draw on traditions of economic organization that resisted the pressures of modern, centralized and audited economic exchange well before the disintegration of Yugoslavia.[14]

Organized crime

With regard to organized crime, the conflicts of the 1990s opened up new opportunities and incentive structures for ruthless, predatory and socially destabilizing mafia networks and corrupt rentiers to gain from clientism, trafficking and black marketeering. As noted above, sanctions busting through Kosovo's borders became a highly lucrative economic strategy. In the post-conflict period, entrepreneurs adapted by expanding the shadow spaces for trafficking in weapons, goods and people. In this project they were inadvertently assisted by the priorities and dynamics of peacebuilding based on the neo-liberal model.[15] The economic priorities of the post-conflict 'protectorate' presented opportunities for further wealth creation among the victors of the conflict.

In particular, arms trafficking has remained a source of income. Dedicated to becoming the army of an independent state, the KLA had formed a separate social, criminal and military structure whose abilities to take over local municipalities were demonstrated after the Yugoslav forces vacated Kosovo.[16] The KLA had also acquired former Yugoslav petrol companies and fuel distribution, and they controlled petrol stations which they used for money laundering.[17] KFOR and the UN Interim Administration Mission in Kosovo (UNMIK) chose not to confront the KLA and enforce disarmament, but instead coerced it into an Undertaking on Demilitarization for arms control and demobilization in June 1999.[18] The policy was dictated by the notion that accessibility to weapons was too widespread to make wholesale disarmament effective.[19] The KLA was officially disbanded and replaced by the Kosovo Protection Corps as a civil emergency force issued with light weapons only. Supposedly under strict international control, the Corps is regarded as an army in waiting. It has participated in violence against minorities, intimidated the Kosovo Police Service and judiciary and is engaged in organized crime and weapons trafficking.[20]

About a third of the half a million weapons looted in Albania in 1997 remain at large, many of them passing through Kukes where they have been sold to

Albanian nationalists in Kosovo and Macedonia. Other Kukes consignments reach the Albanian port of Vlores, a transit centre for weapons taken across the Adriatic into the European Union. Assorted military weapons are found in ordinary homes, and AK47s can be purchased for as little as US$ 35. In 2003, a UN Development Programme (UNDP) flagship initiative aimed to restore public confidence in security through a weapons armistice. Only 155 items were handed in during a short-lived armistice after a year's preparation.[21] Although the murder rate is no worse than elsewhere in central-east Europe, between 330,000 and 460,000 weapons are believed to be in civilian hands and are used more often than elsewhere.[22] Some weapons are held for protection in the event of conflict recurring, as was demonstrated during the ethnic cleansing of Serb, Roma and Ashkali minorities throughout Kosovo in March 2004 in which 19 people died (while the local police and international units took no preventive action).[23] Weapons are also used by youths to demonstrate prowess and by rival KLA factions following the disbandment of the organisation. Murders have as much to do with disaffected youth and gangsterism, as with the politics of ethnicity. Gang warfare directed against a notorious Gashi family in Kosovo was responsible for a car bomb in Sarajevo that killed a Gashi associate in January 2004.[24] Attacks against protectorate personnel also continue – though it was probably inadvertently symbolic that in 2003 a violent affray injured members of a World Bank delegation in a Mitrovica pizzeria.[25]

Corruption

Corruption, the misuse of public office or private business for illegal gain, is perhaps less directly life-threatening than the gangsterism of organized crime. Moreover, surveys and indices of corruption related to the misuse of public office indicate that it may not be pervasive in government processes, and that Kosovo fares better than neighbouring communities on scales of tolerance, practices and the ability of the authorities to deal with it.[26]

Yet the issue remains serious and expert opinion reports endemic corruption, particularly among the legal, medical, educational and other professional classes, and in the power and telecommunications companies. In November 2003 the head of UNMIK, Harri Holkeri, had to set up a new unit to counter corruption in budget-funded enterprises – and within UNMIK's own ranks after a UN official was found guilty of embezzling $ 4.5 million from the power company.[27] The EU and other donors had invested upwards of 700 million in reviving the existing power system, but the system produces less than before the conflict and shortages continue; only about a third of the customers actually pay for what they use. Bribery and corruption concerning building permits and the illegal construction of thousands of buildings had also led to an investigation against local politicians.[28] In 2002, a sacked customs officer claimed that international officials were hiding a major corruption problem, and subsequently the head of the customs service, Ylber Rraçi, was charged with fraud and abuse of power.[29] In addition, the failure to regulate financial activities seems to have made it easy to launder money and engage in lottery fraud.[30] Experts also consider that processes of privatization are prone to abuse and without safeguards could become a 'de facto money laundering operation'.[31] Indeed, there are concerns that privatization will follow the same course as in Bosnia and Herzegovina where it enriched an elite of war entrepreneurs and their political protectors.[32] Former KLA fighters, including the Thaçi family, are prominent among the beneficiaries. In January 2000, UN police raided the apartment of Gani, elder brother of the political leader Hashim, and found 500,000 marks in cash, which he claimed had been paid to him for intermediary services by a Canadian construction firm working in Kosovo (though the firm's director maintained that the fee was in the region of only 120,000 marks).[33]

This issue mobilized USAID and the East-West Management Institute to launch a major anti-corruption programme with a major conference in Priština in March 2002, attended by some 200 people, mainly from cadres of capitalism but also from unions and NGOs.[34] Ordinary Kosovars were increasingly disenchanted with the former KLA's protection rackets, trafficking and deadly power struggles. Disciples of free-market capitalism also regard the widespread fraud and corruption in day-to-day business as detrimental to fair competition. Lack of transparency in business practices and an absence of regulatory frameworks, for example, lead to insider dealing.[35] Confronted by the scale of the problem, the institutions promoting free-market enterprise have paradoxically counselled stricter regulation, oversight and accountability mechanisms, financial disclosure provisions and the engagement of NGOs and civil society in anti-corruption schemes. Such measures would no doubt contribute to transforming the economic environment by removing local resistance to audited exchange and providing equal opportunities to corporate capitalism and foreign investors. Nevertheless, the main obstacle to removing corruption is economic stagnation and low purchasing power.[36] Reducing corruption and fraud, like reducing the shadow economies that enable the poor to cope and survive, is thus contingent on improvement in the general economic situation.

Coping and survival

Shadow economic activity has been a means of coping and surviving for sections of the population throughout south-east Europe. The power of mafia and clientist networks is sustained partly because it performs a social function. For example, in Republika Srpska shadow economies increase personal consumption, productivity and employment, improve the variety of goods and services, and reduce social inequalities, adding more than 50 per cent to the domestic product.[37] The black market may also be considered a kind of 'free' market, or at least 'managed' in a sense not dissimilar from the management of capitalism. For example, as with free markets, successful entrepreneurship depends as much on social networks of assistance, protection and marketing as much as competitive pricing. In this sense, too, the black market provides a social function in underpinning networks of clientism and allegiance: 'self-help groups' *par excellence*.

Equally salient, the anti-crime offensives in Kosovo have been hampered by the inability of the external actors to link such offensives to poverty-reduction and job creation strategies. Failure to comprehend the social functions of 'crime' has led in equal measure to hubris, frustration and self-exoneration on the part of the external actors.

Unaccountable economic governance

In its own lack of transparency and accountability, UNMIK has been widely perceived as a sorry exemplar of institution building. Perhaps because UNMIK has been run from the militarily orientated UN Department of Peacekeeping Operations, the mission to Kosovo has lacked knowledge about the local legal system, shown insufficient respect for local traditions and marginalized locally elected representatives in terms of policy input. By 2003, the unaccountable international agencies were reportedly losing respect.[38]

Implementing an ultimatum

The UN mission seemed to have a relatively uncomplicated palimpsest on which to etch an economic future. Clearly there were considerable difficulties apart from economic resistance in the shadow economies. These included the legacies of discrimination against the Albanians and their lack of property rights; the capture of municipal authorities by the KLA; poor rural infrastructure; a gross imbalance in wealth and opportunity between rural and urban areas; and the creation of parallel Serb structures dependent on Belgrade for security, health, education, welfare and public utilities. Nevertheless, wealth redistribution was facilitated by the small population size and the expulsion or marginalization of previously privileged Serb workers, administrators and professionals. Commercial law, and administrative and financial institutions, could be virtually created from scratch. Moreover, UNMIK simply expropriated state assets. Chief among them was the huge, but decrepit and heavily indebted, Trepča state mining and smelting complex near Mitrovica. UNMIK troops seized the complex from Serb control as a prelude to its transfer to foreign consortia.[39] Yet most of the works remain closed on account of sulphur dioxide discharge, acid pollution and flooded mine workings. A major source of employment is thus denied to Serbs, though UNMIK paid some 1,000 workers to clean up the complex.[40]

Above all, NATO came armed with an economic vision that its most powerful members had already inserted into the Rambouillet ultimatum of 23 February 1999 before the war. The *diktat* that 'the economy of Kosovo shall function in accordance with free-market principles' became integral to the NATO/KLA war aim of securing the territory from Serb authority.[41] The economic principles were not actually spelt out at Rambouillet, but it was assumed that they were valid and should be imposed. Security Council resolution 1244 of 10 June was less presumptive, but supported economic development through the Balkan Stability Pact, which in turn specified free-market economies throughout the region.

The constitutional framework

In keeping with NATO's imperialism, UNMIK then arrogated the right to stipulate in the constitutional framework that Kosovo must adopt a neo-liberal economy.[42] Kosovo's leaders had little choice but to agree if they wanted to gain independence eventually.[43] The constitutional framework was formulated by UNMIK, 'the Quint' (the UK, US, Germany, France and Italy), the Contact Group (including Russia), and the G8 (plus Canada and Japan), and promulgated by the Special Representative of the UN Secretary-General (SRSG) in May 2001. It confirmed that UNMIK had the ultimate authority to decide that Kosovo's economic welfare would be fostered through the development of a market economy. The economy would thus be harmonized with what was loosely characterized as the 'Euro-Atlantic community's developmental standards'. Charged with responsibility for economic reconstruction (Pillar 4 in the UNMIK architecture), the EU operates through its European Agency for Reconstruction, which reports to the European Commission as well as to UNMIK. Indeed, complaints by UNMIK about the parallel structures of the former KLA and the Serb minority lack moral authority when the external actors protect their own parallelism. Completely outside UNMIK, USAID is another influential actor, which at the end of 1999 commanded a regulatory framework for the financial sector in the form of the Banking and Payments Authority.

UNMIK exercised exclusive control and regulation over economic policy and personnel, and over public and socially owned property and enterprises.[44] When some members of the UN Security Council, such as Russia, regarded changes to property rights as an infringement of sovereignty, the head of the EU pillar, Joly Dixon, retorted that UNMIK and not the Security Council would decide the details for administering Kosovo.[45] Development benchmarks were subsequently imposed on Kosovo, including the adoption of the deutschmark and then the euro, without any direct input by Kosovars.[46] Moreover, the constitutional framework specified that the SRSG would decide the parameters of budgetary and monetary policy.[47] The SRSG convened and presided over the Economic and Fiscal Council (operated by Americans and Australians paid by USAID)[48] and appointed its international and Kosovar members. The SRSG appointed the international Auditor General, the international and Kosovar members of the Governing Board of the Banking and Payments Authority (acting as the central bank) and verified the locally elected directors of the Customs Service and Tax Inspectorate.

Industrial control

Following the creation of a Department of Trade and Industry in December 2000, an UNMIK regulation (No. 2002/12 of May 2002) set up the Kosovo Trust Agency as the landlord and trustee of socially and publicly owned property. Exclusively under international control and operated by EU staff and USAID contractors, the Trust Agency aimed to 'preserve or enhance the value, viability, and corporate governance of socially owned and public enterprises in Kosovo'. It does so by selling them off. The legal basis for this project is cloudy because constitutionally Kosovo is part of a state that owns these enterprises, and the ownership of many state enterprises was forcibly taken over by KFOR (in the case of the Trepča complex) or by the KLA. The initial goal was privatization of 500 companies, in the face of trade union and Belgrade's opposition. Socially owned enterprises were operating at a third of capacity, employing 30,000 workers with another 30,000 on unpaid leave, out of Kosovo's total employed labour force of 341,000.[49] Kosovar researchers also accused the Department of Trade and Industry of unwittingly reinstating the badly malfunctioning self-management system of the former Yugoslavia by reviving elected worker's councils. In the absence of a Department of Trade and Industry field presence to exert authority, the councils were permanently locked in disputes with self-appointed KLA strongmen who sold off stock and rented out premises to line their own pockets.[50] According to its critics, the Trust Agency's own lack of transparency adds to perceptions of corruption. It has also displayed limited understanding of the needs of the private sector for access to basic infrastructure and property titles, and it has been unable to tackle the essential prerequisite of reforming registry and ownership. Instead, private enterprise has become parasitic on the ailing infrastructures of state industry.[51]

Crime controls

UNMIK learned the necessity of tackling shadow economies from experience in Bosnia-Herzegovina, where anti-crime measures and institutions had been established slowly. UNMIK Customs was the first public body to be set up, and together with EU Customs Assistance Mission (CAM-K) reformed the collection system, tripling revenues between 1999 and 2003.[52] But with only seven CAM-K officers and a shortage of staff and processing capacity in the Customs Service, the control mechanisms were seriously deficient.[53] It also took two years for the EU to establish a Kosovo Anti-Economic Crime Unit to counter crime and promote intolerance of criminality.[54] Moreover, special processes were introduced for illegal activity by key political figures, which fostered a widely held view that Kosovar leaders benefited from a degree of immunity.[55] In effect, criminality was not seen as a high priority and an economic system was introduced that failed to curtail it.

In contradiction to numerous declarations that Kosovo was to be governed in accordance with democratic principles, economic policy is determined by the EU, the international financial institutions and national aid agencies. Under the constitutional framework, the peoples of Kosovo are entitled to protect their ethnic, cultural, religious and linguistic identities, and to be free of economic discrimination. But they are denied the right to choose their economic future, and the choices made for them are ideologically infused and poorly implemented.

Neo-liberal developmentalism

This does not mean that the external agencies have ignored all earlier experience of defective social protection in Bosnia-Herzegovina. Nor have they been insensitive to the moral obligation to repair the economic damage and social displacement wrought by NATO itself during the war. The neo-liberal credo of Rambouillet and the constitutional framework has been tempered in rhetoric and practice by programmes of social protection.

Social protection

Thus the EU's 2002 Action Programme gave priority to the delivery of public services, institution building, public administration and socially oriented projects.[56] The UNDP emphasized employment generation through training programmes and social justice projects for ending ethnic and gender discrimination.[57] The World Bank provided significant sums for social and public welfare and for poverty reduction through a Trust Fund.[58] Together with the UNDP, the Bank also supported community initiatives for infrastructure rehabilitation and attempted to strengthen the income generation capacity of vulnerable rural families. Even the IMF proposed reform to facilitate long-term planning and stressed the need for investment in education, health and social policy.[59] In Kosovo, therefore, several partners in economic restructuring have acknowledged the importance of social justice, and have undertaken investment in poverty reduction and public services.

Bare-knuckle capitalism

However, in moving from reconstruction to development, the EU, the international financial institutions and the national aid agencies, notably USAID and the UK's Department for International Development (which are not accountable to UNMIK), generally sing variations on the neo-liberal tunes of monetarism, privatization, deregulation and state withdrawal from the economy.[60] The adverse impacts of this agenda, in the view of many informed critics such as Joseph Stiglitz and George Soros, were already evident in central and eastern Europe.[61] Undeterred by experience, the development assumptions of the external protectors were presented in policy reports, laws and regulations. As it was not a state, Kosovo could not qualify for World Bank and IMF loans. This might be deemed a blessing in disguise, but the international financial institutions could still provide advice and, as in the World Bank's case subsidize, 'economic reforms', through the budget ($16 million) and private sector development ($3 million).[62]

An IMF delegation to Kosovo in November 2003 concluded that the main risks to the economy arose from serious governance problems in publicly owned enterprises, an uncertain long-term economic outlook and pressures for rapid expansion in current spending. In spite of slackening growth, rising unemployment and falling purchasing power in 2002–03, the IMF welcomed curbs on consumption power and advised further controls on wages, social welfare, public sector employment and compensation for workers thrown out of work by privatization.[63] Here, then, the IMF expressed its (long-discredited) structural adjustment model of fiscal stringency and deflationary curbs on government expenditure and consumption power. Deficit financing was not part of its lexicon, even in conditions of social distress. In the last quarter of 2001, an estimated 50 per cent of the population lived in poverty and 12 per cent in extreme poverty.[64] In the first quarter of 2003, the unemployment rate was estimated at between 49 and 57 per cent (70 per cent among 16–24 year olds). About 25 per cent of the population were registered as job seekers.[65] Not surprisingly, opinion surveys ranked unemployment and poverty among the greatest problems facing Kosovo.[66] These were not, however, the top priorities of the external agencies.

An investor's charter

International officials have had a seemingly inexhaustible faith in economic growth and jobs through the privatization of small to medium enterprises. Joly Dixon was a zealot for rapid privatization and reportedly wanted to sell off enterprises at a rate of 20 a week.[67] His *White Paper* on Enterprise Development Strategy ran into opposition from the unions and some Kosovar economists, as well as from Serbia and the UN Security Council. However, state laws were introduced to ensure an investor-friendly environment, including regulations on foreign investment, repatriation of capital, the purchase of real estate and the 99-year leases of land formerly controlled by socially owned enterprises. These were deemed essential to wean the territory from its dependence on foreign aid.[68]

Likewise, USAID's credo has been: 'to set in place institutions, practices, and policies that encourage and reward investment', and 'to work directly and intensively with businesses to create a dynamic, competitive and expanding private sector.'[69] USAID therefore fostered a mirror image of the US economy with a kind of investor's charter masquerading as a development strategy. It aimed to:

> provide the framework for market-based economic growth that will permit self-sufficiency and enable Kosovo to achieve its economic aspirations in a free market environment. Under this strategic objective the policy and legal environment will be set in place, export barriers diminished, work will be completed on modern budget, tax and financial systems, and socially-owned assets will be privatized.[70]

Accordingly, USAID focussed on improving business capacity and the ability of business associations 'to provide meaningful input in the development of economic policy and law ... [and to] ensure an operating environment that supports business creation, market expansion, and rational investment'. By August 2003, USAID had contributed $200 million to Kosovo, of which $46 million was spent on 'economic policy', and a further $42 million on private-sector development (including agriculture and a business support programme). An example of Albanian Kosovars able to take advantage of this largesse to become one of the *nouveau riche* was Abdurrahman Konjufca. Dismissed as a consequence of Serbianization policies from the state Shpendaria poultry concern by the Serb administration in 1990, Konjufca was able to invest US$1 million of development loans from USAID via the American Bank of Kosovo to gain control of the business after the war.[71] However, these initiatives have provided little new employment; USAID's substantial business support programme had created a grand total of 635 jobs by August 2003.[72] About half of the small to medium enterprises represent the restitution of traditional micro enterprises – the family or one-person smallholdings, pizzerias and kiosks. The majority were barely surviving, let alone driving economic growth.[73]

Privatization of former state and socially owned companies was unlikely to compensate for the liquidation of decrepit industries and loss of industrial employment.[74] The Trust Agency put six such companies up for tender in May 2003, but interest was weak especially among foreign investors.[75] Without employment alternatives, deindustrialization has encouraged emigration, leading to depletion of the territory's skills pool, and encouraged engagement in informal economic activity. Studies of reliance on foreign direct investment and privatization to stimulate economic growth suggest that productivity does not increase and benefits are heavily skewed towards entrepreneurs who take control of public enterprises.[76] Foreign direct investment appears to make little impact on growth, subject to the level of repatriated profits, but increases the risk of instability in production and consumption because of the volatility of external commitment. Moreover, economic deregulation and withdrawal of the state from the economy contradicts the requirement for strong institutions of public authority. The effort accorded to social protection by the external actors has been consistently counteracted by the attention paid to introducing neo-liberalism. In this context, shadow markets act as a survival mechanism, enabling people to exist at, or just above, the general poverty level.[77]

An alternative conception

The free-market ideology represented as a normative model for post conflict societies suppresses the contradiction inherent in nursing, protecting and subsidizing the investment and business sectors with public funds. In Kosovo, the rhetoric of support for private enterprise may disguise an absence of transformation on property laws and business-oriented infrastructure, but this represents a flaw in implementing the model, rather than a critique of the model itself. The externals ignore the effect of bare-knuckle capitalism in weakening social cohesion and political authority. Institution building and social welfare policies may have received closer attention from the external actors than has been the case in Bosnia and Herzegovina, but this has not deflected policy-makers from dictating an economic model, which was given an unusual constitutional status, to privilege profit-seeking entrepreneurs. The model entails fiscal austerity for a balanced budget and the inhibition of consumption power, while large sums are spent in attempting to create a mirror image of aggressive capitalism and to construct a political balance in favour of entrepreneurs.

Controls over organized crime, and incentives to denounce corruption can certainly be improved, and as indicated earlier considerable effort could be made to deal with the trafficking in people. Alternative strategies do need to confront the deeply immoral aspects of criminal activity. This can be done domestically through tough regulation, the monitoring of officials and draconian sanctions; and also through the mobilization of civil society (including investigative journalism).[78] Because shadow economies profit from the absence of cross-border policing and differential tax rates in south-east Europe, a regional approach to trade is also essential. Macedonia has a free-trade agreement with Serbia that allows imports into Kosovo duty-free, while exports from Kosovo to Macedonia incur a 14 per cent tariff. Imports from Albania attract a tax of 26.5 per cent, while Kosovo's neighbours only pay 15 per cent, thereby creating an incentive to misrepresent the origins and value of goods. However, regulation and policing do not address the functional basis of shadow economies when they are coping and survival mechanisms for the general populace in the absence of formal welfare provision. An emphasis on legal controls and policing is unbalanced in that it criminalizes shadow markets while giving the unaccountable external protectors *carte blanche* to legalize socially stressful policies.

Economic expansion to make the territories less 'crime' dependent requires more openness to alternative approaches on the part of the external actors. An alternative route to growth would be based on fiscal policies that stimulate borrowing to build production capacity. A Keynesian recovery strategy for production and purchasing power would also build up social capital. 'Pump priming', even in the absence of a 'Marshall Plan', and cheaper borrowing would stimulate consumption, savings and domestic investment.[79] Modified forms of the protectionism that have enabled the economies of the US and the EU to flourish should not be denied to south-east Europe. There is an element of fantasy about expecting Kosovo to engage in export-led growth and integrated free trade, especially as expert analysis indicates that growth leads to free trade rather than vice versa.[80] Forms of protection might include *inter alia*: non-tariff barriers and subsidies to protect particularly vulnerable sectors such as agriculture; control of imports while liberalizing those vital for processing and trade; and devaluation only to a competitive exchange rate level. Economic priorities would thus shift to fostering production using underemployed resources, easing the demise of ailing industries, strengthening social capital, and providing a firmer basis for a long (perhaps fifteen-year) transformation to freer trade and integration with the EU.

Conclusion

The archiving of the economies of the protectorates in south-east Europe as 'criminal' overlooks the social welfare elements in shadow economies in the absence of state safety nets. The dominant international partners present in south-east Europe appear to have learned something of the importance of social protection from their experience of rubbing neo-liberal salt into Bosnia's war wounds. However, the investment in social projects and poverty reduction does not compensate for the ideology of aggressive neo-liberalism that perpetuates the dependence of the poor on shadow economies and keeps the mafiosi and war entrepreneurs in business.

The protectorate powers allowed no debate on the most appropriate economic systems to foster. NATO members went to war with an economic strategy already cast, and the EU and the international financial institutions were delegated a completely free hand to impose it. Consequently, the UNMIK and associated authorities have ultimate control over finance and budgets; there has been limited transfer of ownership over economic policy.

The strategy may be summarized as macroeconomic stability to promote investor confidence, and the use of public money derived from government revenues in Kosovo and government budgets in aid donor countries to subsidize private capital acquisition and investment for profit. The intention may not only be to achieve macroeconomic stability, install a free enterprise culture and make Kosovo safe for foreign investment. Given concerns about organized crime, corruption and the shadow economies, UNMIK has exercised caution in relinquishing the levers of the economy to Kosovar leaders and has invested in a degree of social protection. However, this has also meant that a meaningful role in economic decisions is denied to civil society and it is difficult for the population to hold Kosovar politicians responsible for the country's economic welfare. This may be justifiable in so far as civil society is likely to have limited influence on economic policy, but it also seems to be the case that the international protectors define civil society in the narrow terms reminiscent of Adam Smith, as private enterprise to be given every assistance to counter the economic claims of the rest of civil society. Moreover, the international protectors seem to discount the extent to which an imported economic model, especially if rigorously imposed, reinforces the need for communities to protect themselves from the adverse impacts of neo-liberalism and to spend as much as they think advisable on public infrastructure projects and public services.[81]

Dependence on governmental support to private enterprise contradicts the neo-liberal ideology of the free market that the strategy claims to represent and reproduce. In addition, it may be seriously doubted whether subsidizing business generates strong public institutions and economic growth in post-conflict contexts. Privatization is likely to further reward the war entrepreneurs who claimed the spoils of peace. At the same time, the neo-liberal economic model inhibits the prospects for legitimate work, taxable economic exchange and an increase in consumption power. In the absence of alternative sources of income generation, dependence on shadow activity has therefore been a necessity for many workers and their families.

Acknowledgement

I am indebted to Claire Heristchi, Neil Cooper and other colleagues who commented on the draft, and to the ESRC-funded research programme on the Transformation of War Economies, RES-223–25–0071.

Notes

1 Robert Corker, Dawn Rehm and Kristina Kostial, *Kosovo: Macroeconomic Issues and Fiscal Sustainability* (Washington, DC: IMF, 2001), p. 24.
2 Gross national product (GNP) exceeded GDP by about 25% (GNP = GDP + income of Kosovars employed by international donors + diaspora remittances). IMF estimates cited by the Banking and Payments Authority of Kosovo, *Annual Report: 2002*, Pristina, 2002, p. 8 (www.bpk-kos.org/publications/Annual%20Report%2002.pdf).
3 Ibid; Sven Gunnar Simonsen, 'Nation-building as Peacebuilding: Racing to Define the Kosovar', *International Peacekeeping*, 11, 2 (Summer 2004), pp. 289–311; United Nations Development Programme (UNDP), 'Factsheet 4: Security', Communications and Advocacy Team, UNDP, May 2003 (www.ks.undp. org); UNDP, 'Kosovo Early Warning Report N0.4', May–August 2003, p. 10. Donor commitments for budget support, peace implementation and reconstruction were 2.5 billion for 1999–2003. This excluded humanitarian assistance and funds for the international police. Diaspora remittances were worth an estimated 400–500 million euros annually. Office for South East Europe, European Commission and the World Bank, 'Donor Pledges and Commitments and Spending in Kosovo', June 2003. (www.seerecon.org/kosovo/documents/kosovo_report_june_2003.htm).
4 European Stability Initiative, *The Ottoman Dilemma: Power and Property Relations under the United Nations Mission in Kosovo*, Priština: UNMIK Lessons Learned Unit and European Union Pillar in Kosovo, 8 August 2002.
5 Carl-Ulrik Schierup (ed.), *Scramble for the Balkans: Nationalism, Globalism and the Political Economy of Reconstruction* (Basingstoke: Macmillan, 1999); European Stability Initiative (n.4 above).
6 Branka Magaš, *The Destruction of Yugoslavia: Tracking the Break-up, 1980–92* (London: Verso, 1993), pp. 96–7. See also, George Macesich (ed.) with Rikard Lang and Dragomir Vojnić, *Essays on the Yugoslav Economic Model* (New York: Praeger, 1989).
7 World Bank estimate cited in Alexandros Yannis, 'Kosovo: The Political Economy of Conflict and Peacebuilding', in Karen Ballentine and Jake Sherman (eds), *The Political Economy of Armed Conflict: Beyond Greed and Grievance* (Boulder CO: Lynne Rienner for IPA, 2003), p. 173.
8 See, e.g., Xavier Bougarel, *Bosnie: Anatomie d'un conflit* (Paris: La Découverte, 1996), p. 125; Peter Andreas, 'The Clandestine Political Economy of War and Peace in Bosnia', *International Studies Quarterly*, 48, 1 (2004), pp. 29–51; David Cortright and George A. Lopez, *Sanctions and the Search for Security: Challenges to UN Action* (Boulder, CO: Lynne Rienner for IPA, 2002), p. 98.
9 Francesco Strazzari, 'Between Ethnic Collusion and Mafia Collusion: The "Balkan Route" to State Making', in Dietrich Jung (ed.), *Shadow Globalization, Ethnic Conflicts and New Wars: A Political Economy of Intra-state War* (London: Routledge, 2003), p. 145.
10 The US Drug Enforcement Agency estimated in 1997 that the Kosovo mafia's finances were worth treble the GDP of the Albanian state, cited in ibid., pp. 141–2.
11 See, generally, Tim Judah, *Kosovo: War and Revenge* (New Haven: Yale University Press, 2000), pp. 135–62.
12 See, e.g., Michel Chossudovsky, 'The Criminalization of Albania', in Tariq Ali (ed.), *Masters of the Universe? NATO's Balkan Crusade* (London: Verso, 2000), pp. 285–316.
13 'BiH is a centre of organized crime', *Nezavisne Novine* (Banja Luka), 2 December 2003, p. 2. [OHR trans.]; Foreword by Henrik Kolstrup, UNDP Resident Coordinator, *Human Development Report: Bosnia and Herzegovina, 2002* (Sarajevo: UNDP, 2002).
14 Christopher A. Corpora, 'The Gas Station Blues in Three Parts: The Effects of Organized Crime on Stability and Development in Southeast Europe', Paper presented at the ISA Conference, New Orleans, 23–27 March 2002.

15 Yannis (n. 7 above).

16 Marcus Brand, *The Development of Kosovo Institutions and the Transition of Authority from UNMIK to Local Self-Government,* Priština/Geneva: Centre for Applied Studies in International Negotiations, January 2003, p. 25.

17 Adriatik Kelmendi, 'Kosovo: Fuel Smugglers Flourishing', Institute for War and Peace Reporting (BCR No.321), 28 February 2002 (www.iwpr.net/in...rchive/bcr2/bcr2_20020228_3_eng.txt).

18 David Rohde, 'Kosovo Seething', *Foreign Affairs*, May/June 2000, pp. 65–79.

19 Neil Cooper, 'Security Sector (Lack of) Transformation in Kosovo', in Keith Krause and Fred Tanner (eds), *Arms Control and Contemporary Conflicts: Challenges and Responses*, PSIS Special Studies No. 5, Geneva: Programme for Strategic and International Security Studies and Geneva Centre for Security Policy, 2001, pp. 65–127.

20 William G. O'Neill, *Kosovo: An Unfinished Peace*, (Boulder, CO: Lynne Rienner for IPA, 2002) pp. 117–23; John Cockell, 'Joint Action on Security Challenges in the Balkans', in Michael Pugh and Waheguru Pal Singh Sidhu (eds), *The United Nations and Regional Security: Europe and Beyond* (Boulder CO: Lynne Rienner, 2003), pp. 124–7.

21 Robert Piper, UNDP Kosovo Resident Representative, 'Moving from Reconstruction to Development', Press Conference, 17 December 2003 (www.ks.undp. org).

22 Graduate Institute of International Studies, Geneva, *Small Arms Survey 2004: Rights at Risk* (Oxford: Oxford University Press, 2004), p. 197.

23 See the Human Rights Watch Report, *Failure to Protect: Anti-minority Violence in Kosovo*, March 2004, 16, 6 (D) (July 2004) (www.hrw.org/reports/2004/kosov00704); ICG, 'Collapse in Kosovo', International Crisis Group report no.155, Pristina/Belgrade/Brussels, 22 April 2004.

24 The deceased, Taib Torlaković, specialized in extortion. Agim Gashi, a drug baron in Milan until his arrest there in 1999, had supplied his brothers in Kosovo with weapons for the war. 'One of Sarajevo Mafia leaders killed', *Nezavisne Novine* (Banja Luka), 19 January 2004, pp. 1,3; BBC, 'Correspondent', broadcast 7 December 2003.

25 Coincidentally the Prime Minister, Bajram Rexhepi, was also present and may have been the main target of the violence. UNMIK News release, 8 December 2003 (www.unmikonline.org/news).

26 Bertram I. Spector, Svetlana Winbourne and Laurence D. Beck (for Management Systems International), 'Corruption in Kosovo: Observations and Implications for USAID', 10 July 2003. and SELDI Corruption Index Report April 2002 in USAID, p. 12.

27 'UN forms anti-corruption unit in Kosovo', *Agence France-Presse*, 5 November 2003.

28 Nheat Islami, 'Mayor to Lift Lid on Kosovo Corruption', Institute of War and Peace Reporting, BCR No.332, 19 April 2002 (www.iwpr.net/in...rchive/bcr2/bcr2_20020419_1_eng.txt).

29 Zoran Culafic, 'Customs in Kosovo', UNMIK on Air, 4 February 2002 (www.unmikonline.org/radio/scripts/Englsh/february04/021604.htm).

30 Arben Qirezi, 'Kosovo: Lottery Arrests Highlight Growth in Fraud', Institute of War and Peace Reporting, BCR No.328, 4 April 2002 (www.iwpr.net/in...rchive/bcr2/bcr2_20020404_5_eng.txt).

31 Spector et al. (n. 26 above), p. 19.

32 See, Michael Pugh, 'Postwar Political Economy in Bosnia and Herzegovina: the Spoils of Peace' *Global Governance*, 8, 4 (Autumn 2002), pp. 467–82.

33 Lutz Kleveman, 'Brothers in arms fall out over spoils of Kosovo', *Daily Telegraph* (London), 12 June 2000.

34 East–West Management Institute, 'Report on Fighting Corruption in Kosovo: Lessons from the Regional Conference', Pristina, 4–5 March 2002 (www.ng02ngo/pdf/ReportAnti-CorruptionConference_21.pdf).

35 Muhamet Sadiku, 'The Impact of Corruption on Kosovo's Economy', Survey conducted in December 2001 by the Riinvest Institute for Development Research, Priština (a partner of the Washington-based Center for International Private Enterprise) (wwww.cipe.org/publications/fs/articles/article1e35.htm).
36 Spector et al. (n.26 above).
37 Rajko Tomaš, *Analysis of the Grey Economy in Republika Srpska*, Banja Luka: UNDP, March 1998.
38 See, Brand (n. 16 above), pp. 19, 30–4; Simon Chesterman, *Kosovo in Limbo: State-building and Substantial Autonomy* (New York: International Peace Academy report, August 2001); International Crisis Group [ICG], *Two to Tango: An Agenda for the New Kosovo SRSG*, ICG Europe Report No. 148, Priština/Brussels, 3 September 2003, p. 18; Robert Muharremi et al., *Administration and Governance in Kosovo: Lessons Learned and Lessons to be Learned*, Priština/Geneva: Centre for Applied Studies in International Negotiations, January 2003.
39 The aggregate debts were over 80 million. At its peak in the 1970s it had employed 22,800 workers, but this had diminished to 7,000 by 1995. Michael Palairet, 'Trepča, 1965–2000', report for the Lessons Learned and Analysis Unit, EU Pillar of UNMIK, European Stability Initiative (available at www.crisisweb.org); UNMIK news release, 14 August 2000 (www.un.org).
40 Palairet (n. 39 above).
41 'Interim Agreement for Peace and Self-Government in Kosovo', Rambouillet, 23 February 1999, ch. 4a 'Economic Issues', Art. 1(1). Article II specified the reallocation of ownership and resources of government-owned assets, pensions and social insurance, revenues and any other matters relating to economic relations.
42 Regulation No.201/9 on a Constitutional Framework for Provisional Self-Government in Kosovo, Promulgated by the Special Representative of the Secretary-General Hans Haekkerup, 15 May 2001.
43 Susan J. Henders, 'The Road to Kosovo and Kurdish Iraq: The Internationalization of Minority Autonomy Arrangements', Paper presented at BISA 28th annual conference, University of Birmingham, 15–17 December 2003.
44 Muharremi et al. (n. 38 above), p. 39.
45 He denied that his early departure from the job was related to this. Interview with Joly Dixon *Koha Ditore*, (Priština) 2002, p. 11. (www.unmikonline.org/press/mon/lmm200200.html); 'Analysis: Kosovo investment – an acceptable risk?', *Reuters* report, Priština,18 June 2000 (www.UNMIKonline.org/press/wire/im190600.html).
46 ICG (n. 38 above), p. 16.
47 Regulation No.201/9 (n.42 above), ch.8.1 (c),(d).
48 Muharremi et al. (n. 38 above), p. 39.
49 UNDP, 'FactSheet 1: Unemployment', Communications & Advocacy Team, UNDP, May 2003 (www.ks.undp. org).
50 Muharremi (n. 38 above), pp. 40–1.
51 Ibid., pp. 42–3; European Stability Initiative, 'The Ottoman Dilemma' (n.4 above).
52 Richard Caplan, 'Partner or Patron? International Civil Administration and Local Capacity-building', *International Peacekeeping*, 11, 2 (Summer 2004), pp. 229–47.
53 World Bank, 'Kosovo: Economic and Social Reforms for Peace and Reconciliation', Washington DC: World Bank, 1 February 2001 (www.seerecon.org/kosovo/documents/wb_econ_report)
54 Yannis (n. 7 above).
55 Brand (n. 16 above), pp. 16–17, n.42. However, in 2002 arrests by KFOR of high profile Albanian Kosovar leaders, including Rustem 'Remi' Mustafa, led to a brief spell of nationalist rioting. Paul Mitchell, 'Kosovo: UN forces arrest former KLA commanders', 4 September 2002 (www.wsws.org).
56 European Agency for Reconstruction, '2002 Annual Action Plan', press release EAR/REG/03/01, 14 February 2003 (www.ear.eu.int/publications/news-a1a23gc4.htm).

57 UNDP Kosovo, 'Job-creation and minority programming' 17 December 2003 (www.ks.undp. org/flagship).

58 In 2002–03 the Bank's affiliate, the International Development Association, allowed UNMIK grants of up to $15 million with a focus on poverty alleviation. From 2000 to 1 July 2002 the Bank's $60 million Trust Fund had financed $4.2 million for social protection, $6 million in social funds, $4.4m in education and health, and $14.7m for agriculture. World Bank 'Kosovo Brief', September 2002 (http://Inweb18.worldbank.org/ECA/ko...9496D385256B3C005EEA54?Opendocument). The World Bank's Post-conflict Reconstruction Unit has produced pro-poor diagnostics and appears to accept that a linear model of transition is generally unviable. World Bank Post-Conflict Unit, 'Conflict Prevention and Post-Conflict Reconstruction: Lessons Learned' (Washington DC: World Bank, 1998).

59 IMF, 'Staff Visit to Kosovo, Concluding Statement', 3–14 November 2003 (www.imf.org/external/np/ms/2003/111403.htm).

60 The World Bank, for example, placed privatization well ahead of social protection in its main strategy document (n. 53 above). Like some aid donors including the European Commission and the UK, the IFIs often make development aid conditional on privatizing utilities, which then fail to deliver quality services to the poor. Peter Hall and Robin de la Motte, 'Privatisation and Conditionalities in Six Countries', Report by the Public Services International Research Unit, Greewich University, for War on Want, February 2004.

61 George Soros, *The Crisis of Global Capitalism: Open Society Endangered*, Oxford: Public Affairs, 1998; Joseph Stiglitz, *Globalization and its Discontents (*London: Penguin, 2002); Amy Chua, *World on Fire: How Exporting Free-Market Democracy Breeds Ethnic Hatred and Global Instability* (New York: Doubleday, 2002).

62 European Commission and the World Bank (n.3 above).

63 IMF (n. 59 above). An agreement with the Unions allows 20 per cent of proceeds of sales of socially owned enterprises to go to workers employed for the past 3 years. Spector et al., (n.26 above), p. 19.

64 USAID strategy paper September–December 2001 survey (www.usaid.gov/missions/kosovo/pdf/kosovo_strategy_2001_2003.pdf).

65 UNDP, 'Factsheet 1: Unemployment', Communications, Advocacy Team and Policy Team, May 2003 (www.ks.undp. org); 'Early Warning Report' No.4, table 2.1, p. 11 (www.ks.undp. org).

66 UNDP, 'Early Warning Report', (n. 65 above), Table A10, p. 31.

67 Interview with Joly Dixon, *Koha Ditore* [Priština], 2002, p. 11 (www.unmikonline.org/press/mon/lmm200200.html).

68 Stefan Armbruster, 'UN launches Kosovan sell-off', BBC News, 23 May 2003 (http://news.bbc.co.uk/1/hi/1business/2932328.stm).

69 USAID Kosovo Mission, *Strategic Plan 2004–2008*, Priština, July 2003, p. 15.

70 Ibid., p. 16, strategic objective 1.2.

71 International Center for Soil Fertility and Agricultural Development, 'Kosovar Agribusinessman's Investment in Poultry Farm Pays Off', (available at: www.ifdc.org/SuccessStories/Kosovar%2520Agribusinessmen.pdf).

72 USAID/Kosovo, *Newsletter*, 1, 2 (Priština, August 2003), p. 4.

73 Muharremi (n. 38 above), pp. 41–2.

74 Simonsen (n. 3 above).

75 The UNDP explained this as a combination of factors: lack of economic reform in the business environment, lack of UNMIK transparency in the process; absence of trade union consensus; disputes over legislation and ownership of land in municipal and social ownership; and concern about the use of proceeds. UNDP (n. 65 above), pp. 16–18.

76 Massimo Florio, *The Great Divestiture* (Cambridge, MA: MIT Press, 2004); Béatrice Hibou (ed.), *Privatizing the State* (New York: Columbia University Press for CERI, 2004).

77 Michael Pugh and Neil Cooper with Jonathan Goodhand, *War Economies in a Regional Context: Challenges of Transformation* (Boulder CO: Lynne Rienner, 2004).
78 Spector et al. (n. 26 above).
79 Stiglitz (n. 61 above).
80 Kamal Malhotra et al., *Making Global Trade Work for People* (London: Earthscan, 2003).
81 Henders (n. 43 above). See also, Susan L. Woodward, 'Economic Priorities for Successful Peace Implementation', in Stephen Stedman, Donald Rothchild, and Elizabeth Cousens (eds), *Ending Civil Wars: The Implementation of Peace Agreements* (Boulder, CO: Lynne Rienner, 2002), pp. 183–214.

8 Administering membership of international society

The role and function of UNMIK

Rasmus Abildgaard Kristensen

The United Nations Interim Administration in Kosovo (UNMIK) is the most radical contemporary manifestation of an old idea, namely that the administration and sovereignty of failed states and contested territories could be entrusted to international organizations and powerful states acting on behalf of international society.[1] The practice of international administration has a long history stretching back at least to the end of the First World War. Some of the most prominent examples have been the League of Nations Mandates System and its successor, the UN Trusteeship System. However, during the period of decolonization, the practice lost its legitimacy and seemingly died. For that reason, it was somewhat unexpected that international administrations should resurface in the 1990s. Beginning in 1995 with the administration of Bosnia, under the auspices of the Office of the High Representative, and culminating in 1999 with the UN administrations of Kosovo and East Timor, international organizations have taken on responsibility for governing entire peoples and territories.

The new administrations have drawn a great deal of scholarly attention in academic journals, but the vast majority of this literature has focused on technical issues related to the design and conduct of particular administrations.[2] These issues are important, but – as argued by Roland Paris – there is a need for analyses that relate these administrations to larger theoretical debates within the discipline of International Relations.[3] However, with a few exceptions, this call has gone unheeded.[4] Drawing on the international society approach, this chapter offers a theoretically guided analysis of international administrations by examining their role and function as an institution of contemporary international society.[5] This means that the practice of international administration should be understood as an institutionalized example of collective action to promote and uphold common norms and values in the society of states.[6] More specifically, the chapter will look at the relationship between some of the fundamental norms and values that have informed the contemporary revival of the institution. Are they compatible or do they conflict with one another? On that basis, I seek to explain the underlying normative reasons for UNMIK's difficulties in implementing and reconciling its two main purposes, namely to resolve the delicate question of Kosovo's final status while creating democratic institutions of self-government.

At the theoretical level, I argue that international administrations are not only established to rebuild collapsed governance structures in failed states, as has been the traditional understanding in the literature on the contemporary cases, but may also be used to address sovereignty problems stemming from disputes over the status of the territories put under administration.[7] More importantly, I argue that we need to examine the nexus between these two functions and relate them to more general norms and values of international society. I further posit that the principle of self-determination (including the debates about positive versus negative sovereignty and national versus territorial self-determination) is critical in understanding the role and function of international administration as well as the institution's inbuilt dilemmas. Referring to UNMIK's difficulties in Kosovo, I show that the problems cannot be explained merely as the result of international mismanagement or the fact that two conflicting parties – each supported by different great powers – make rival territorial claims. Rather, UNMIK's predicaments reflect a much deeper normative inconsistency in the society of states. The case of Kosovo clearly demonstrates the inherent difficulty in promoting positive sovereignty and internal self-determination (democratic and humanitarian government) while defending a restrictive territorial definition of the right to external self-determination (the right to claim sovereign statehood). Finally, I suggest a way out of the dilemma in Kosovo and discuss how normative consistency can be restored in the society of states without jettisoning its fundamental ordering principles.

The chapter is organized as follows. The first section outlines the theoretical debate about international administrations and what this fails to account for. Section two presents a loose genealogy of changes in the definition of the right to self-determination from the interwar period to the post-Cold War order. Sections three to five look at UNMIK's role in Kosovo and examine the practical and normative dilemmas encountered. The final section discusses the problems and potential of international administration as an institution in contemporary international society.

The theoretical debate about international administrations

While a number of academic articles have tried to pin down the role and function of the new international administrations, the overwhelming majority of these analyses have been confined to listing specific functions, such as the promotion of human rights, the provision of law and order, or the establishment of electoral systems.[8] Approached from a more abstract perspective, international administrations are used to displace local actors who – normally – would have been responsible for the governance of a particular territory. In other words, international administration challenges the principle of self-determination – that is, the right of a people to determine its own affairs.[9] Why, then, are international administrations established? Ralph Wilde suggests that the institution should be seen as a device to address two perceived problems with the normal model of state sovereignty.[10] I will add that the best way to understand the character of these problems is to start with the two component parts of the principle of self-determination. Following Robert Jackson, 'determination' refers to the way people are to govern themselves, while 'self' refers to the identity of the people who are to govern themselves.[11]

First, international administrations can be seen as a response to problems with the quality of governance being exercised by local actors. The problems arise when the political authority in a particular territory is unable or unwilling to maintain order within its borders and govern with some degree of legitimacy and consent from the local population. An international administration responds to this problem by taking over the responsibility for such failed or collapsed states in order to create or restore basic domestic conditions of security and freedom before sovereignty is returned to the local population.[12] This function often consists of two tasks. The first and most immediate task is to fill a governance vacuum. The second and more long-term task is to reform the local administrative structures in order to remove the problem that led to the establishment of an international administration in the first place. This is typically understood to imply the furtherance of democracy and good governance through various institution-building activities.

Second, international administration can be deployed to address problems related to the identity of certain local actors who exercise or might exercise administrative control over a particular territory (that is, problems related to the collective 'self'). In this case, the problems arise when it is disputed who has the right to exercise sovereign authority in a given territory. Unfortunately, there are very few discussions of this aspect in the literature on international administrations. This is remarkable given that all contemporary examples of international administrations have been established in the context of a territorial dispute: Bosnia had been the scene of a devastating territorial conflict among its three constituent groups; Kosovo's Albanian majority had struggled for ten years to secede from Serbia; and in East Timor, the local population had overwhelmingly voted for independence after a prolonged guerrilla war against Indonesia. In the literature, these territorial disputes have either been seen as part of the background which led to the uncivil conditions that prompted the establishment of an international administration, or they have been treated as a contextual factor complicating the implementation of the operation.[13] However, currently it is not being considered that responding to territorial problems is in fact an integral part of the rationale behind the administrations.

The only comprehensive treatment of this aspect in the literature – to my knowledge – is an article by Ralph Wilde.[14] From a cursory analysis of historical and contemporary cases, Wilde provides a categorization of the various functions of international administrations, including different ways in which the institution may address problems in connection with territorial disputes. For example, an international administration can provide neutral administration of a disputed territory while negotiations about the status are being conducted among the affected parties. Alternatively, after an agreement, an international administration can facilitate the transfer of a territory from one state to another by taking over the administration for a transitional period and thereby provide a face-saving alternative to a direct handover.[15]

Wilde points in the right direction, but I will argue that his analysis is underdeveloped for two reasons. First, although Wilde has closed an important gap in the literature by describing how international administrations have been set up to deal with not only governance problems, but also with sovereignty issues, he does not consider how the two functions might be related. Of course, it is entirely possible that international administrations are deployed to address only one of the two types of problems – that is, to solve either governance problems or sovereignty problems. However, as will be argued in the following analysis, UNMIK was in fact set up to deal with both aspects at the same time. Therefore, we need to examine whether the fact that the administration was also established to address a sovereignty problem had any influence on its ability to solve the governance problems at hand. In other words, has the function of addressing the territorial dispute constrained UNMIK's ability to promote democratic practices and prepare the local population for self-government?

Second, Wilde does not relate the two functions to more fundamental international norms on 'how' sovereignty should be exercised or which 'selves' are entitled to claim sovereign statehood. Therefore, his categorization remains at the practical level while it can tell us little about international administrations as an institution of international society. Thus, on the one hand, differences between specific approaches to solve territorial disputes may be less important because they reflect the same international norms. On the other hand, one particular way to address a territorial dispute may in fact reflect vastly different norms depending on the territorial status that is being envisaged and therefore have equally different implications for the organization of international society. For example, if an international administration is used to promote a certain territorial status, it matters a great deal whether this implies that an ethnic group is allowed to secede from an existing state or not, as this would tend to either affirm or deny the existence of a right to secession. Without examining the normative background, we cannot understand the role and function of international administration as an institution of contemporary international society and we cannot engage in a discussion on its problems and potentials.

The normative background

As argued in the previous section, international administration is best understood in terms of what it is not, namely self-determination. Consequently, this section will examine how the interpretation of the two component parts of the right to self-determination has changed before, during, and after the Cold War.

Before the Second World War, norms governing the right to independent statehood presupposed not only the existence of a people willing to govern themselves, but also a demonstrated capacity for capable and civil government. The implication was that those people unable to meet these criteria were relegated to the inferior status of protectorates, mandates, or trusteeships administered by more developed nations.[16] During the period of decolonization, the positive sovereignty doctrine came under pressure from the growing number of Third World countries in the UN who considered the inequality and paternalism inherent in the system unacceptable. This resulted in an unqualified right to self-determination which did not presuppose any demonstrated capacity for self-government.[17] At the broader normative level, the society of states sought to establish juridical sovereignty – the mutual recognition of sovereignty, territorial integrity and non-intervention – as the new basis for international order.[18]

While the normative characterization of the two periods described above is relatively uncontroversial, the post-Cold War order is more disputed. However, I will argue that there is clear evidence of a renewed focus on positive sovereignty. Such evidence is: new guidelines for the recognition of states, the character of UN peace operations, and political conditionality in assistance programmes. The first example is the recognition of successor states to Yugoslavia and the Soviet Union. In this context, both the EC and the US issued guidelines which listed a number of domestic characteristics, including a democratic form of government, as a precondition for recognition.[19] Although, as demonstrated by Per Bredholt Christensen, these guidelines were not consistently applied, the very fact that these criteria were enunciated signalled a departure from the strict adherence to the negative sovereignty doctrine that had characterized the Cold War period.[20]

As another example, the basis of UN peace operations changed from traditional, interpositional peacekeeping to a broader doctrine of political peacebuilding. This latter doctrine, which has found expression in a number of UN operations during the 1990s, implies that international society should give assistance to rebuild and reform governmental institutions and processes after civil wars in order to create democratic and secure states.[21] At the broader normative level, this doctrine reflects a renewed belief among states that empirical sovereignty underpins international order. This is also illustrated by the fact that the UN Security Council has adopted an expanded definition of what constitutes a threat to international peace and security so that it now includes internal conflicts which may generate humanitarian crises and regional instability.[22] Finally, in the aftermath of the Cold War, Western donors began to present Third World states with demands for democracy and good governance as a condition for financial and technical assistance.[23] This exceptional interference in the domestic affairs of other states indicates that full membership of international society has once again become conditional on a demonstrated capacity for self-government.

Having examined the changing interpretations of political 'determination', we shall proceed to explore the question of which 'selves' were entitled to exercise self-determination in the form of sovereign statehood. After the First World War, the principle of national self-determination acquired considerable legitimacy in deciding which claims to statehood should be recognized.[24] The essence of the principle was not so much to ensure perfect congruence between states and nations, but rather that the creation of new states or the redrawing of borders should be based on the 'will of the people'.[25] The process of decolonization fundamentally transformed this interpretation of the collective 'self' since the borders of the new states were not based on ethnic or national identity, but instead conformed to existing colonial boundaries. This was partly because the principle of national self-determination had been discredited in the Second World War, partly because the principle would have been impossible to apply in the context of decolonization.[26] Therefore, the right to self-determination was given a territorial interpretation based on the principle of *uti possidetis juris* which stipulated that the entity demanding self-determination needed to have a pre-existing juridical existence in order to be elevated to independence.[27] While national self-determination had been seen as conducive to international order in the interwar period, the principle was now considered disruptive. Instead, the new normative framework sought to establish the sanctity of existing borders on the basis of mutual recognition of sovereignty and territorial integrity.[28] For that reason, there was no recognized right to secession outside the colonial context.

What then about interpretations of the collective 'self' in the post-Cold War order? The disintegration of the Soviet Union and Yugoslavia reopened the debate about the meaning of the right to self-determination.[29] However, the recognition process has reaffirmed the existing and restrictive interpretation of which 'selves' have the right to claim sovereign statehood. Thus, the great powers came to agree that the internal boundaries of Yugoslavia and the Soviet Union should be elevated to international borders. In Bosnia, this agreement was challenged by Serbs and Croats who launched a war to carve out territories mainly populated by their ethnic group. However, the society of states refused to recognize such redrawing of borders and the internationally imposed Dayton Peace Agreement upheld the territorial integrity of Bosnia from 1995. In sum, the 'selves' entitled to self-determination are still given a territorial definition while there is no recognized right of ethnic minorities to demand independence.[30] In the words of the Badinter Committee, this was motivated by the wish to 'maintain the basic parameters of the state system and avoid the proliferation of centrifugal tendencies and claims'.[31] This indicates that the society of states still believes that international order is best maintained by the principle of territorial integrity and the colonial practice of legitimating inherited boundaries.

In conclusion, while the norms legitimating statehood in the post-Cold War order have changed from negative to positive sovereignty (that is, democratic and humanitarian government) on the dimension of political 'determination', international society has retained its restrictive interpretation of which 'selves' have the right to claim sovereign statehood (that is, the principle of *uti possidetis juris*). In the following sections, we shall see how UNMIK's activities in Kosovo relate to this normative framework.

UNMIK and state-building in Kosovo

The challenge facing UNMIK upon its establishment on 10 June 1999 was enormous. In addition to filling the void after the withdrawal of the Serbian administration, UNMIK was tasked with 'organizing and overseeing the development of provisional institutions for democratic and autonomous self-government pending a final settlement'.[32] This involved rebuilding and reforming local political and administrative institutions according to international standards and the development of indigenous capacity to administer these institutions in the future.[33] While some authority was transferred to the municipal level in 2000, the process of transferring authority to the local stakeholders did not seriously begin until the adoption of the Constitutional Framework for Provisional Self-Government in May 2001 and the Kosovo-wide elections in November the same year. This process has been guided by the principle that authority will only be transferred to local officials and politicians when they have shown the will and capacity to govern in a responsible way. For example, in December 2002, the head of the UN Security Council, Ole Peter Kolby, stated that 'UNMIK has reached a stage of transferring responsibility to Kosovo's provisional institutions; the more the institutions can demonstrate they can execute the responsibilities they already have, the more they will be given'.[34] This principle has also underpinned the 'standards before status' policy, which entails that local institutions have to meet certain benchmarks for democracy, human rights and good governance before discussions can be initiated on the final status of the province.[35] At the time of writing, the local entities have not demonstrated full compliance with these standards and UNMIK therefore retains significant executive and legislative authority.

From this brief review it should be clear that the international administration of Kosovo was established to address problems related to the quality of governance being exercised by the local actors. Belgrade's atrocities had demonstrated its unwillingness to safeguard minimal civil conditions for the people of Kosovo. For that reason, international society had to intervene and take over the responsibility for administering Kosovo in order to restore basic conditions of freedom and security. However, UNMIK was not only established because of Serbian unwillingness to provide security and good governance, but also because the Kosovars lacked the capacity to govern themselves. In that way, the administration clearly demonstrates the renewed focus on positive sovereignty after the end of the Cold War. This focus is also evidenced in the 'standards before status' policy. Local institutions have to demonstrate capacity for self-government before international society will grant independence or full autonomy to Kosovo. More generally, the international administration was not only established to secure a lasting humanitarian outcome of NATO's intervention, but also to safeguard the regional security interests of the West by preventing resumption of violence. In both ways, however, UNMIK reflected new post-Cold War international norms which stress that domestic order underpins international order. However, as I will argue in the following sections, solving governance problems was not UNMIK's only function and this significantly changes our understanding of its normative rationale.

The territorial status of Kosovo

When adopting Resolution 1244, the Security Council left the delicate question of Kosovo's final status open. This, however, did not mean that the great powers fundamentally disagreed over what status options they would prefer. In fact, international society has maintained a surprisingly consistent line on the status question. Moreover, this position has been informed by the wish to uphold existing and restrictive norms on how international boundaries may change. This argument is already demonstrated by the fact that Resolution 1244 reaffirmed the UN's commitment to the principles of sovereignty and territorial integrity and established that, pending a final settlement, Kosovo was still formally a part of the FRY.[36] In the following section, I shall examine international society's position on Kosovo's final status by discussing the five options normally put forward in diplomatic discourse, namely restoration of full Serbian sovereignty, unilateral secession, partition of the province, a loose federation, and Belgrade's acceptance of independence.

As to the first option, international society has clearly signalled that it would be unrealistic to give Belgrade full control over Kosovo, as this would inevitably lead to a new war.[37] At the other end of the continuum, international society has been equally unwilling to allow Kosovo to secede unilaterally from Serbia. Contrary to what is normally argued, it is important to realize that the West has no more appetite for the independence option than Russia and China. The European Union has continually rejected the idea of independence for Kosovo and even in the US, where sympathy for the Kosovar Albanian aspirations is significantly higher than in Europe, there has been no clear support for independence at the governmental level.[38] The basic reason for rejecting independence is the collective determination not to create any bad precedents. In the words of the British Foreign Minister, independence for Kosovo provides 'an unpalatable model in Europe for violent secession along ethnic lines'.[39] More specifically, it is feared that independence for Kosovo could provoke secessionist demands from the Croats and Serbs in Bosnia, the Muslim and Hungarian minorities inside Serbia as well as the Albanian minority in Macedonia and thereby further destabilize these countries.[40] At the broader normative level, secession challenges the principles of sovereignty and territorial integrity and the existing restrictive interpretation of the right of self-determination based on the principle of *uti possidetis juris*. The problem is that Kosovo – so the argument goes – does not qualify for independence after this criterion, because it did not have the status of a republic in the former Yugoslavia.[41]

The option of partition has been floated by Serbia on several occasions, but has been readily denounced by the US, EU, and UNMIK.[42] In July 2002, Michael Steiner, the UN Special Representative (SRSG) from January 2002 to September 2003, said in a briefing to the Security Council that 'there will be no partition and no cantonisation. The outcome cannot be mono-ethnic, but must be multi-ethnic'.[43] While peaceful and agreed border changes are allowed for in the Helsinki Final Act, and as such compatible with the existing normative framework, the line of reasoning seems to be that partition has the potential to provoke instability in the entire region by opening a Pandora's Box of rival territorial claims.[44] More generally, the reluctance to accept partition – even by agreement – and Steiner's comment that the result has to be multi-ethnic rather than mono-ethnic, demonstrate that international society is determined to ensure that the existing territorial justification for sovereign statehood is not put under further pressure.

As to the option of a loose federation, the October 2000 regime change in Belgrade suggested that some sort of autonomy arrangement might be possible within the FRY, perhaps with Kosovo enjoying a similar status to Montenegro. Officially, this idea was first floated in a policy paper on Kosovo's final status written by the UN Secretary-General and circulated to the Security Council in October 2000. Here it was argued that the international community should direct its efforts 'towards the gradual establishment of a Republic of Kosovo equipped with the same degree of sovereignty that we can foresee for the Republic of Montenegro and the Republic of Serbia in a future arrangement'.[45] According to Hans Hækkerup, the SRSG in Kosovo from January to December 2001, this idea commands widespread support among the members of international society.[46] Initiatives to improve relations with Serbia, such as the establishment of the UNMIK/FRY Common Document from November 2001, and the international efforts to avert Montenegro's bid for independence, can be taken as further indications that international society is indeed striving to incorporate Kosovo in a democratized and reformed version of the Yugoslav federation.[47] This option is not without problems since Kosovo would never have obtained a similar degree of autonomy without the international intervention. However, while it challenges the principle of absolute state sovereignty, the normative attraction of this option is that it leaves the more important principle of territorial integrity uncontested.

The final option for Kosovo's future status is to secure Belgrade's acceptance of independence. While international society has been disinclined to contemplate unilateral secession, the opposition would be less strong if Belgrade were to approve of independence. Moreover, agreed border changes would not significantly challenge the existing restrictive principles guiding the right to sovereign statehood. However, while being an acceptable solution at the broader normative level, independence by agreement does not seem to be the preferred option of international society, as it is feared that this solution may still provoke instability and create bad precedents at the regional level.

UNMIK's role in addressing the status question

What role has UNMIK played in relation to the status question? In essence, the administration has been used as an instrument to handle the dilemma arising from the need to ensure that the Kosovars can enjoy substantial autonomy under conditions of freedom and security while at the same time preventing any changes to existing borders. Resolution 1244 is therefore best understood as an attempt to buy time. By keeping the question of final status open while insisting on the formal preservation of FRY sovereignty, the international administration does not significantly challenge the principles of sovereignty and territorial integrity. Moreover, it is painstakingly clear that none of the preferred options for the future status of Kosovo can be implemented overnight. Serbia is not at present ready to accept independence, and the option of reintegrating Kosovo in the FRY is even more problematic as the Kosovo Albanians vigorously oppose it.[48] Nevertheless, international society seems to believe that this opposition can be overcome in time, provided that the process of democratization in Serbia and Kosovo continues unabated.[49] Therefore, in order to prevent the status question from erupting prematurely, which would result in demands that cannot be met, international administration will have to continue at least into the medium term.

According to Resolution 1244, UNMIK was mandated to facilitate 'a political process designed to determine Kosovo's future status, *taking into account the Rambouillet Accords*'.[50] Thus, apart from the reference to Rambouillet, the Resolution did not mention any specific timeframe for the settlement of the status question. However, if we look at the Accords from February 1999, the relevant paragraph states that '*three years* after the entry into force of this Agreement, an international meeting shall be convened to determine a mechanism for a final settlement for Kosovo'.[51] In other words, it seems fair to argue that the timeframe implicit in UNSCR 1244 for the resolution of Kosovo's final status was three years. The most important international document pertaining to Kosovo after UNSCR 1244 is the Constitutional Framework for Provisional Self-Government in Kosovo, which was imposed by the SRSG in May 2001.[52] This document proclaimed that Kosovo's future status would be determined 'through a process *at an appropriate future stage*'.[53] In other words, the status question now appeared to have been deferred indefinitely while the international administration would be prolonged correspondingly.

However, this prolongation of the international administration had to be legitimized and the means to do so was the so-called 'standards before status' policy. In fact, this policy had already been in place before it was officially formulated. In June 2001, for example, Hækkerup stated that 'a decision on the future status of Kosovo requires a level of political maturity and readiness to compromise that the parties have not yet attained'.[54] When Steiner took over as SRSG in February 2002, this policy was formalized and further elaborated. Speaking in April 2002, Steiner declared that it would not be possible to discuss the question of final status 'until Kosovo's society and institutions show that they are ready'. 'Therefore,' he continued, 'we must spell out what is required in order to get there. This is why I have devised a series of benchmarks that will identify what needs to be done before we can launch the discussions on status. First standards then status'.[55] According to the International Crisis Group, the primary rationale behind the 'standards before status' policy has been to defer the status question and legitimize the continuation of the international administration.[56] There are a number of indications that this interpretation is correct.

First, as repeatedly pointed out by the Kosovo Albanians, many of the standards actually pertain to areas within the reserved powers of the SRSG, making it impossible for the Kosovars to create progress by themselves.[57] Second, in the year following their announcement UNMIK made no effort to clarify the meaning of the standards or assess how far Kosovo was from meeting them.[58] Then, after severe criticism from the Kosovo Albanians, UNMIK presented a report in January 2003 that sought to clarify the benchmarks by adding a number of subgoals and indicators. Despite this clarification, the benchmarks still remained too vague to serve as operational guidance for the provisional institutions.[59]

This stalemate was finally brought to an end in December 2003 when UNMIK issued a revised version of the standards followed by an implementation plan in March 2004. At the same time, UNMIK promised a review of final status in mid-2005.[60] However, SRSG Harri Holkeri was quick to underline that there was nothing inevitable about this decision and that the review would happen later, if sufficient progress on the standards were not made. 'There is only one route to final status,' Holkeri explained, 'and that is through progress on standards'.[61] Holkeri's successor, Søren Jessen-Petersen, who was appointed SRSG in June 2004, has expressed more will to contemplate talks on the status question, but along with his predecessors, he insists that it will only happen if the standards are successfully implemented.[62] Therefore, as pointed out by several observers, it is hard to escape the conclusion that this new policy has been yet another temporizing measure. While the publication of a provisional expiry date may serve to calm Albanian frustrations, a number of observers have expressed doubts as to whether the standards are attainable in the short run.[63]

I am not arguing that the benchmarks are irrelevant as an instrument to promote fully functioning institutions of self-government on the basis of democracy, human rights and good governance. However, everything seems to indicate that the benchmarks have been used more to legitimize the continuation of the international administration and defer the discussion of final status than to build democratic institutions of self-government. This also means that we have to revise the normative interpretation of the 'standards before status' policy. Contrary to its traditional representation, the policy cannot simply be understood as an indication of the new preoccupation with empirical sovereignty after the Cold War since it also served the purpose of preventing premature discussions of the status question.

Territorial status and the promotion of democratic institutions of self-government

Having argued that the international administration of Kosovo was not only established to solve governance problems, but also to address the question of Kosovo's territorial status, we need to investigate how the latter function has impacted on the former. According to UNMIK, the sovereignty issue is more symbolic than substantive. In order to formally preserve FRY sovereignty, UNMIK could not issue laws, but only regulations, and Kosovo could not have a parliament, but only an assembly. In other words, the effects have merely been on the language used by the administration, while the day-to-day issues of governance in Kosovo have not been seriously affected.[64] In this passage, I will suggest that this argument is flawed. The question of Kosovo's territorial status, and the way the international administration has addressed it, has profoundly shaped and constrained UNMIK's state-building efforts. Below, we shall investigate the nexus between the two functions in relation to what is probably the most important aspect of state-building, namely the promotion of democratic institutions of self-government. Specifically, UNSCR 1244 committed UNMIK to promote 'the establishment of substantial autonomy and self-government in Kosovo'.[65] Following that, the Constitutional Framework envisaged the further development of 'meaningful self-government' through the transfer of responsibilities to 'Provisional Institutions of Self-Government in the legislative, executive and juridical fields'.[66] Does this mean that the Kosovars can now enjoy 'meaningful self-government'?

Commenting on the Constitutional Framework, the International Commission on Kosovo argued that this is not case. On the contrary, the Kosovars 'will have the illusion of self-rule rather than the reality'.[67] Indeed, looking at the text it seems clear that authority of the institutions of self-rule is circumscribed by the vast powers accorded to the UN Special Representative. The SRSG is empowered to dissolve the assembly, appoint and remove judges, appoint all senior economic officials, set financial and policy parameters for the budget, and oversee all external relations. In addition, he has final authority with regard to law enforcement, customs, and monetary policy. Furthermore, he retains control over the Kosovo Protection Corps, and the administration of public property and enterprises.[68] Finally, in case the argument may have been understated, it is explicitly decreed that the Constitutional Framework 'shall not affect or diminish the authority of the SRSG to ensure full implementation of UNSCR 1244, including overseeing the Provisional Institutions of Self-Government and taking appropriate measures whenever their actions are inconsistent with UNSCR 1244'.[69] In other words, the reserved powers of the SRSG, as specified in chapter eight of the Constitutional Framework, significantly limit the scope of the PISG. Despite these restrictions, the PISG were supposed to assume a number of significant responsibilities, including control over basic governance functions, such as health and education. Yet, the transfer of these so-called 'chapter five' competencies to the new local government has been extremely slow.[70] This has given rise to severe criticism from the Kosovars who argue that UNMIK is deliberately holding on to its powers. In response to this criticism Michael Steiner explained that 90 per cent of the competencies had been successfully transferred by May 2003. As pointed out by the International Crisis Group, this seemed like a gross exaggeration considering that the so-called Transfer Council, established in January 2003 to assess whether UNMIK had sufficiently handed over chapter five competencies, identified 44 areas where UNMIK retained authority although they belonged to PISG's mandate. Moreover, UNMIK subsequently declared that its readiness to hand over all chapter five competencies would depend on whether the PISG 'works more seriously'.[71] This climate of hostility was not improved until after the March 2004 turmoil, which brought pressure upon UNMIK to devolve more powers to the local institutions. As a result, an agreement concerning the transfer of more economic control to the local bodies was finalized in December 2004. However, while local institutions have gained more power recently, the UN still retains the last word on all major issues.[72]

This brief review highlights that the authority of the PISG has been circumscribed by the reserved powers of the SRSG and effectively diminished by the slow transfer of competencies. In sum, it seems fair to conclude that the international administration is holding on to its powers. We then need to investigate why this is the case. I will argue that this should not be seen primarily as the result of imperial condescension or bureaucratic turf fighting, as the International Commission on Kosovo has argued, but rather as a result of a deliberate political strategy devised by UNMIK and the Security Council.[73] In the words of Michael Steiner, 'the pace at which UNMIK can transfer further authority to the Provisional Institutions depends on their readiness to assume real responsibilities'.[74] The argument seems to be that the Kosovars still lack the capacity to direct their own affairs. However, taken at face value, this argument is unpersuasive. Certainly, Kosovo is not a harmonious social-democratic welfare state, but any doubts about the political maturity of the Kosovar Albanian people have proven groundless in recent elections. People have generally chosen to cast their votes for the moderate LDK, led by Ibrahim Rugova, while radical parties like the PDK, a successor to the KLA, have been unable to gain substantial support. As for administrative capacity, the executive branch of the PISG undoubtedly lacks experience, but through international assistance and monitoring it should be possible to enhance indigenous capacity and ensure good governance while at the same time leaving significant responsibilities in the hands of the Kosovars. In sum, while the Kosovars may not be ready to direct their own affairs without supervision, it is simply not clear why UNMIK requires the full panoply of administrative powers described above.

The real dilemma of UNMIK and international society is that the more successful the building of democratic institutions of self-government is, the more quickly the delicate issue of Kosovo's territorial status will surface. In other words, there are limits as to how much authority can be delegated to the Kosovars without precipitating a premature decision on the status question. Specifically, there are two reasons why more power cannot be transferred to Kosovo's provisional institutions. The first reason is symbolic in nature. While it may be possible to formally preserve FRY sovereignty when authority firmly resides with a neutral international administration, this fiction becomes much harder to maintain if local institutions of self-government have control over matters such as external relations, customs, and monetary policy, as these areas define some of the core attributes of statehood.

The second reason is more substantive in character. The more power that is vested in Kosovo's institutions, the more power they will have to challenge the territorial agenda of the international community. According to the former UN Special Representative, Hans Hækkerup, Russia and the Western powers were already concerned at the outset that the Kosovar Albanians would use a duly elected and internationally recognized assembly as a platform to make decisions in violation of UNSCR 1244 – that is, to proclaim independence or in other ways address the status question directly.[75] As argued by several observers, this concern was also one of the reasons why international society decided to hold municipal elections before Kosovo-wide elections.[76] Moreover, these fears turned out to be well-founded, as the Assembly on several occasions since its formation passed resolutions which have addressed the status question and thus acted outside the powers and responsibilities of the PISG. In May 2002, for example, the assembly passed a resolution on the 'Territorial Integrity of Kosovo'. Again in November, the Assembly passed a resolution which condemned the inclusion of Kosovo in the preamble of the Serbia-Montenegro Constitution. The then SRSG, Michael Steiner, immediately declared these resolutions null and void and they were later condemned by the Security Council and the EU.[77] The damage has been limited only because such declarations are non-binding in the sense that they are outside the scope of authority vested in the assembly in accordance with the Constitutional Framework and thus belong to the reserved powers of the SRSG.

However, it has become increasingly difficult for UNMIK to transfer more authority to the Assembly, as a unilateral declaration of independence is looming. Moreover, going any further would alienate Belgrade which is carefully looking out for any signs that its formal sovereignty is being compromised. The problem appears to be well understood by the SRSG. Thus, in August 2002, responding to the suggestion that the transfer of powers should be speeded up, Michael Steiner said that: 'The Albanian political elite, and the public opinion, are not prepared for this. In any case, they should get rid of the illusion that the transfer of powers from UNMIK to local institutions paves the way toward independence'.[78] In other words, more extensive self-government cannot be entrusted to the Kosovars because it would precipitate a decision on the question of final status, and thereby endanger international society's long-term goal of reintegrating Kosovo in a federation with Serbia and Montenegro or at least obtaining Belgrade's acceptance of independence.

What are the long-term political repercussions of this dilemma? If the international administration holds on to its powers, and self-government becomes an illusion, there is a considerable risk that the already strained relationship between UNMIK and the Kosovo Albanians could evolve into an open crisis.[79] Although the riots in the spring of 2004 were more spontaneous than planned, they can also be attributed to the failings of the international administration in the sense that UNMIK's efforts to prevent any discussion of final status have allowed tension to be built up.[80] Moreover, the fact that UNMIK clings to its authority makes democratic learning ineffective because voters can change their local politicians far more easily than they can change policies. At the end of the day, the important political decisions in the province are taken by international officials and not by the elected local representatives. As a result, the electorate is unable to hold the decision-making authorities accountable for their policies. The ultimate risk, in the words of Ivan Krastev, 'is not a sudden, but a slow death of democracy through a gradual process or erosion and delegitimation that destroys democratic regimes even when institutions are still in place'.[81] In fact, the International Crisis Group has recently argued that institutional life in Kosovo is already dangerously detached from the rest of the Albanian Society.[82]

The counter-argument to this critique, often made among UNMIK officials, is that the international administration has been able to use the unsettled status question to put pressure on Kosovar Albanian politicians to persuade them to concentrate on creating viable institutions of self-government and improving inter-ethnic relations. However, UNMIK has clearly failed to persuade local politicians to focus on 'standards'. In the absence of any formal process to tackle the issue, the status question has completely dominated the agenda and thereby shifted focus away from more ordinary problems which might otherwise have been addressed.[83]

The question of final status has profoundly constrained UNMIK's ability to establish democratic institutions of self-government and to transfer competencies to these institutions. This is not to argue that Kosovo is ready for full autonomous self-government, let alone independence. In fact, UNMIK and KFOR will be needed in Kosovo for years to come, as the establishment and entrenchment of democratic institutions and a robust civil society will take time. However, the preservation of vast powers in the hands of the international administration will only lead to more instability and effectively undermine efforts to further democratic practices in the province.

The normative inconsistency of international society

Departing from an analysis of UNMIK's activities in Kosovo, this chapter has explored the role and function of international administration as an institution of international society. The case of Kosovo demonstrates that international administrations are not only established to rebuild collapsed governance structures in failed states, as has been the traditional understanding in the literature on the contemporary cases, but may also be used to address sovereignty problems stemming from disputes over the status of the territories put under administration. At the broader normative level, UNMIK's activities have been constitutive of the international normative framework which emerged after the end of the Cold War. On the one hand, the rehabilitation of collapsed governance structures has reflected and reinforced the new norms which emphasize the importance of positive sovereignty. On the other hand, UNMIK has sought to defend the principle of territorial integrity and the existing restrictive interpretation of which 'selves' have the right to self-determination. Finally, the function of addressing sovereignty problems severely constrained the ability of UNMIK to solve the governance problems at hand.

More generally, does the case of Kosovo demonstrate that international administrations cannot carry out both functions at the same time? Clearly, the restoration and promotion of democratic institutions of local self-government is potentially more difficult when the administration is established, not only to solve governance problems, but also to address a territorial dispute. In the latter case, it is not possible to downgrade the administration to an assistance model because it is the very fact of administrative control that enables the administration to address the sovereignty problem.[84] However, the scope of this problem clearly depends on the circumstances under which the administration is established and the specific way in which it is addressed. In Kosovo, the dilemma has been exacerbated by the fact that the administration was established to 'freeze' the status question and prevent the local population from declaring unilateral independence. It has therefore been impossible to delegate substantial authority to the local stakeholders since they would use this authority to challenge the territorial agenda of the international administration. Alternatively, had the administration promoted a territorial status compatible with the aspirations of the local population (that is, independence), the dilemma would have been less pronounced.

In a broader perspective, therefore, UNMIK's problems can be attributed to the fact that the normative setting of international society after the Cold War has displayed a curious inconsistency with regard to the principle of self-determination. Political 'determination' has been redefined in the sense that legitimate statehood has become conditional on a democratic and humanitarian form of government. In other words, the people of a territory have become the source of state sovereignty.[85] In contrast, international society has retained a restrictive interpretation of which 'selves' have the right to exercise self-determination in the form of sovereign statehood. This right does not pertain to any self-defined 'peoples', but only to pre-existing territorial jurisdictions. However, as demonstrated in the case of Kosovo, it is difficult to insist that the 'will of the people' is the source of state sovereignty and then qualify this proposition by arguing that it only applies internally in the relations between rulers and the ruled and not externally in defining the boundaries of the political community. The two issues cannot be separated, as they both address the question of who is to govern.

Put differently, UNMIK's predicaments draw attention to a dilemma built into the revitalized institution of trusteeship. On the one hand, the UN Security Council and others have gradually come to insist that sovereignty should be exercised in a responsible way and cannot be a cover for misrule, anarchy and the repression of minorities. On the other hand, there has been considerable unwillingness to draw the logical conclusion of these new norms and bestow sovereignty on ethnic minorities that have been subjected to severe oppression. As a result, UNMIK may develop democratic institutions in Kosovo, but be unable to complete the task and also transfer its sovereign powers to the local population.

This finding indicates that normative consistency has to be restored in the society of states if the practice of international administration is to play a constructive role in creating a more just and stable international order. More specifically, the society of states has to accept a less restrictive interpretation of which 'selves' have the right to self-determination in the form of sovereign statehood. The traditional rejoinder to this argument is that a less restrictive regime would undermine international order. Expanding the right to self-determination would make borders tremble and cause even more instability and violence. However, this argument has to be made, not just asserted. We have to weigh the consequences of accepting a less rigid interpretation of the right to self-determination with the consequences of not doing so. As we have already seen, the existing restrictions in the normative regime governing state-sovereignty may cause instability and undermine the legitimacy of international administrations, but is the alternative really chaos? Alexander Downes argues that this fear is overestimated since accommodating international norms neither restrain nor encourage minority groups in advancing secessionist claims.[86] On the contrary, such demands are almost completely determined by domestic factors. Therefore, international borders are hardly going to tremble if the existing normative regime is softened. That being said, I am not arguing that we should go to the opposite extreme and allow the principle of national self-determination and a right to secession to take precedence over the principles of sovereignty and territorial integrity in every case. What I am arguing, however, is that the existing normative framework operates with an unnecessarily restrictive interpretation of which 'selves' have the right to claim sovereign statehood. Therefore, what is needed is a more pragmatic approach.

The case of Kosovo can be used to demonstrate that there is actually plenty of room to soften the existing regime without jettisoning the fundamental ordering principles of international society. One option could be to allow Kosovo to become independent by reference to the principle of *uti possidetis juris*. Considering that the province was an autonomous entity in Yugoslavia with almost the same rights as the republics, is hard to see why the aforementioned principle cannot be applied.[87] Moreover, this justification for independence would only change the existing regime marginally. Alternatively, international society could accept the more radical argument that Belgrade has lost its sovereign rights over Kosovo as a result of its own misrule. This justification for independence would clearly challenge the current normative framework, but not seriously. The Albanians in Macedonia or the Bosnian Serbs, for example, could not use it as a basis for secessionist claims.[88] Besides, if the society of states were to accept the idea of 'sovereignty as a licence' it would actually put pressure on repressive governments to improve their treatment of ethnic minorities. In my view, the latter option is preferable to the former since it draws toward the logical conclusion of new international norms which give emphasis to democratic and humanitarian government, and thereby restores normative consistency in the society of states. At the same time, such a change in the normative framework would eliminate the present dilemma of trusteeship since sovereignty could then be transferred to the people whom the administration is set up to protect – irrespective of their identity – once they are ready to assume that responsibility.

One might argue that Kosovo would be the obvious place to begin this much needed normative revision, but it is questionable whether international society will adopt a more pragmatic approach. However, it is certain that UNMIK will encounter serious problems if the status question is not settled in the near future and in a manner acceptable to the Kosovars. In the final analysis, the continuance of an international presence in Kosovo depends on the consent of the local population. Anything else is a recipe for discord.

Acknowledgement

The author would like to express his considerable thanks to Tonny Brems Knudsen, Carsten Bagge Laustsen and Chris Freeman for their many valuable comments on earlier drafts of this article.

Notes

1 For the purposes of this chapter, international administration refers to the situation where a state, a group of states, or an international organization assumes full responsibility for conducting the affairs of government in a foreign territory. Such administrations should be contrasted with operations where the international community acts as an independent advisor to existing local governments. See Jarat Chopra, 'Introduction', in Jarat Chopra (ed.), *The Politics of Peace-Maintenance* (Boulder: Lynne Rienner Publishers, 1998), pp. 13–14.

2 See, for instance, Michèle Griffin and Bruce Jones, 'Building Peace through Transitional Authority: New Directions, Major Challenges', *International Peacekeeping*, 7, 1 (2000); William O'Neill, *Kosovo: An Unfinished Peace* (Boulder: Lynne Rienner Publishers, 2002); Simon Chesterman, 'East Timor in Transition: Self-determination, State-building and the United Nations', *International Peacekeeping*, 9, 1 (2002), pp. 45–76; Simon Chesterman, 'Walking Softly in Afghanistan: the Future of UN State-Building', *Survival*, 44, 3 (2002), pp. 37–46; and Richard Caplan, 'A New Trusteeship? The International Administration of War-torn Territories', *Adelphi Paper, No. 341*, 2002.

3 Roland Paris, 'Broadening the Study of Peace Operations', *International Studies Review*, 2, 3 (2000), pp. 29, 44.

4 See, for example, Robert Jackson, *The Global Covenant* (Oxford: Oxford University Press, 2000), pp. 294–315; William Bain, 'The Tyranny of Benevolence: National Security, Human Security, and the Practice of Statecraft', *Global Society*, 15, 3 (2001), pp. 277–94; and William Bain, 'The Political Theory of Trusteeship and the Twilight of International Equality', *International Relations*, 17, 1 (2003), pp. 59–77.

5 The international society approach is also referred to as the English school of international relations. In this chapter, the term international society will be used in two ways. First, it refers to the abstract idea that there is a societal element to the international system. Hedley Bull, in his classical formulation, defined international society as existing when 'a group of states, conscious of certain common interests and common values, form a society in the sense that they conceive themselves to be bound by a common set of rules in their relations with one another and share in the working of common institutions'. Hedley Bull, *The Anarchical Society: A Study of Order in World Politics* (London: Macmillan, 1995), p. 13. Second, I will use the term as an euphemism for the great powers and other important international players whose collective action in the case of Kosovo may be said to represent the will of international society.

6 Here I draw on the English School's notion of an institution. Bull explains that 'by an institution we do not necessarily imply an organization or administrative machinery, but rather a set of habits and practices shaped towards the realisation of common goals.' Bull further tells us that institutions 'are an expression of the element of collaboration among states in discharging their political functions'. Bull (n.5 above), p. 71. Bull mentions war, diplomacy, international law, and the idea of the great powers as examples of fundamental institutions. Recent writings within the international society tradition have added humanitarian intervention and trusteeships as other examples of fundamental institutions. See, for example, Tonny Brems Knudsen, 'Humanitarian Intervention and International Society: Contemporary Manifestations of an Explosive Doctrine', Ph.D. dissertation, University of Aarhus: 1999; Barry Buzan, *From International to World Society? English School Theory and the Social Structure of Globalisation* (Cambridge: Cambridge University Press, 2004).

7 See, for instance, Griffin and Jones; Chesterman, 'East Timor'; Caplan (all n. 2 above).

8 Ibid.

9 Kamal S. Shehadi, 'Ethnic Self-determination and the Break-up of States', *Adelphi Paper No. 283*, IISS 1993, p. 4.

10 Ralph Wilde, 'From Danzig to East Timor and Beyond: The Role of International Territorial Administration', *American Journal of International Law*, 95, 3 (2001), pp. 586–7.
11 Robert Jackson, *Quasi-States: Sovereignty, International Relations and the Third World* (Cambridge: Cambridge University Press, 1990), p. 75.
12 Jackson (n. 4 above), pp. 300–1.
13 See, for instance, Ibid., pp. 306–7; Caplan (n. 2 above), pp. 17–18; Alexandros Yannis, 'Kosovo under International Administration', *Survival*, 43, 2 (2001), pp. 31–48.
14 Wilde (n. 10 above).
15 Wilde (n. 10 above), pp. 587–97.
16 Jackson (n. 11 above), pp. 72–4; see also Bain, 'The Political Theory' (n. 4 above).
17 Jackson (n. 11 above), p. 75; Jackson (n. 4 above), p. 304.
18 Michael Barnett, 'The New United Nations Politics of Peace: From Juridical Sovereignty to Empirical Sovereignty', *Global Governance*, 1, 1 (1995), pp. 80–3.
19 'EC Declaration on the Guidelines on the Recognition of the New States in Eastern Europe and the Soviet Union', 16 December, 1991. See Roland Rich, 'Recognition of States: The Collapse of Yugoslavia and the Soviet Union', *European Journal of International Law*, 4 (1993), p. 43.
20 Per Bredholt Christensen, *Anerkendelse af stater* (København: Jurist- og Økonomforbundets Forlag, 2002), pp. 175–94.
21 The term peacebuilding was coined by the former UN General Secretary, Boutros Boutros-Ghali, in his influential report *An Agenda for Peace* (New York: United Nations, 1992). See also Andrea Kathryn Talentino, 'Intervention as Nation-Building: Illusion or Possibility', *Security Dialogue*, 33, 1 (2002), p. 28; Paul Taylor, 'The United Nations in the 1990s: Proactive Cosmopolitanism and the Issue of Sovereignty', *Political Studies*, XLVII (1999), pp. 539–44.
22 Barnett (n. 18 above), pp. 83, 90–1; Taylor (n. 21 above), pp. 545–6.
23 Peter Viggo Jakobsen, 'The Transformation of United Nations Peace Operations in the 1990s', *Cooperation and Conflict*, 37, 3 (2002), p. 272.
24 Jackson (n. 11 above), p. 60.
25 The plebiscite was the preferred solution to implement this principle in practice. James Mayall, *World Politics: Progress and its Limits* (Cambridge: Polity Press 2000), p. 45.
26 Samuel J. Barkin and Bruce Cronin, 'The state and the nation: changing norms and the rules of sovereignty in international relations', *International Organization*, 48, 1 (1994), p. 125.
27 Martyn Rady, 'Self-determination and the dissolution of Yugoslavia', *Ethnic and Racial Studies*, 19, 2 (1996), p. 381; Robert Jackson, 'Boundaries and International Society', in B.A. Roberson (eds), *International Society and the Development of International Relations Theory* (London: Pinter, 1998), pp. 161–2.
28 James Mayall, 'Sovereignty, Nationalism and Self-determination', *Political Studies*, XLVII (1999), p. 476.
29 Ibid., p. 474.
30 Jackson (n. 27 above), p. 168; Mayall (n. 28 above), p. 484.
31 The Badinter Committee was established in autumn of 1991 to facilitate an orderly dissolution of Yugoslavia. Quoted in Rady (n. 27 above), p. 385.
32 UNSCR 1244 (1999): Article 10.
33 International Crisis Group, 'A Kosovo Roadmap (II) Internal Benchmarks', *Balkans Report No. 124 (II)*, March 2002, pp. 3–4; Yannis (n. 13 above), pp. 36–7.
34 International Crisis Group, 'Two to Tango: an Agenda for the New Kosovo SRSG', *Balkans Report No. 148* (September 2003), p. 18.
35 UNMIK Press Release, 'Standards before status' (April 2002); UNMIK Benchmarks, January 2003.
36 UNSCR 1244(1999): Article 10 (my italics).

37 Michael Steiner, the former UN Special Representative to Kosovo, has stated on numerous occasions that there can be 'no return to status quo ante 1999.' UNMIK News, 30 July 2002.
38 See, for example, statement by the Belgian Foreign Minister, Louis Michel, speaking for the Belgian Presidency of the EU following the Kosovo-wide elections in 2001, 'We have not changed our minds. We are not in favour of independence'. Quoted in International Crisis Group, 'A Kosovo Roadmap (I) Addressing Final Status', *Balkans Report No. 124 (I)* (March 2002), p. 19. See also remarks by US Secretary of State, Madeleine Allbright, delivered to the Council of Foreign Relations, New York, 28 June 1999, 'Belgrade's withdrawal has altered the reality within which the people of Kosovo will formulate their aspirations. Until now, independence has seemed the only alternative to repression. But in the future, the Kosovars will have something they have never had, which is genuine self-government'.
39 Quoted in Justin Eldridge, 'Kosovo: Land of Uncertainty', *European Security*, 10, 2 (2001), p. 43; see also United States Institute of Peace, 'Kosovo Final Status: Options and Cross-Border Requirements', *USIP Special Report No. 91*, July 2002, p. 3.
40 See Eldridge, Ibid., p. 43; United States Institute of Peace, *USIP Special Report No. 91*, p. 8; International Crisis Group, *Balkans Report No. 124 (I)* (n. 38 above), p. 1; Jacques Rupnik, 'Yugoslavia After Milosevic', *Survival*, 43, 2 (2001), p. 21.
41 See Jackson (n. 4 above), p. 332.
42 International Crisis Group, 'Kosovo's Ethnic Dilemma: The Need for a Civic Contract', *Balkans Report No. 143* (September 2003), p. 8; Institute for War and Peace Reporting, *Balkan Crisis Report No. 266* (July 2001) and No.405, February 2003.
43 UNMIK News, 30 July 2002.
44 International Crisis Group, *Balkans Report No. 124 (I)* (n. 38 above) p. 10; International Crisis Group, *Balkans Report No. 143* (n. 42 above), p. 4.
45 SG (2000) 0990 (NATO-version): Para.8.
46 Hans Hækkerup, *Kosovos mange ansigter* (København: Lindhart & Ringhof, 2002), pp. 254–5.
47 UNMIK/FRY Common Document, 2001. Montenegro cannot be allowed to secede because UNSCR 1244 refers to Kosovo's continuing place in the FRY. Consequently, if the federation were dissolved, Kosovo would be cast adrift which would make it much harder to negotiate a new agreement compared to simply elevating Kosovo to the status as a third republic within the current framework. See Institute for War and Peace Reporting, *Balkan Crisis Report No. 404* (February 2003); Rupnik, 'Yugoslavia', p. 24; International Crisis Group, *Balkans Report No. 124 (I)* (n. 38 above), p. 15.
48 International Crisis Group, *Balkans Report No. 143* (n. 42 above), p. 8.
49 International Crisis Group, *Balkans Report No. 124 (I)* (n. 38 above), p. 10.
50 UNSCR 1244, Article 11e (my italics).
51 Rambouillet Agreement, Chapter 8.3 (my italics).
52 Simon Chesterman, 'Kosovo in Limbo: State-building and Substantial Autonomy', International Peace Academy (August 2001), pp. 6–7.
53 UNMIK/REG/2001/9, Preamble (my italics).
54 Quoted in Chesterman (n. 52 above), p. 6; See also International Crisis Group, *Balkans Report No. 124 (I)* (n. 38 above), p. 2.
55 UNMIK Press Release, 'Standards before status', April 2002.
56 International Crisis Group, *Balkans Report No. 148* (n. 34 above), p. 16.
57 Ibid., p. 17.
58 International Crisis Group, *Balkans Report No. 143* (n. 42 above), p. 1.
59 It is difficult to see how the local entities can demonstrate compliance with requirements such as 'sustained efforts by the PISG to promote values of rule of law' or 'support the establishment of a solid economic framework'. UNMIK Benchmarks, January 2003.

60 UNMIK Press Release, 'Standard for Kosovo', 10 December 2003; Kosovo Implementation Plan, 31 March 2004.
61 UNMIK Press Release, 10 December 2003, UNMIK Press Release, 6 February 2004.
62 'Young and wanted', *Economist*, 29 December, 2004.
63 International Crisis Group, *Balkans Report No 155* (April 2004), pp. 2, 5–6; Institute for War and Peace Reporting, 'UN Lays Down Conditions', *Balkan Crisis Report No. 491*, April 2004.
64 International Crisis Group, *Balkans Report No. 143* (n. 42 above), p. 2.
65 UNSCR 1244(1999): Article 11(a).
66 UNMIK/REG/2001/9, Preamble.
67 International Commission on Kosovo, *The Follow-Up of the Kosovo Report* (New York: Oxford University Press, 2001), p. 20.
68 UNMIK/REG/2001/9, Chapter 8.
69 UNMIK/REG/2001/9, Chapter 12.
70 Refers to chapter five of Constitutional Framework. International Crisis Group, *Balkans Report No. 155* (n. 63 above), p. 2.
71 International Crisis Group, *Balkans Report No. 143* (n. 42 above), pp. 18–19.
72 'A protectorate as divided as ever', *Economist*, 25 October 2004; Artan Mustafa, 'UN Chief Restores Faith in Kosovo Mission', Institute for War and Peace Reporting, *Balkan Crisis Report No. 536*, January 2005.
73 International Commission on Kosovo (n. 67 above), p. 20.
74 UNMIK News, 30 July 2002.
75 Hækkerup (n. 46 above), p. 96.
76 See, for instance, Institute for War and Peace Reporting, *Balkan Crisis Report No. 96*, November 1999.
77 International Crisis Group, *Balkans Report No. 148* (n. 34 above), pp. 6–7.
78 UNMIK Press Release, 'UNMIK Exit Strategy', August 2002.
79 Rupnik (n. 40 above), p. 24.
80 International Crisis Group, *Balkans Report No. 155* (n. 63 above), pp. 2, 42.
81 Ivan Krastev, 'The Balkans: Democracy without Choices', *Journal of Democracy*, 13, 3 (2002), pp. 44, 51.
82 International Crisis Group, *Balkans Report No. 155* (n. 63 above), p. 2.
83 International Crisis Group, *Balkans Report No. 143* (n. 42 above), p. 3.
84 See also Wilde (n. 10 above), p. 587.
85 See 'The Responsibility to Protect', Report of the International Commission on Intervention and State Sovereignty (December 2001).
86 Alexander Downes, 'The Holy Land Divided – Defending Partition as a Solution to Ethnic Wars', *Security Studies*, 10, 4 (2001), pp. 87–8.
87 Rady (n. 27 above), p. 286.
88 International Commission on Kosovo (n. 67 above), p. 30.

9 From UNMIK to self-determination?

The puzzle of Kosovo's future status

Tonny Brems Knudsen

With the adoption of UN Security Council Resolution 1244 on the 10 June 1999, NATO's humanitarian intervention in Kosovo gave way to the establishment of the United Nations Interim Administration in Kosovo (UNMIK) and the Kosovo Force (KFOR), which provides the military back-up for the UN and its many partners in the ongoing attempt to reconstruct the province.[1] The creation of this multi-organizational administration of Kosovo led by the UN, an arrangement which amounts to 'an international trusteeship in everything but name',[2] seemed to be constructive in a number of respects, at least in the short term.

First, the adoption of resolution 1244 brought the international intervention to stop the atrocities and civil war in the province back on solid legal grounds, at least in so far that the international involvement was now based on a clear mandate from the UN Security Council, and not just on NATO's appeals to international humanitarian law, the practice of UN-sponsored humanitarian intervention in the 1990s and standards of international morality.[3] With the adoption of Resolution 1244, the international attempt to bring an end to ethnic cleansing and obtain a lasting peace could now continue inside the machinery of the UN.

Second, the UN-decision to assume control over the province and its reconstruction brought Russia and China, in various degrees, back into the framework of collective crisis management, and Russia was even able to join NATO in KFOR following the brief dispute over Russia's bold advancement to Pristina Airport without prior consultation.

Third, the joint enterprise of UNMIK and KFOR offered an attractive answer to the acute question of how to proceed from NATO's victory in the 'humanitarian war' to a lasting peace. For a number of political, legal, humanitarian and moral reasons, a genuine NATO occupation of the province was not a viable option, and a return of authority to Belgrade or an immediate move to independence or self-rule for the province was out of the question as well given the background of atrocities and civil war. Under these circumstances, a UN trusteeship in everything but name was arguably the only practical solution to the problem.

However, the lack of clarity in Resolution 1244 regarding Kosovo's future status – something that was constructive to begin with in so far that it made it possible for all the main actors to join in – soon became a problem for the international administration of the province. The Albanian majority has become more and more unwilling to accept a state of affairs in which there is no guarantee that the dream of independence will ever become a reality. The question is whether the Albanian community can accept any other decision concerning the future of the province than full independence, and if not, how long its leaders will wait before they start not only to see UNMIK (and the international community) as a part of their problem, but also to work actively against it. On the other hand, how can the Serb community in Kosovo – whose extremely difficult situation was plain to see during the 2004 March riots[4] – survive if the province obtains its independence from Serbia and Montenegro? Furthermore, is such a solution possible at all in light of the resistance from Belgrade, Moscow and Beijing? It is these difficult questions that are to be solved in troublesome negotiations to be arranged by the UN in late 2005 and 2006.

To UNMIK, the problem remains that any solution to the question of Kosovo's future status, including a (non-)decision to cling on to the policy of 'constructive uncertainty', is likely to cause resentment in either the Albanian or the Serb community, or in both of them. To that come some delicate legal questions concerning Serbia and Montenegro's possible loss of sovereignty and the risk of setting a precedent for secession with rebellion, humanitarian intervention, and international trusteeship as stepping stones.

This chapter examines these puzzles by discussing the various options regarding the future status of Kosovo and their likely consequences. It is argued that nothing less than full *de facto* independence for Kosovo will satisfy the Albanian majority which is a precondition of success. However, political conditions and legal qualifications must accompany the international recognition of this independence and this points to the need for a continuation of elements of a UN trusteeship arrangement for years to come.

International trusteeship, national self-determination and pragmatic peacebuilding

Can an international trusteeship arrangement, be it formal or informal, lead to independence for the concerned territory and people? The promotion of 'well-being and development' for the inhabitants of the mandated territories was certainly the main justification of the mandate system established under the League of Nations after the First World War, and preparation for self-government or independence became one of the stipulated goals of the post-war UN trusteeship system provided for in Chapters XII and XIII in the UN Charter.[5] However, the UN trusteeship system – an obvious starting point for the discussion of this question in spite of the fact that Kosovo is governed by an interim administration under the auspices of the UN Security Council and the UN Secretary-General as provided for in Resolution 1244, instead of being a formal trusteeship under Chapters XII and XIII – was intended for (1) former mandates of the League of Nations, (2) territories detached from enemy states in the Second World War and (3) colonial territories placed under the trusteeship system by states responsible for their administration.[6]

In other words, the system was, in reality, intended for territories with an unclear or problematic status as of 1945, and for colonies or similar territories which the sovereign state at some point would be prepared to send on the road towards self-rule and independence. Trusteeships were not to be established against the will of the relevant sovereign state, and territories that progressed to independence were not supposed to fall under outside administration again. Moreover, the system itself became redundant with the wave of de-colonization in the 1960s and 1970s, and with the adoption of the 'Declaration of the Granting of Independence to Colonial Countries and Peoples' in the UN General Assembly in 1960, which stressed that backwardness could never be an excuse for the rejection of independence.

From a legal and institutional point of view, then, it is easy to see that international administration of a territory and its population is problematic when we talk about a political unit which is already an established state or a part of such a state. Even if the formal UN trusteeship system was functioning, Kosovo could not have fallen under it without a highly creative interpretation, at least not without the explicit and un-coerced consent of Belgrade. Moreover, if an imposed trusteeship arrangement – which is a suspension and international appropriation of sovereignty – is followed by independence for a part of the territory of a sovereign state, it becomes legally and institutionally speaking controversial, to say the least. In the case of Kosovo, the imposition of a *de facto* trusteeship arrangement was already in itself a recognition of minority rights and a right to self-rule as also stated directly in Resolution 1244. If minority protection and self-rule is followed by independence, we are talking about the termination of the sovereign rights of the mother-state as a consequence of a process of humanitarian intervention and international administration: trusteeship as a mid-way station to independence.

For these reasons, it is a very delicate question as to whether a trusteeship arrangement not wanted by the original holder of sovereign power over the territory in question can give way to independent statehood. On the other hand, there is still such a thing as a right of national self-determination which might be invoked in favour of the independence of Kosovo, there is still a duty not to turn against ones own population as the Yugoslav authorities did against its Albanian population in 1998–9, and there is still a historical and political logic of international trusteeship saying that the goal of outside administration is to prepare the people in question for self-rule. If orderly and civilized conditions of governance had been a fact at the outset, a kind of international administration could hardly have become a subject at all.

Theoretically, the complicated relationship between the revitalized trusteeship institution and other basic norms and institutions of international society, first of all state sovereignty and non-intervention on the one hand and national self-determination, humanitarian intervention and international peacebuilding on the other, can be discussed by means of the distinction between a 'pluralist' and a 'solidarist' conception of international society.[7]

According to the pluralists, order, justice and the rule of law in international society hang first of all on the ability of states to provide for these qualities in their *own* societies, and in accordance with their own values. In other words, 'the good life' is to be defined and provided by the state meaning that there can be many different versions of the good society in the world at a given point in time. Hence the term 'pluralism'. To pluralists like Robert Jackson, the international trusteeship institution is problematic because of the fact that for all its good intentions, outside administration of a given territory and population can hardly take place without compromising such basic principles of the contemporary international order as sovereignty, non-intervention and the self-determination of states.[8] Moreover, international trusteeship inevitably brings back memories of colonialism, paternalism and imperialism, and since governance requires a set of values, principles and institutional habits, it might also lead to a clash of civilizations.

The following pluralist rules of thumb regarding contemporary international trusteeship might thus be tentatively formulated: (1) international trusteeship should be avoided when possible. (2) When it is applied at all, it should be based on the consent of the affected sovereign authorities, and the sovereign powers should be returned to that government (provided that governmental structures exist at all) as soon as this is possible in a responsible way. (3) The international administration of the territory in question should be organized as a temporary helping hand rather than a genuine *de facto* trusteeship, and the responsibility of domestic order and justice should be canalled back to local and state authorities as quickly as possible. (4) For practical and possibly moral reasons, an international trusteeship might pave the way for autonomy, but it cannot be allowed to lead to a full application of the right of national self-determination in its classical meaning: independence.

With a Grotian or 'solidarist' approach to the question of international trusteeship and its relationship to the principle of national self-determination, a different picture materializes. The heart of the solidarist conception of international society is the assumption of international solidarity and collective security, the endorsement of institutions of global governance, a high degree of attention to non-state actors, and a belief that state sovereignty should be seen as qualified by standards of international law including international humanitarian law.[9] In this perspective, it is sometimes necessary that the international community as represented by the UN takes responsibility for populations at risk. Furthermore, in solidarist thinking claims of national self-determination which are well founded on ethnicity, language, history and practical circumstances tend to find some support when such claims are put forward in the context of atrocities committed against the national minority. This is also reflected to some degree in recent state practice as evident from the partial success of claims put forward by the Iraqi Kurds (who were able to transfer the security zone established after the war over Kuwait in 1991 into *de facto* autonomy), the Muslims of Bosnia, the people of East Timor and the Albanians of Kosovo, who would hardly have found themselves in a situation in which their future status is a choice between self-rule or independence, if it had not been for the campaign against them in 1998–9.[10] In the solidarist perspective, humanitarian intervention, international trusteeship and possibly also some openness towards claims of national self-determination must be a part of the international machinery exactly because the inter-state order has its weak points and occasional breakdowns.

In other words, the questions concerning the trusteeship of Kosovo and what comes after – in reality a question of what degree of self-determination it will lead to – cannot be answered in any definitive way solely on the basis of theoretical and historical insight into the requirements of international order. However, it is such a calculation of internally conflicting concerns for order, justice and progress that must be made in the negotiations over Kosovo's future status, along with a careful sensibility to the specific circumstances, primarily the Albanian majority demand for self-determination on the one hand, and the extremely difficult situation for the Serb and other minorities, both before and after a decision regarding future status has been taken, on the other.

Kosovo's unclear status and the problem of solving it

It is hardly surprising that Kosovo's status has remained unclear since the resort to UN trusteeship. The problem with an announcement of a decision regarding the future status of Kosovo is that this will, by implication, also be an announcement of winners and losers: the Kosovar Albanians and the Serbs of Kosovo and Serbia cannot obtain their goals unless at the expense of the other side.

To the Kosovar Albanian population, NATO's humanitarian intervention and the establishment of Kosovo as an international trusteeship in everything but name appeared to set the track for an inevitable move to independence.[11] The Albanians do not seem to be prepared to accept anything less than independence,[12] and considering the mass deportations in 1999 and the background to these, this is perhaps an understandable position.

To Kosovo's considerably diminished Serb minority, the situation remains very difficult as evident from the 2004 March riots. The Serbs live in fear of attacks in isolated enclaves, they are not free to work and they do not enjoy freedom of movement. Moreover, they find it very hard to accept that they have now become a national minority within a predominantly hostile political entity with all that this implies in loss of identity and national self-esteem.[13] Thus, the Serbs of Kosovo cling on to the hope of the re-establishment of the rule of Belgrade, and so does Serbia herself, although a more realistic view on Serbia's limited possibilities appears to have gained ground in Belgrade. Still, anything less than the degree of sovereign power in and over Kosovo that would follow from autonomy or status as a republic alongside Serbia and Montenegro is likely to be seen as a (final) defeat of Serbian hopes and aspirations.

In their favour is the fact that Russia and China have been against any solution that takes any more sovereignty away from Serbia than was stipulated in Resolution 1244,[14] something that seems to rule out independence and conditional independence, but not self-government inside the state union of Serbia and Montenegro. The reasons for this are well-known: the resentment over NATO's resort to force in 1999 without their consent in the Security Council, Russia's close relations with Serbia, and the widely shared concern that the establishment of an independent Kosovo might set a precedent for armed secession by means of outside interference.

For these reasons academic observers, politicians, diplomats and representatives of the involved international organizations argued extensively that it is better to leave the question of Kosovo's future status aside until the local and international climate becomes more conducive. Why push for a solution which will inevitably put either the Albanian or the Serbian side in the loser's position and thus turn one of the parties against UNMIK and the international community, which must in any case continue its work with the reconstruction of the province? Why open up the delicate questions of national self-determination and sovereignty at a time when two of the five great powers in the UN Security Council are still resentful over the prospects that an, in their view, unlawful intervention will lead to the creation of a new state or substantial autonomy in a way not consistent with the established international rules and norms in this field? Inside academia, Alexandros Yannis has even argued that the status of Kosovo should be frozen and 'Kosovo should enter a deep winter in which Resolution 1244, with all its ambiguities, will be the only guiding light for both Kosovar Albanians and Serbs as well as for the international administration'.[15] In an apparent acceptance of the arguments behind this position, the Kosovo Commission stated in its report from 2000 that 'there are occasions ... where parties can be induced to take the first steps towards political reconciliation only if the final destination of the process is not disclosed prematurely',[16] and with the 'standards before status' policy, this has been the position of successive UN administrators of Kosovo as well.

However, for the sake of the population of Kosovo and for the ability of UNMIK to maintain its legitimacy in the eyes of the great majority of the population, it is imperative that an answer to the delicate question of future status is found in the near future.[17] In the absence of a decision, both sides are likely to become more and more impatient and worried about the future status of Kosovo and the role that UNMIK might play in that respect. Sadly, the 2004 March riots can easily be interpreted as an explosion of Albanian frustration over the lack of results concerning their main ambition. On the Serbian side, the attempt to institutionalize the *de facto* division of the province along the Ibar River seems to be a logical and popular answer to the uncertainty about the future status of the province.[18] For both parties, there has been and remains an unfortunate wisdom in trying to change the political, economic and demographic conditions in the province before a potentially unwarranted decision about future status is taken in the Security Council.[19]

For these reasons, a decision concerning the future has to be taken as soon as possible, as has also become clear in the UN Security Council and beyond. However, it does not have to be *implemented* immediately; on the contrary, there is no alternative to a continued international management or at least surveillance of Kosovo in the short term.

Kosovo's future status: full independence under international trusteeship surveillance

As we have seen, the UN Security Council has committed itself to a promise of substantial self-rule for Kosovo at a minimum. In reality, it is also the international community and the UN Security Council that must take the final decision. Belgrade has neither the moral integrity nor the political power to hold on to its sovereignty over the province following the campaign against the Kosovar Albanian people in 1998–9 and the lost wars during the 1990s. As for the Albanian side, it cannot transfer its final victory in the struggle against the rule of Belgrade in 1999 and its relatively favourable present position into full independence without the political and financial support of the international community.

What can the UN Security Council and in particular the great powers do? In principle, a whole range of possibilities can be imagined, but following the report from the Kosovo Commission published in 2000, most accounts discuss the following: (1) the indefinite continuation of Kosovo as an international protectorate, (2) partition of the province, either by means of a canton arrangement or by setting up a new border along the Ibar River which is *de facto* separating the Albanian and Serbian populations, (3) autonomy within Serbia and Montenegro, (4) conditional independence, and (5) full independence.[20]

As recognized by the UN's sitting administrator of the province Søren Jessen-Petersen, an indefinite continuation of Kosovo as an international trusteeship in the sense discussed so far is hardly an option for the very same reasons that the decision concerning future status has to be taken now: the main goals of the Serb and the Albanian sides are mutually exclusive and uncertainty only invites speculation on both sides as to how to exploit the weaknesses of the trusteeship arrangement to their own advantage.

For legal and political reasons, partition seems to be the worst of all possible solutions to the international community, since this would run counter to some of its most fundamental rules and beliefs, namely that if borders are to be changed along ethnic lines or as a result of armed conflict at all (in itself a critical precedent to set) then it must be along established internal borders, as in the case of former Yugoslavia in the early 1990s. Furthermore, international society has invested too much in avoiding a settlement built directly and completely on a combination of ethnicity and military power to accept such an outcome today. Add to this the fact that Kosovo can hardly exist as a political unit without the north being included.

A return to Serbian rule is impossible too, both because Serbia has lost its moral right to rule over Kosovo in the eyes of much of international public opinion, and because of the fact that the Albanian community is not going to accept such a solution under any circumstances. Most likely, it would be prepared to resist such an outcome by force. More than 15 years of hardship – as they see it – after a bloody civil war, destruction of villages in 1998 and mass deportation in 1999 for the cause of freedom and national self-determination – only to give it all up? As has been indicated by the Kosovo Commission, this would be unthinkable.[21] It is also unlikely that the Kosovar Albanians would accept even substantial autonomy while still ultimately under the control of Serbia.

However, status as a third state in a new state union alongside Serbia and Montenegro might be acceptable to Kosovar Albanian leaders, but only if this would mean independence in everything but name, and only if full independence (including UN membership) is not ruled out in the long term.[22] In practice, then, this option would be difficult to distinguish from independence, and full independence as a recognized sovereign state with UN membership would be likely to follow from this scenario within a few years, unless we imagine that the Albanians – in spite of the present state of advanced self-government – are somehow forced to accept an element of substantial Serbian or federal sovereignty over the province.

This leaves, in reality, a controversial choice between conditional independence or full independence. Needless to say, the solution that the international community – led by the great powers in the Security Council – must work out in the near future (and then prepare for and implement over a period of some years) has to be as just, prudent and practical as possible to provide an acceptable answer to the many problems pointed to in this chapter: *just* in terms of the events that have taken place in the province over recent years, but also in terms of minority rights and protection which is acutely needed for Serb, Roma and other minorities; *prudent* in terms of the possible ramifications for the regional and international order (the risk of setting a precedent for armed secession and a change of borders, and the need to maintain the common understanding between the great powers); *practical* in terms of the requirements of a continued international administration of Kosovo, or at least the assistance, surveillance and initially also armed protection of minorities at risk.

With its acceptance of the practical realities (first of all the understandable rejection by the Albanians of Serbian rule, and the fact that Kosovo can never be reconstructed successfully against the will of its 90 percent Albanian population) on the one hand, and a much needed concern for the Serb, Roma and other minorities on the other, *conditional independence* as suggested by the Kosovo Commission and International Crisis Group[23] seems to be the best solution. The problem is how to put some real and permanent substance into such conditions and qualifications in order to avoid repeating the experiences with Slovenia and especially Croatia when these states were recognized by the international community in the beginning of the 1990s. Back then, the granting of minority guarantees was set up as a formal condition for recognition in a legal context, but it was in reality entirely up to the new states themselves how and to what degree they were going to live up to the promises. Both the Kosovo Commission and the International Crisis Group are aware of this problem, but the proposals of the former seem to rely primarily, although not exclusively, on guarantees given and steps taken in Kosovo before the granting of independence, and the proposals of the latter seem to be imagining a system of guarantees and surveillance based on the continuation of the far-reaching powers of the Special Representative of the UN Secretary-General, powers that have become increasingly unacceptable to the Albanian side.

In any case, there is no doubt that a system of minority protection must be an un-negotiable condition for a qualified recognition of independence for Kosovo. The situation of the Serbs and the Roma remain very difficult especially following the 2004 March riots.[24] A treaty-based promise by the new Kosovar Albanian leaders that the new 'state' will respect the rights of minorities is not enough at all, and neither is a temporary surveillance of these matters by UNMIK as suggested by the Kosovo Commission. A human rights inspection regime with permanent offices in the province, most obviously in Pristina and in areas with Serb enclaves, a legally binding bill of minority rights, and a system for minority protection must be established. Furthermore, by UN Security Council resolution, this permanent inspection regime must be given the power to take action against abuses and violations of this bill of rights, and the possibility of sanctions in case of such violations must be openly stated. We might conceive of such an arrangement much in the way that some European diplomats were discussing the possible creation of a permanent weapons inspection regime with its own buildings, staff and equipment for Iraq, before the US and its allies resorted to force.

In other words, what is suggested here is that full independence for Kosovo, and an international recognition of the country as a sovereign state and a member of the UN, is accompanied by the set-up of a permanent trusteeship arrangement under the UN Security Council and the Secretariat whose responsibilities will be much more restricted than those of UNMIK today, but whose powers will remain potent in a few specific areas, first of all that of minority protection. An element of trusteeship will thus continue indefinitely, but there will be no uncertainty with respect to Kosovo's status.[25] Apart from the surveillance of minority protection based on human rights inspection centres around the province, the new trusteeship arrangement could act as the guarantee of Kosovo's borders and a mediator in disputes in such matters with the power to take decisions or to propose decisions to be taken by the UN Security Council. Furthermore, the new trusteeship arrangement might deal with other central aspects of state creation, consolidation and regional order such as arbitration in property disputes and access to places, buildings and monuments of historical or religious significance.

First of all, however, the new trusteeship arrangement as suggested here would become an institutionalized framework for a permanent guarantee that legitimate Serb interests will be taken care of in spite of the granting of full independence to Kosovo, and it would also become a forum for persistent dialogue and cooperation between Kosovo, Serbia (or Serbia and Montenegro at the federal level) and the international community represented by the UN. The idea is not that Serbia and Montenegro should give up all influence on Kosovo in return for international guarantees and surveillance. The idea is that Serbia and Montenegro should take direct part in that institutionalized system of trusteeship herself, so that any impression that the plight of the Serbs in Kosovo, and the legitimate interest of the former sovereign power, are completely out of the hands of Belgrade can be repudiated.

Ramifications for the parties and international society

Against this proposal it might be argued that conditional independence is not realistic due to international concern for the respect of established sovereignty and borders, the likely resistance from China and Russia and the need to respect UN Security Council resolution 1244 and its reference to the Rambouillet Accords which refers to 'the will of the people' as only one of a number of elements as the basis of a decision concerning Kosovo's future status. However, as indicated above, developments over the last couple of years have made anything but *de facto* independence or full independence almost unthinkable. Authorities and competences are furthermore already transferred to the elected bodies in Kosovo and not to Belgrade on a scale and with a speed which makes substantial integration into Serbia, or even Serbia and Montenegro, unrealistic and also increasingly pointless. What UNMIK is preparing the people of Kosovo for is, in reality, to run all internal affairs by themselves.

In that context, it is better to work out some substantial and permanent arrangement for the protection of Serbian interests than to insist on a mainly symbolic status for Serbia which would not give the Serbs of Kosovo anything of real value. It should be possible to convince Serbia and Montenegro as well as Russia and China of the wisdom of this, especially when it is plain for all parties to see that Kosovo has in reality become independent already and that this state of affairs is likely to create a permanent problem for the Serb and Roma minorities, as well as for the legitimate interests that Serbia has in the province. Furthermore, UNMIK cannot continue on the current basis without running into greater and greater difficulties in its relations with the local authorities and the Albanian majority. It would be much better for UNMIK to continue on the basis of a clarification of the end status, first as an administrating body which will increasingly become a helping hand as in Bosnia, later as a permanent institution under the UN Security Council with the task of on the spot surveillance of minority rights, border issues, the access of Serbia and Serbs to places and monuments, and arbitration in matters concerning property rights between Kosovo and Serbia.

This would in the longer (and relatively permanent) run be a trusteeship arrangement in a new and much less interfering variant which has, however, a potential as an institution capable of handling the specific challenges pointed to above. The experience of Kosovo shows that crisis management and comprehensive peacebuilding in the context of secession and state dissolution take more than just good will and plentiful resources. International rules and institutions must be adjusted as well. More specifically, under special circumstances like those of Kosovo, it is necessary to apply a less strict interpretation of sovereignty and the right of national self-determination, especially when this right is invoked in the context and background of atrocities and massive forced displacement. However, as indicated above the solidarist calculation is much more complicated than this, since the Serb minority could, in principle, make the same claim with reference to the more recent atrocities against it. If it is accepted that neither reintegration into Serbia (and Montenegro) nor partition are viable options, a hitherto unseen trusteeship arrangement acting primarily as a relatively permanent framework for potent minority protection could be the institutional solution.

The principles of international law, international morality, prudence and pragmatism must be blended according to circumstances. In Kosovo, it is time for a decision for full independence under permanent international supervision in the form of a permanent trusteeship arrangement with (after a longer period of scaling down) limited responsibilities, but strong powers to implement them in order to avoid a destruction of the Serb community in the country. In international society, it is time to restore the trusteeship institution as such, but along principles and practices that prevent it from being exploited as a vehicle for great-power ambitions, as argued elsewhere in this book.[26]

Acknowledgement

I am grateful to Chris Freeman and Lene Mosegaard Søbjerg for helpful comments on draft versions of this chapter.

Notes

1 On the background, see the Independent International Commission on Kosovo (the Kosovo Commission), *The Kosovo Report* (Oxford: Oxford University Press, 2000), Part I.

2 See Robert Jackson, *The Global Covenant* (Oxford: Oxford University Press, 2000), p. 307.

3 On humanitarian intervention see Tonny Brems Knudsen, *Humanitarian Intervention*, (forthcoming on Routledge).

4 On the riots see Human Rights Watch, *Failure to Protect: Anti-Minority Violence in Kosovo, March 2004*, 16, 6 (D) July 2004.

5 See Peter Lyon, 'The Rise and Fall and Possible Revival of International Trusteeship', *The Journal of Commonwealth and Comparative Studies*, 31, 1 (1993), pp. 96–110 and James N. Murray Jr., *The United Nations Trusteeship System* (Urbana: The University of Illinois Press, 1957).

6 Lyon (n. 5 above) 100–105. See also Søbjerg's contribution for this book.

7 Hedley Bull, 'The Grotian Conception of International Society', in Herbert Butterfield and Martin Wight (eds), *Diplomatic Investigations* (London: Allen and Unwin, 1966), pp. 51–73; Jackson (n. 2 above). For a development of this distinction, see Knudsen (n. 3 above).

8 Jackson (n. 2 above), pp. 301–315. In the following I refer to the ideas of Robert Jackson.

9 Knudsen (n. 3 above). Here, I build on Hersch Lauterpacht's comprehensive authorship. See also Lyon (n. 5 above) and the discussion of the ideas of Mervyn Frost in Jackson (n. 2 above), pp. 299–301.

10 On national self-determination see also Rasmus Abildgaard Kristensen, 'Minoriteters krav om selvbestemmelse og det internationale samfund', *Politica*, 33, 3 (2001), pp. 191–208 and his contribution to this book.

11 Alexandros Yannis, 'Kosovo Under International Administration', *Survival*, 45, 2 (2001), pp. 31–48, see p. 36.

12 Kosovo Commission (n. 1 above), p. 260–262.

13 Ibid., p. 260; Yannis (n. 11 above), p. 37–38.

14 Yannis (n. 11 above) p. 35; Kosovo Commission (n. 1 above), p. 260.

15 Yannis (n. 11 above), p. 44.
16 The Kosovo Commission (n. 1 above), p. 260.
17 This was also the position of the Kosovo Commission by 2001. See '*The Follow-up on the Kosovo Report: Why Conditional Independence*, 2001 (www.kosovocommission.org), pp. 20–22.
18 International Crisis Group (www.crisisweb.org), 'UNMIK's Kosovo Albatross: Tackling Division in Mitrovica', *Crisis Webnews*, 3 June, 2002, pp. 1–21.
19 Kosovo Commission (n. 17 above), pp. 19 and 21; International Crisis Group, *A Kosovo Roadmap (I): Addressing Final Status*, ICG Balkans Report No. 124, March 2002, pp. i–iv.
20 See the Kosovo Commission (n. 1 above), chapter 9, and 2001 (n. 17 above); International Crisis Group (n. 19 above), pp. 1–17; Dana H. Allin et al., 'What Status for Kosovo?', Chaillot Paper 50, Institute for Security Studies, WEU, October 2001; and United States Institute of Peace, 'Kosovo Final Status. Options and Cross-border Requirements', Special Report No. 91, July 2002.
21 Kosovo Commission (n. 1 above), pp. 261–2.
22 Ibid., pp. 24–5. See also International Crisis Group (n. 20 above), pp. 10–11, and Dana H. Allin et al., 'What Status for Kosovo?', Chaillot Paper 50, Institute for Security Studies, WEU, October 2001, pp. 32–5.
23 The Kosovo Commission (n. 1 above), chapter 9; and 2001 (n. 17 above), pp. 25–31; International Crisis Group (n. 19 above), pp. 6 and 12–17.
24 Kosovo Commission (n. 1 above), p. 260; Human Rights Watch (n. 4 above).
25 The International Crisis Group has proposed something similar, but sees the arrangement as temporary. See International Crisis Group (n. 19 above), p. 12 and 'Kosovo: Towards Final Status', Europe Report n. 161, 24 January 2005.
26 As this book goes into press, the UN Security Council (S/PV.5290 of 24 October 2005) has decided to open the negotiations concerning future status (to go on for most of 2006) as called for by the UN administrator in Kosovo, Søren Jessen Petersen, with the (not entirely convincing) claim that progress has been made and UN standards are being met.

10 Liberal trusteeship

The convergence of interest and ideology in international administration

Christopher P. Freeman

In terms of peacekeeping, international relations theory has been lurking in the basement, treated like a 'phantom of the opera', as one writer has put it.[1] Certainly, looking at the spectrum of operational developments from the Suez UN Emergency Force in 1956, to the UN Assistance Mission in Afghanistan today, it is near impossible to ignore the manner in which these missions have become politicized and bound up with a greater world order project. This preoccupation has framed both current political practice as well as international relations theory to function within an uncritical promotion of a liberal 'peacebuilding consensus' drawing on solidarism as a justification for humanitarian intervention and transitional administration to institute liberal democracy.[2] At its most extreme, the UN, or so called 'coalitions of the willing', have occupied and administered sovereign territories in the name of a new, liberal international order and morality.

This chapter comparatively examines international administration both in UN-led operations since the 1990s and those conducted under the 'war on terror'. International interventions in the Balkans, East Timor, Afghanistan and even Iraq have all been construed to various degrees as humanitarian actions for the good of local constituents, not dissimilar to the purifying Arthurian search for the Holy Grail. The question is whether the re-emergence of international governorships – the so called 'new trusteeships' – is evidence of just such a Quest?[3] Have the Western organisers been trying to bring about a just international society, or merely exploiting the political currency of humanitarianism to build a new world order determined more by the traditional concerns of security and economic interests? In modern form the contours of such a Quest are visible in the militarization of liberal state-building through intervention in 'failed' and non-liberal and non-cooperative 'rogue' states. Perhaps we should remember, however, that the crucible of the Knights of the Round Table was not purely to suffer for the sins of Camelot, but to save it. The virtue of the Quest was as much bound up with the pursuit of the Grail as in moral salvation of the Knights themselves, and thus of Camelot. The Quest, in the end, becomes a goal in itself.[4] Is successful conclusion of these missions elusively evading its pursuers, or could it be that in current practice, 'peace' is an ideological phantom?

Arguably, the function of international peace maintenance has become an increasingly permanent one. First, this chapter posits that, in selected cases, liberal inclusion of war-torn and rogue states has become securitized, prompting military intervention and beyond into international administration. Second, it forwards the concept of *liberal trusteeship* as confirming the political aspirations of international administration. Third, it critically explores the limitations of liberal trusteeship, whether in some cases there can actually be a successful exit within the remit of current strategy? Finally, the chapter reflects constructively on how state-building operations, as they appear increasingly necessary for managing globally occurring state fragmentation, could be improved. While the importance of 'strengthening local ownership' is often mentioned, deeper exploration is lacking. The preceding analysis suggests an approach built upon the constraints and opportunities of local culture and its political aspirations.

The securitization of liberal inclusion

The UN's operations in East Timor and Kosovo have been the largest and most ambitious in scope, but smaller scale operations over the past decade have collectively pointed in a clear direction of interest. Affecting the process of government in places seen as chaotic or threatening is increasingly becoming part of the *raison d'être* of the UN's activity in maintaining international peace and security. A defining feature of post-Cold War security is the transformation of the formerly neutral task of military peacekeeping into country-wide 'peace operations'. In Western eyes local ideologies, having descended into repression or violent competition, are disenfranchised and systematically de-legitimized as part of the greater global 'human rights revolution'. Compliance with 'international standards' is enforced through a 'new radical interventionism'.[5] The ambition of these interventions is one aimed at social transformation of societies into liberal states[6] through a range of measures, with trusteeship as its most extreme tool, surpassing even war but often preceded by it.

What Mark Duffield terms 'liberal peace' is embodied in the re-engagement between 'zones of safety' and 'zones of chaos', occurring as part of a renewed venture of postcolonial regulation. The aim of liberal peace is 'to [selectively] transform the dysfunctional and war-affected societies that it encounters on its borders into cooperative, representative and, especially, stable entities'.[7] Selective inclusion of failed and rogue states into the liberal zones of peace has now become securitized,[8] in so far that such states are treated in discourse and policy as an existential threat to human security and to international order. Bringing them into the international system is a new public policy for peace, both for the UN and liberal states.[9] Adam Roberts observes that, in the cases of Afghanistan and Iraq, humanitarian and security justifications clearly overlap.[10] Security policy is no longer limited to the manipulation of the territorially sovereign state. It extends to the penetration of the state, the socialisation of its polity and the administration of its rule of law to groups and individuals within it.

However, convergence of motives does not imply that state-building through the UN or the war on terror will absorb every non-liberal or war-torn country. Clearly this has not happened globally. But constitutional pluralism is discredited by a core group of liberal states using solidarism to legitimize the militarized replication of their political system. However, this should not lead to lofty assumptions such as Michael Mazarr's polemic in *International Affairs,* 'George W. Bush: Idealist'.[11] While solidarism remains important for mobilizing support for interventions, national agendas remain the key to discerning the nature and commitment to a liberal international order, or 'peace'.

Recurrence of shifting measures of involvement in UN peace operations appear to reflect the changing geometry and levels of interests on behalf of the intervening parties. Strategies depend on a blend of realism and externally defined idealism. For example, the Office of the High Representative (OHR) in Bosnia-Herzegovina is on a tight leash under the scrutiny of the 'Peace Implementation Council' (PIC), dominated by European states but also including Japan and the US, all the primary donors to the OHR budget.[12] The PIC, as its mandate makes clear, is responsible for giving the High Representative 'political guidance'.[13] A similar arrangement existed in East Timor, where, according to Jarat Chopra, the UN failed in a democratic sense because of its failure to live up to its essential obligation to the Timorese, instead prioritizing internal politics and the desires of the donor nations.[14]

Strong ambiguities also exist between international rhetorical support for state-building in Afghanistan and the thin financial lifeline intended to facilitate democracy. While it is clear – at least in rhetoric – that renewed state failure would be a strategic failure in the war on terror,[15] reasons underlie non-delivery on donor commitments and expansion of security outside Kabul. One such reason, and certainly not an idealist one, could be that keeping Afghanistan off-kilter allows Coalition Forces to prosecute open war against Islamist militants, enlisting the Afghan National Army in this task without questions being asked about the limits and legality of the use of force. While removal of the Taliban regime as a catalyst for terrorism was securitized post-September 11, Afghanistan's relevance to the expansion of the liberal peace remains peripheral.[16] Thus regime change and subsequent escalation of the globally more consequential Iraq crisis, led to the desecuritization of Afghanistan on the international agenda, even if consolidation of democracy remains unfinished.[17]

Full state-building, including under UN auspices, has always strongly reflected the national security and economic interests of contributing states. As Jean-Marie Guehenno suggests, national agendas come first, with regional considerations second and global ones a distant third.[18] In the more traditional realms of UN operations in the Balkans, the external appearance of unified efforts owe in no small part to the coherence of national objectives in regional stability, particularly given the accelerated process of EU accession. However, in Afghanistan and Iraq the widely varying degrees of interest by national actors explain themselves more clearly in the 'bilateralization' of both economic and security assistance. Coalition operations against Al Qaeda and Islamist militancy in Afghanistan remain independent of the more internationalized process of state-building, while in Iraq coherence of US and UK political strategies has ensured their continued commitment, as well as reluctance by nations that opposed the war to embroil themselves in the operation. However, the transnational nature of insecurity makes the likelihood of future operations where the UN operates the functions of government high,[19] even if the task of military intervention may be commandeered by coalitions of the willing, not always with UN approval. Kosovo and Iraq have shown that a humanitarian crisis can be manipulated by both substate and state actors so as to provoke intervention or gain *post facto* approval for political engagement by the UN, which can hardly maintain a non-interventionist policy when faced with great-power proposals for addressing human suffering.[20]

The aspirations: international regulation via liberal trusteeship

'Liberal trusteeship' as a political tool is a means of socialisation, and of transformation. Its aim is one of *pacification* rather than subjugation and direct resource exploitation,[21] as was often associated with colonialism. Consequently, it is not intended to result in imperialism – though it may be driven by it – and its expression when operative is more akin to a democratic authoritarianism imposed by internationals; it negates temporarily the principle of self-determination for the peace dividend it is intended to pay. As Robert Jackson argues, the administration of war-torn or rogue states may not be permanent in ambition as in an earlier era of international trusteeships, mandates and protectorates, but in the assumption that self-government shall be restored is vested an expectation that it takes place in a pacific manner with integrative intent toward the liberal peace.[22]

Regulation occurs to varying levels across the system, through conditional development aid and structural adjustment on the lower end of the scale to UN trusteeship and occupation in its highest form. These mechanisms of international governance are increasingly becoming permanent features of the post-Cold War system. Cyprus, Bosnia, Kosovo, Afghanistan and Iraq all operate on an international supporting machinery to varying extents, as do an array of 'developing' Third World states, often in conflict.[23] In his peace maintenance thesis, Jarat Chopra outlines a hierarchy of international engagement in war-torn societies, which includes not only UN governorships but the full spectrum of humanitarian and military activities to provide a 'unified concept' of operations. These include: preventive deployment and monitoring missions, internal conflict resolution measures (such as mediation or Disarmament, Demobilization and Reintegration of former combatants), assistance to civil authorities (such as refugee returns), protection of humanitarian relief operations (humanitarian corridors and 'safe areas'), and guarantee and denial of movement (such as the no fly zones in Iraq).[24] These connect upwards to the phenomenon of transitional administrations, in which Chopra sees four operational categories, and horizontally into civilian policing (such as the International Police Task Force and UN Civilian Police), international criminal tribunals and all manner of human rights work.

The operational categories range from 'light' to 'heavy' footprint through 1) *Assistance* (public administration support and advice); 2) *Partnership* (the UN acts as an auditor with a final veto in a democratization or decolonization mission); 3) *Control* (the UN deploys into local ministries and institutions with the executive ability to overturn policy decisions and dismiss officials); and 4) *Governorship* (the UN subsumes the full task of government, for example in a failed state situation).[25] Such international administrations have the capacity and remit for (a) creation and enforcement of new legal systems, (b) the management and rebuilding of local economies, (c) the appointment and dismissal of officials, (d) the reconstruction and operating of public utilities (including the subcontracting of these functions to foreign firms), (e) the establishment of effective customs and police services, and (f) the provision of public security.[26]

In practice, the two intermediate levels of Partnership and Control are less frequent – most trusteeships are either governorships or broadly mandated assistance missions, and as major donors to reconstruction *all* are supervisory. Transitional administrations such as the UN Interim Administration Mission in Kosovo and the UN Transitional Administration in East Timor reign somewhere around the Governorship level, with a lessening role as they attempt to localize government in preparation of exit. The UN Assistance Mission in Afghanistan, as its title foretells, is in the Assistance category, but its influence in terms of convening the Loya Jirga, civil registration and electoral organization, and auditing government reform – especially in areas such as gender representation and mainstreaming, press freedom and the constitution – betray it as having, if not mission creep, then certainly routine incursions into the realms of Partnership and aspects of Control. The Coalition Provisional Authority in Iraq, on the other hand, transcends the scale even for what Chopra terms Governorship, in the sense that his concept includes a multilateral vision and the external veto of at least the UN Security Council. In Bosnia, Kosovo and Iraq the aspirations of the regulatory agenda now extend as far as including provisions for a free-market economy in new national constitutions, and in East Timor to negotiating deals with multinationals for economic exploitation of national oil resources in the Timor Gap.[27]

Liberal trusteeships operate according to three component ambitions: peace maintenance, economic restructuring/discipline and socialisation. In the liberal ideology all three are seen as inseparable, and human rights makes the project morally admissible and often desirable to liberal publics.

Peace maintenance

In theory, military intervention separates or quells belligerents and prevents the dominance of a single domestic agenda predicated on force. Instead normalcy is to be determined via an institutionalist vision of justice based on democratic representation, majority rule and multiculturalism. The function of peace maintenance at its most basic then is to effect a 'negative peace' in which local war is simply absent, while trusteeship attempts to bring about a permanent basis for international and domestic cooperation. The construction of a space in which to 'build' or mediate peace, even if it does not succeed, can prevent or lessen conflict while in process. As such, regardless of the merits of UNMIK or the UN Transitional Administration in East Timor (UNTAET) in facilitating democracy and reconciliation in Kosovo or East Timor, their jurisdiction have lessened conflict which could otherwise cause greater regional disturbance through conflict spillover or refugee flows. Similarly, international administration attempts to prevent and punish the development of revolutionary extremist doctrines and assists in the solidification and protection of borders, effectively underwriting territorial sovereignty.

Economic restructuring and discipline

International administration implies an agenda for transformation of domestic political economy into one governed by neo-liberalism and the rule of law. Current doctrine replicates prevailing economic thought in liberal societies as regards the potential of neo-liberalism to deliver development and thus the added stability that comes with its logic and incentives.[28] Regional integration is important, with EU membership consistently employed as conditionality for conformity and economic discipline in the Balkans and Eastern Europe. Robert Axelrod, in his seminal work on cooperation and game theory, argued that 'for cooperation to prove stable the future must have a sufficiently large shadow', provided by a stable set of relationships and expectations.[29] In the case of former Yugoslavia, the dividend for cooperation is regional integration and economic development through membership of the EU and added security by, for example, Serbian entry to NATO's pre-membership club, the Partnership for Peace. Economic and political carrots of this sort are key elements of peacebuilding strategy and societal regulation. They provide the leverage necessary to bend the will of former belligerents, pacifying them into cooperation and regional politics rather than localized violence. There is also the added agenda of rule of law. Endemic criminality, political corruption and porosity of borders have typified post-war situations, facilitating convergence into a 'crime-terror nexus' [30] In Republika Srpska this resulted in illegal transfers of long range missile engines and chemical weapons munitions to Libya and Iraq, and the international indictment of senior officials including the resignation of the Serb member of the Bosnia-Herzegovina presidency, Mirko Sarovic.[31] Thus the need to regulate borders and control resource flows have connected the war on terror to multilateral 'humanitarian' peace operations.

Socialisation

Trusteeship maintains or aspires to create a human rights regime where it is absent or lacking in domestic institutional or normative support, an 'international responsibility to protect'. Human rights provides the political currency to enforce an embracement of the liberal agenda in its entirety including banning of local parties, dismissal of non-compliant officials, and imprisonment of national leaders (such as Milosevic, Karadizic and Mullah Omar) together with a paternal veto on all domestic political developments. To the extent that such a peace is desired by local constituencies, and workable in that the local domestic space can be connected to the global via international facilitation, temporary regulation gathers legitimacy. As Joseph Nye argues, 'soft power', the proselytizing quality of Western ideas and institutions could 'make other people want what we want',[32] by socializing nations and individuals globally into the American dream. However, if intervention is not wholly desired by occupants of a 'host' society because it is divided or sceptical of its aims, absorption of a society into the liberal peace is problematized. Legitimacy comes into question in the perception of those asked to trust an international administration of their country and the fundamental complications of state-building are encountered, shifting 'trusteeship' into open-ended occupation and resistance.

The limitations: no exit even with strategy?

The new liberal trusteeships have been characterized by many of the same features and dilemmas as the UN Trusteeship System (1945–94), which replaced the League of Nations mandates (1920–45). One of these has been the defining notion of the 'sacred trust of civilisation' meant to exist between 'backward native peoples' and 'the family of nations'.[33] This concept, the 'dual mandate' as Burke coined it, became the guiding parable not only for effective governance, but for the administrative and civic education required to progress to national self-government.[34] Under the occupying powers in Iraq, we see a reversion to principles and practices of the national mandate system, and the problems of local rebellion and terrorism which beset it and eventually led to a forced British retreat from Palestine. However, the post-Cold War operations run under the UN banner, which appear more similar to the relatively successful international trusteeships run under the UN Trusteeship Council in the first decades after the Second World War, have been facilitated by at least the initial perception on behalf of local actors that a genuine dual mandate exists. Indeed, as Berdal and Caplan point out there is much to be learned from the wealth of colonial period literature on international governance of dependencies and trusteeship territories,[35] even if this is a comparison many in the business of transitional administration are still uncomfortable making.

Greater focus on the local dimension in peace operations and international administration has only recently begun to emerge fully into the research and policy agenda. Chopra, for example, argues from the experience of East Timor 'that the idea of international administration has not matured democratically' because it 'has not been subjected downward to the will of a local population as a constituency.'[36] To a considerable extent, this echoes the past. As J.M. Lee points out from the British colonial enterprise, 'good government' became a slogan in colonial affairs because it implied that 'self-government' meant 'incompetent administration'.[37] The term in fact said more about the prejudices, prevailing attitudes and political education of colonial officials than it may have about the societies they administered.[38] While these trusteeships aspired through a process of 'tutelage' to instil the civic sprit, ethos of public service and bureaucratic competency, they themselves did not make use of the 'Westminster model' in the societies they governed.

Colonial administrations were not accountable to a set of rules of administrative morality enshrined in a national code, nor to a supreme court, council of state or other auditory body or to scrutinize public decisions.[39] The sole requirement was the annual submission of a completed 'questionnaire' to the Trusteeship Council similar in modern form to the Secretary-General's Reports to the Security Council.[40] 'Good government,' according to Lee, 'was a collection of political attitudes accepted by consent among those in positions of authority'.[41] Similar issues plagued the early UN administrations of the 1990s, but today aims and efforts to develop constitutions accordant with 'Islamic principles' in Afghanistan and Iraq and co-opting local traditions such as the Loya Jirga point to the development of, at least on the surface, a more culturally informed approach. The challenge, then, is how to develop a form of 'participatory intervention' that ensures justice – as far as possible – for the constituent parts of the host nation and that 'resonates with local social reality'.[42]

In a comprehensive study of international administrations in the 1990s, Richard Caplan points out that success is contingent on two variables: operational aims and contextual factors.[43] The clarity and convergence of these are one way of discerning whether an operation will achieve its stated objective and whether local political dynamics will follow. For example, in the successful cases of the UN Transitional Administration in Eastern Slavonia (UNTAES) and the UN Transitional Administration in East Timor (UNTAET), it was clear that the envisaged end-state was largely unavoidable. Due to the strategic context of the war in former Yugoslavia and lack of interest from Serbia, Eastern Slavonia would be returned to Croatia – any autonomy agreement for Croatian Serbs would have to be negotiated within those politically determined constraints. Likewise in East Timor the violent and illegal nature of Indonesian occupation, its sponsoring of West Timorese and indigenous militias, destruction of Timorese infrastructure and the circumstances of international intervention, meant the territory would have to gain its independence to be governable.[44]

In Kosovo on the other hand, the international community's own uncertainty and likely unwillingness to contravene the Helsinki doctrine of peaceful change of borders[45] and act as final executioner of the former Yugoslavia, led it to mandate UNMIK to promote 'substantial autonomy and self-government' for Kosovo, despite the Kosovo-Albanian majority's demand for independence.[46] This has worsened prospects for cooperation by not satisfying either Kosovar-Albanian or Serbian demands for absolute sovereignty, and complicated UN withdrawal, making it a more or less permanent prop for peace and security in Kosovo – and potentially in south-east Europe.

In Afghanistan, a similar dilemma is emerging, where initially in the post-Taliban era a widespread enthusiasm existed for the idea of a new, unified Afghanistan.[47] Failure to deliver on donor commitments, security and the problematic alliances of intervention led to the entrenchment of unpopular warlords and a Tajik dominated government which politicized ethnicity, alienating the Pashtun majority.[48] The fallout has been increased Taliban resurgence and a diminishing political space for cooperation, reform and extension of the central government. In an opposite sense the same has occurred in Iraq. Early withdrawal of the Coalition Provisional Authority and calling of elections has been precipitated by Baathist and jihadist terror tactics which have inflamed anti-American nationalist sentiments and caused dangerous mass mobilization along sectarian faultlines, presumably hoping to trigger civil war. Such scorched-earth tactics by 'spoilers', alienated segments of the polity, would hold less currency in situations where missions were entered into with broad, locally-led political goals and operational strategies. Judging from history it appears that success, defined as achievement of an intended and sustainable political outcome, has been determined this way.

Looking to the successful efforts of liberal trusteeship, Germany, Japan, Eastern Slavonia and East Timor, the instrumental factors have been those of legitimacy and totality of control.[49] Even in cases where international engagement has begun as military occupation following unconditional surrender, the relation of trusteeship has developed over time, hinging on the effectiveness and manner of administration. According to Annika Hansen, 'political legitimacy is to a large extent a matter of expectations and performance, where the population's perception of performance is conditioned by the degree to which security and stability are provided'.[50]

However, Simon Chesterman concludes that the problem in UN-led operations has been that the means are inconsistent with the ends. To Chesterman, assertions that transitional administrations are dependent on 'local ownership' are inaccurate and have created misleading expectations among local populations adding or even creating a crisis of legitimacy that undermines state-building efforts[51] by forcing internationals to 'sell' policies essential for the monopoly of the state to local populations. Some of these actors may, as in Afghanistan and Iraq, not share the aims of the international community even in the broadest sense,[52] profiting directly from maintenance of the war economy as a source of status and power, or even of survival.[53]

Resistance is enforced by domestic codes of loyalty and kinship which can be invoked along patrimonial, ethnic or religious lines and which add to the difficulty of an international administration penetrating society and affecting lasting change. As Jennings points out, US efforts in Japan and Germany faced a domestic context where internal fractures were mainly political and not underscored by religious or ethnic divisions – military occupation was country-wide and borders were controlled internally as well as externally by allies. To this was added the national acceptance of defeat, war-weariness and the international climate of reconciliation and physical reconstruction that followed the Second World War.[54] It is comparable in an international sense, to elements of Zartman's 'ripe moment' arising from the sustained losses of a hurting stalemate between competing actors, creating space for negotiation and generating will for a political settlement.[55]

In contrast, current efforts in Iraq and Afghanistan are only partially matched to these criteria. 'De-Baathification' may appear similar to the post-war process in Germany of 'de-Nazification', but suffers from the added complication that political re-education is not sufficient as the Sunni ruling class prepares to take its place in Iraq, recast as a disempowered minority under a Shia-dominated democracy. Such prospects may be sufficient to create incentives among some for armed struggle against 'the new Iraq', especially as it is subsumed under the greater banner of a global *jihad* against a Western-dominated liberal peace. Also in Afghanistan, incentives for inclusion under a centralized government have been weakened by the absence of a profitable 'licit' economy. For local warlords who give up their fiefdoms and control over cross-border trade routes, the value of their current assets will not be matched by reconstruction.[56] In Kosovo, the continued difficulties in convincing stakeholders to abandon political war aims and to dismantle the shadow economy has heightened uncertainty and allowed space for the Kosovar-Albanians to rearm.[57] In these cases, conflict has been exacerbated by external, often regional conflict connections – so called 'bad neighbourhoods' – where flows of resources, arms and combatants from interested parties abroad have fed conflict domestically.[58]

Post-war porosity of borders and a preponderance of shadow networks and economies make control over resistant populations near impossible. Entrenchment of lawlessness in the immediate post-conflict period has hampered state-building efforts to a point where it has, at one time or another, been the primary strategic security issue in all three theatres.[59] Moreover, failure of neo-liberal reforms to deliver on social welfare and withdrawal of the state from the economy via privatization creates a reverse incentive system where war entrepreneurs hold most of the cards when it comes to commanding loyalty and services.[60] Inability to attain decent standards of living from employment within the licit economy constitutes an implicit disincentive for legal economic activity and an explicit incentive for perpetuating drug trafficking or mafia sponsored corruption, especially among the security services and legal personnel. This increases the centrifugal forces exerted by private actors eroding the sovereignty of the state,[61] a serious problem if the control of the state is seen as synonymous with the norms and mechanisms of liberal peace. The concern of these isolated governments, then, becomes not day-to-day governance of society, but maintenance of power in a fractured and impoverished state and assurance that donor channels remain open to facilitate governing authority, 'it actually destroys the state's physical capability to act alone – the emperor is not naked, but he is wearing hired clothes'.[62]

International administration and mediation has become a supporting machinery without which protectorate states and their regional orders may well collapse. Partly due to the longevity of the international presence, inter-ethnic competition and animosity have become institutionalized and socialized into a new political culture, without the administration having the experience of controlling it and where little capacity or will exists to perform this function in an impartial manner. It could be that within the remit of current thinking there is no exit, even with strategy. The solution may well be vested in the shadow of the future – one which Michael Ignatieff argues is present in the heavier footprint of an 'imperial commitment to stability' on behalf of the US.[63] But the question remains, whether such a shadow is projected by the presence of foreign troops and motorway billboards promising eventual EU membership, without conclusively resolving the original grievances that first led to conflict and transformation of networks that perpetuate conflict into ones that support peace.

The way forward: conclusive reflections

Operational lessons remind us that such a shadow may be more deeply cast if pursued according to a more 'restrained approach', with a clear hierarchy of operational priorities sensitive to the political nature of state-building.[64] Amitai Etzioni posits that many of the failures in recent operations have been due to the pursuit of an overambitious and too widely defined socio-normative agenda.[65] In Iraq for example, de-Baathification of society alienated local stakeholders in the ruling and middle class, bringing the very claim of 'trusteeship' into question among its constituents.[66] This dilemma was deepened by lack of a strategy for law and order in the immediate post-conflict phase, one which could have been built around a regionally assembled 'policekeeping' force of Arab and Muslim gendarmes, with international advisors and specialists.[67] Such an approach would have carried a lighter footprint, lessening the perception of Western occupation, improved communication and through its reliance on multilateralism, made intervention conditional on generating consent in the Muslim world.

Current approaches contradict the factors considered to have made efforts in Germany and Japan successful. According to Etzioni, a restrained approach to a narrower agenda allows greater and more focused commitment, lowers expectations and increases the scope for success.[68] This would involve working initially with the institutions and bureaucracy in power – though removing the top leadership – and pushing gradual reform by creating incentives for mid-level leadership to support the new state. Recognizing local power dynamics and economic networks is essential to create a system that can affect their transformation into politics and a peace economy through an intelligent incentive system. This means analysis of the role of local actors and their agendas must be objective, not ideological. Condemnation of 'warlords' and Baathists neither exploits nor removes their interests in maintenance of power and the shadow economy that sustains it. If anything, alienating power-holders is likely to cause resistance to transformation or even rebellion, as in Iraq and parts of Afghanistan.

In addition, though theory and practice have evolved, more often than not operations have been entered into without a clear, robust hierarchy of priorities to which locals can attach their expectations. Graham Day, an old salt of the Balkan and Timor missions, argues that such a hierarchy should proceed on the basis of establishing order and gradually building governance, with an emphasis on 'policekeeping' – robust civilian policing with military backup if necessary. This, what he calls an 'incubator model', entails 1) Cessation of warfighting – imposition of martial order; 2) Creation of law and order – via immediate policekeeping (ideally in the first 100 days of intervention) of both economic and violent crime to instil the confidence necessary for peaceful interaction and development of a licit economy; 3) Building governance – restoration or construction of public institutions and internal security architecture, including courts, judiciary and a culturally appropriate body of law, for example, a possible mix of civil and sharia law or constitutional principles; 4) Handover of sovereignty – to a functioning society which runs its own courts and security system, but continued development and democratization assistance.[69] The end goal is a state of what Michael Dziedzic describes as a condition of 'law and order with justice', through internalized judicial processes, public accountability of institutions and a durable peace based on popular sovereignty.[70]

Moreover, as Michael Pugh argues, accelerated privatization and electioneering is likely to increase polarization in a post-war society and is inappropriate in a setting where the state is already weak. Western states were consolidated under periods of large state ownership. Centralisation of authority under a new government could be better assisted through more protectionist Keynesian economics, stimulating local employment and stakes in peace through reconstruction contracts and state managed industry.[71] To aid development and avoid donor dependency such initiatives must be followed up by substantial debt relief.

This framework could be broadly drawn upon in state-building situations and serve both to lessen the international burden and produce exit strategies with greater prospects for a sustainable outcome. However, there is a danger of externalizing justice processes overly, which may satisfy appetites for an international morality, but not necessarily the practical or ideological demands of those inhabiting post-conflict societies.[72] To foster reconciliation and a sustainable regime of law and order which survives international withdrawal, judicial processes must take place – and be seen to take place – primarily within society, rather than exclusively through international tribunals or protracted 'policekeeping'. Sensitization to local traditions of justice and administration essentially subcontracts the process to society itself, representing not only a start to the return of sovereignty, but a system that is culturally understood and therefore functional, while lessening the international footprint and drain on resources.

Everywhere life occurs there is a social logic of interaction that determines action and expectations of reaction. When reflected on formally in the human setting, it interchangeably takes the name of 'culture' or 'civilization'. Civilization usually refers to legally enshrined codes of behaviour, while culture refers to normative social codes. But legislation does not make society, though it can sometimes change it. Laws that work are those that respond to social codes and values already ingrained, or which can be enforced without tipping the political balance into oppression: this is the art of good governance. While state-building should entail greater state involvement in the economy and security sectors – enlarging its shadow and presence – maximizing consent by staying out of social engineering or making reform efforts more gradual might be a way out of the no-exit dilemma.

In East Timor, the internationalized justice process faced severe difficulty, not only because the widespread illiteracy among the Timorese complicated usage of a written civil law system based on foreign understandings and codes of behaviour, but because the lack of passable roads made a centralized legal system based on courts in the capital Dili unworkable. However, employing traditional village councils functioning on a peer jury system and consensus-based decision making was highly successful, not only removing the need for a 'travelling policeman' or court, but as a tool for reconciliation where village members who had joined the militias were often forgiven and allowed to rejoin their village, thus directly fulfilling the goal of demobilization and reintegration.[73] This approach was also employed with child soldiers in Mozambique, to good effect, and is now in employed Afghanistan to broker greater unity through the village level National Solidarity Programme. Traditional councils may be subject to the cultural prejudices of host-societies, especially as regards views on gender, codes of honourable behaviour and punishment. However, even if the price of law and order and the dividend it pays in human security means a toll on liberal values and cosmopolitan views on justice, it could be a necessary task.

Creating space for political action and expression *is* within the remit of international administration, while determining the ideological character of politics are more treacherous waters. Distinctions between 'hardliners' and 'moderates' have proven over time to be unreliable as political tactics on behalf of external and local actors change.[74] Likewise banning parties that do not sit well with Western sensibilities but reflect indigenous dispositions has not proven to be effective,[75] and can contribute to the cause of extremists by alienating a disaffected youth.[76] Despite Western charges of barbarism, radical movements are a product of the political ecology in which they evolved,[77] and they express real sentiments within society.[78] Resistance to reform in Afghanistan and Iraq reflect the partial consent under which intervention was originally undertaken. It may be, that to encourage more liberal tendencies in host-societies, extremist parties need to be allowed space to fail. This is the most likely way of enacting a democratic pressure towards centre-field politics, in which those that would be spoilers could be absorbed. The role of international administration in a post-conflict setting is to seize upon such popular sentiments and support them, and this is the likely explanation for the success in Germany, Japan, Eastern Slavonia and East Timor. In Bosnia and Kosovo the problem has been a mixture of the two: consent as far as it has suited factional interests and entrenchment of the shadow economy, sustaining and empowering those that would breach the peace.

These challenges do not mean that peacebuilding should be abandoned, merely that liberal trusteeship might be more successful if it focused more on fulfilling the conditions of trusteeship and less on the immediate creation of societies in its own image. The greatest obstacle to successful state-building is the shifting perception among those governed from trusteeship to occupation. In Iraq, Baathist resistance to the Coalition Provisional Authority has allowed other global actors with a local agenda, what Sir Jeremy Greenstock calls the 'Al Qaeda franchise', to exploit a fragile political situation and inflame it into open conflict and rebellion.[79] If as the liberal logic holds, sovereignty is vested in the people and not the state, then designing an inclusive governance framework which incorporates 'spoilers' – the former Timorese militias, the Kosovo Liberation Army, Baathists and Taliban – can ultimately be the only remedy for resistance, and the best defence against external manipulation of the political process.

An international administration, despite its merits, will enjoy less political currency for public leadership than a domestic movement. A restrained approach could lower transaction costs of other activities, increase local tolerance for foreign administration, and translate into a more self-determined, and thus sustainable, local order. As Peter Galbraith suggests, Iraq must allow its respective constituencies to realize their political demands. Loose confederacy which builds on Kurdish autonomy, the Shia religious movement and Sunni nationalism allows society to organize itself, rather than impose the dominance of one agenda over another.[80] Such a solution safeguards communal self-determination rather than attempting to construct it, in this case through centrally imposed secular, liberal nationalism. It would be likely to lose foreign militants to many local allies. Similarly, with flagging consent for trusteeship in Kosovo, the only remaining option now that appears workable is 'conditional independence' on the basis of minority rights and protection.[81]

State-building, these days, need perhaps be more about trusteeship and less about the fulfilment of an ideological vision. The recurring problem is that in international politics a commitment to human rights tends to be subservient to a commitment to self-interest and security, which in itself is subject to states' perceptions of threat and approaches to counter them. Realism is a well-worn concept in international relations that exposes problems, but cannot always formulate solutions effectively. The cooperative logic of liberalism is cancelled if constituents of 'host' nations do not want to be liberals, at least in a political sense. Over time internationals might be able to improve the technical quality of governance, but there could be limits to social transformation. Shaped by the background of conflict and international intervention, particularist nationalisms and spreading Islamism may represent more than an error of judgement on behalf of locals, that will be overcome by protracted waiting for 'political maturity' to arise. The secret of soft power, making 'other people want what we want', may be that 'to get what we want', internationals to a greater degree need to 'give them what they want'. Until participatory strategies for intervention are clearly and sincerely pursued, peace will remain a phantom, elusive, immaterial and increasingly bloodstained.

Acknowledgement

I am grateful to Tonny Brems Knudsen, Carsten Bagge Laustsen, Michael Pugh and Guido Galli for indispensable comments on draft versions of this chapter.

Notes

1 Michael Pugh, 'Peacekeeping and International Relations Theory: Phantom of the Opera?', *International Peacekeeping*, 10, 4 (Winter 2003), pp. 104–5.

2 See Oliver Richmond, 'UN Peace Operations and the Dilemmas of the Peacebuilding Consensus', *International Peacekeeping,* 11, 1 (Spring 2004).

3 See Richard Caplan, *A New Trusteeship? The International Administration of War-Torn Territories,* Adelphi Paper 341 (London: International Institute for Strategic Studies, 2002).

4 'Ancient Voices: Search for the Holy Grail', *BBC2,* 29 March 2004.

5 Jens Stilhoff Sørensen, 'Balkanism and the New Radical Interventionism: A Structural Critique', *International Peacekeeping,* 9, 1 (Spring 2002), pp. 8–9.

6 Mark Duffield, *Global Governance and the New Wars: The Merging of Development and Security* (London: Zed Books, 2001), p. 11.

7 Ibid., p. 11.

8 On securitization and de-securitization see Ole Wæver, "Security and Desecuritization", in Ronnie Libschutz (ed.), *On Security* (New York: Columbia University Press, 1995).

9 The British Defence White Paper of 2003 identified failed and rogue states as primary security threats together with a blueprint for structural reform of British armed forces to meet them through global power projection, 'the expeditionary strategy'. Likewise, the US National Security Strategy (2002) explicitly sets out policy to, (V) 'Prevent Our Enemies From Threatening Us, Our Allies, and Our Friends With Weapons of Mass Destruction' (including pre-emptive strike), (VI) 'Ignite a New Era of Global Economic Growth through Free Markets and Free Trade', and (VII) 'Expand the Circle of Development by Opening Societies and Building the Infrastructure of Democracy'. The International Commission on Intervention and State Sovereignty (ICISS) have overtly sought to deterritorialize the concept of sovereignty to allow for an international 'responsibility to protect' persecuted populations through normalization of humanitarian intervention and peace operations. For the White Paper see: http://www.mod.uk/publications/whitepaper2003/index.html; the NSS, http://www.whitehouse.gov/nsc/nss.html; Report of the ICISS, http://www.dfait-maeci.gc.ca/iciss-ciise/report2-en.asp; and Kofi Annan, 'Democracy as an International Issue', *Global Governance,* 8, 2 (April–June 2002).

10 Adam Roberts, 'Intervention Without End?', *The World Today,* 59, 4 (April 2003), p. 10.

11 Michael J. Mazarr, 'George W. Bush: Idealist', *International Affairs,* 79, 3 (May 2003), pp. 503–23.

12 The PIC comprises 55 states and international organizations, but the Steering Board of 10 include Canada, France, Germany, Italy, Japan, Russia, the United Kingdom, United States, the European Commission, and the Organization of the Islamic Conference, which is represented by Turkey. The 21 million Euro budget of the OHR in 2004 is funded as follows: EU 53%, USA 22%, Japan 10%, Russia 4%, Canada 3.03%, OIC 2.5%, others: 5.47%. Information from the OHR website, http://www.ohr.int/ohr-info/gen-info/#pic.

13 This is the explicit role of the Steering Board, which funds the OHR. OHR website, ibid.

14 Jarat Chopra, 'Building state failure in East Timor', *Development and Change,* 33, 5 (2002), p. 998.

15 The construction of a representative and open state in Afghanistan is explicitly stated as the strategic aim of the Coalition strategy in the war on terror. See Richard N. Haas, 'Future of Afghanistan', Testimony Before the Senate Committee on Foreign Relations, Washington DC, 6 December 2001, http://www.state.gov/s/p/rem/6757.htm.

16 As Heristchi argues, Al Qaeda is not a state and war against the Taliban made the war on terror more tangible to Western publics. Claire Heristchi, 'Winning the War on Terror? The Contradictions of Counter-terrorism and Implications for the Pursuit of Peace Operations', 'Challenges of Peace Operations: Into the 21st Century', Stockholm Conference 23–25 May 2003, p. 4.

17 On the war against Iraq and Iraq as a military trusteeship see also the introductory chapter in this book.
18 Jean-Marie Guehenno, 'The Current and Future Challenges of UN Peacekeeping', 18 June 2003, London: Royal Institute of International Affairs.
19 Simon Chesterman, 'East Timor in Transition: Self-determination, State-building and the United Nations', *International Peacekeeping*, 9, 1 (Spring 2002), p. 48.
20 Attempts by the KLA to internationalize their conflict via the media and precipitating reprisals from Serb forces played into an international climate where Serbia was widely seen as the aggressor of the Yugoslav wars, leading to (illegal) NATO intervention and later a UN administration. Likewise, the deepening security crisis in Iraq and dilapidation of public services positions the UN under obligation of its mandate to alleviate human suffering and assist maintenance of international peace and security, rather than taking a principled political stance against involvement on the legal basis of how intervention was originally conducted.
21 Duffield (n. 6 above), p. 34.
22 Robert Jackson, 'International Engagement in War-torn Countries', *Global Governance*, 10, 1 (January-March 2004), p. 23.
23 Examples include the Democratic Republic of Congo and Sudan, where international medical agencies and relief aid perform the essential functions of the state where this is unable or unwilling to provide for its own population.
24 Jarat Chopra, 'Introducing Peace-Maintenance', in Jarat Chopra (ed.), *The Politics of Peace-Maintenance* (Boulder, CO: Lynne Rienner, 1998), p. 5.
25 Ibid., pp. 13–16.
26 Mats Berdal and Richard Caplan, 'The Politics of International Administration', *Global Governance*, 10, 1 (January–March 2004), p. 2.
27 See OHR Mission Implementation Plan, 30 January 2003, http://www.ohr.int/ohr-info/ohr-mip/default.asp?content_id=29145; the 'Bulldozer Initiative' to remove obstacles to privatization http://www.ohr.int/ohr-dept/econ/bulldozer-initiative/index.asp; *UNMIK at Two: From Reconstruction to Economic Development*, UNMIK public information pamphlet; 'Law of Administration for the State of Iraq for the Transitional Period' (Interim Constitution), Coalition Provisional Authority, March 2004: contains provisions for the 'sacrosanct' right to property and liberty, available at http://www.cpa-iraq.org/government/TAL.html; 'The Timor Gap Treaty: Independent East Timor', Oxfam Briefing Paper No. 25, February 2000, http://www.oxfam.org.au/publications/briefing/timor_gap_treaty/east_timor.html.
28 Michael Pugh and Neil Cooper, with Jonathan Goodhand, *War Economies in A Regional Context: Challenges of Transformation* (Boulder, CO: Lynne Rienner, 2004), pp. 196–7.
29 Robert Axelrod, *The Evolution of Cooperation* (New York: Basic Books, 1984), p. 174. Cited in Mark Baskin, 'Between Exit and Engagement: On the Division of Authority in International Administrations, *Global Governance*, 10, 1 (January–March 2004), p. 121.
30 Such cooperation includes trading expert knowledge in counterfeiting, bomb making, fire arms and military training, or operational support through access to smuggling routes, safe houses or contact networks, sometimes in government. Tamara Makarenko, 'A model of terrorist-criminal relations', *Jane's Intelligence Review*, 30 July 2003, http://www.janes.com/security/international_security/news/jir/jir030730_1_n.shtml
31 See International Crisis Group, *Arming Saddam: The Yugoslav Connection*, ICG Balkans Report, No. 136, December 2002, pp. 1–7; 'High Representative Comments on Resignation of Mirko Sarovic from BiH Presidency', Office of the High Representative, Sarajevo, 2 April 2003, http://www.ohr.int/ohr-dept/presso/pressr/default.asp?content_id=29615.
32 Joseph Nye, *The Paradox of American power: Why the World's Only Superpower Can't Go It Alone* (Oxford: Oxford University Press, 2002), pp. 1–8.

33 H. Duncan Hall, *Mandates, Dependencies and Trusteeship* (London: Steven and Sons for the Carnegie Endowment for International Peace, 1948), p. 105.
34 Ibid., p. 97.
35 Berdal and Caplan (n. 26 above), pp. 1–2.
36 Jarat Chopra (n. 14 above), p. 990.
37 J.M. Lee, *Colonial Development and Good Government: A Study of the Ideas Expressed by the British Official Classes in Planning Decolonization 1939–64* (Oxford: Clarendon Press, 1967), p. 6.
38 Ibid., p. 6.
39 Ibid., p. 2.
40 'Rules of Procedure for the Trusteeship Council', UN Doc T/I/Rev. I, 23 April, 1947, para XII, reprinted in Annex XV in Hall (n. 33 above), pp. 379–80. See also Annex IX, '"B" Mandates: Questionnaire Intended to Facilitate the Preparation of the Annual Reports from the Mandatory Powers', UN Doc T/44, 8 May, 1947, pp. 319–22.
41 Lee (n. 37 above), p. 2.
42 Chopra (n. 14 above), p. 999.
43 Caplan (n. 3 above), pp. 17–21.
44 Ibid., p. 17.
45 See *Helsinki Final Act* (1975), Article 1(a): Section I-IV. Section I asserts that members 'consider that their frontiers can be changed, in accordance with international law, by peaceful means and by agreement' and that (Section IV) 'participating States will likewise refrain from making each other's territory the object of military occupation or other direct or indirect measures of force in contravention of international law ... No such occupation or acquisition will be considered as legal'. OSCE website, http://www.osce.org/docs/english/1990–1999/summits/helfa75e.htm#Anchor-29952.
46 Caplan (n. 3 above), pp. 17–18. See also International Crisis Group, 'Kosovo's Ethnic Dilemma: The Need for a Civic Contract', ICG Balkans Report No.143, 28 May 2003, http://www.crisisweb.org/home/index.cfm?id=1625&l=1; Security Council Resolution 1244 (1999), esp. Article 10 on the aims of the international civil presence, p. 3, http://ods-dds-ny.un.org/doc/UNDOC/GEN/N99/172/89/PDF/N9917289.pdf?OpenElement.
47 Remarks by Barnett Rubin, 'Afghanistan: Two Years After Bonn', Conference organized by the Swedish Committee for Afghanistan, Stockholm, 20 November 2003.
48 See International Crisis Group, *Afghanistan: The Problem of Pashtun Alienation*, Asia Report No. 62, August 2003, http://www.crisisweb.org/home/index.cfm?id=1641&l=1; Pugh and Cooper, with Goodhand, *War Economies in A Regional Context*, p. 48.
49 See for example David Harland, 'Legitimacy and Effectiveness in International Administration', *Global Governance*, 10, 1 (January–March 2004), pp. 17–19.
50 Annika S. Hansen, 'International Security Assistance to War-Torn Societies', in Michael Pugh (ed.), *Regeneration of War-Torn Societies* (London: Macmillan Press, 2000), p. 36.
51 Simon Chesterman, *You, The People: The United Nations, Transitional Administration and Statebuilding*, Final Programme Report, International Peace Academy, November 2003, pp. i, 7.
52 Caplan (n. 3 above), p. 46.
53 Pugh and Cooper, with Goodhand (n. 28 above), pp. 47–8, 58–71, especially the layered concept of combat, shadow and coping economies as a means of differentiating incentive structures of local actors.
54 Ray Salvatore Jennings, *The Road Ahead: Lessons in Nation Building from Germany, Japan and Afghanistan for Post-war Iraq*, United States Institute of Peace, Peaceworks Report No. 49, May 2003, pp. 65–70.
55 See I. William Zartman, *Ripe for Resolution: Conflict and Intervention in Africa* (Oxford: University Press, 1989), pp. 263–7.
56 Pugh and Cooper, with Goodhand (n. 28 above), p. 52.
57 Caplan (n. 3 above), p. 17.

58 Defined as conflicts linked 'through a variety of negative processes, including invasion, subversion, collapse of state capacities, cross-border ethnic or religious solidarities, smuggling, looting, arms trafficking, and forced population movements'. Barnett Rubin in 'Regional Approaches to Conflict Management in Africa', Seminar Report, International Peace Academy, 2001, p. 1, http://www.ipacademy.org/PDF_Reports/REG_APPR.pdf.
59 See 'Good Intentions Will Not Pave the Road to Peace', Afghanistan Policy Brief, CARE International/Centre for International Cooperation, 15 September 2003, http://www.careusa.org/newsroom/specialreports/afghanistan/09152003_afghanistanbrief.pdf; 'Iraq: The Need for Security', Amnesty International Special Report, 4 July 2003, http://web.amnesty.org/library/print/ENGMDE141432003; 'Measures to Re-establish Security and Build Peaceful Co-existence in Mitrovica', UNMIK Press Release, UNMIK/PR/161, 16 February 2000, http://www.unmikonline.org/press/press/pr161.html.
60 Pugh and Cooper, with Goodhand (n. 28 above), pp. 160–76.
61 Ibid., p. 52.
62 Rhys Dogan and Michael Pugh, *From Military to Market Imperatives: Peacekeeping and the New Public Policy*, Plymouth International Papers, No. 8, 1997, p. 9.
63 Michael Ignatieff, 'Nation-building Lite', *New York Times Magazine*, 28 July 2002.
64 See Kirsti Samuels and Sebastian Einsiedel, 'The Future of UN State-Building: Strategic and Operational Challenges and the Legacy of Iraq', Policy Report, International Peace Academy, November 2003.
65 Amitai Etzioni, 'A Self-restrained Approach to Nation-building by Foreign Powers', *International Affairs*, 80, 1 (January 2004), pp. 1–18.
66 A poll in March/April 2004 registered 46% of Iraqis as agreeing the Coalition had done 'more harm than good' and 17% believed 'it is acceptable to attack Coalition forces,' the latter figure translates roughly into 4 million people. Quoted by Tim Sebastian on BBC *Hardtalk*, 22 June 2004.
67 Graham Day and Christopher Freeman, 'Policekeeping is the Key: Rebuilding the Internal Security Architecture of Post-war Iraq', *International Affairs*, 79, 2 (March 2003), pp. 335–49.
68 Etzioni, 'A Self-restrained Approach to Nation-building by Foreign Powers', pp. 14–15.
69 Graham Day, *Policekeeping: A Field Guide to Law and Order Operations in Failed States*, Washington, DC: Unites States Institute of Peace Press, forthcoming.
70 Michael Dziedzic, 'Introduction', in Robert Oakley, Eliot Goldberg and Michael Dziedzic (eds), *Policing the New World Disorder: Peace Operations and Public Security* (Washington, DC: National Defence University Press, 1998).
71 Pugh and Cooper, with Goodhand (n. 28 above), pp. 180–5.
72 See Chandra Lekha Sriram, 'Universal Jurisdiction: Problems and Prospects of Externalizing Justice', in Martti Koskenniemi and Jarna Petman (eds), *Finnish Yearbook of International Law*, XII (Boston: Martin Nijhoff, 2001), pp. 47–9.
73 Day (n. 69 above).
74 For example, Baskin argues that 'moderates' and 'hardliners' are 'defined by the momentary needs of the international community' – 'a hardliner is someone with the capacity to maintain a distinct agenda ... and will not cooperate on terms exclusively defined by international officials'. Given shifting attitudes to Slobodan Milosevic pre- and post-Kosovo, Saddam Hussein from Cold War ally, to post-Cold War 'rogue dictator' and Afghan President Hamid Karzai's former affiliation as a Taliban supporter, these distinctions do appear arbitrary and fluctuating in tact with national interests. Baskin (n. 29 above), pp. 130–1.
75 Caplan (n. 3 above), p. 57.
76 Executive Summary, 'Islamic Extremists: How Do They Mobilize Support?', Special Report No. 89, United States Institute of Peace, July 2002, http://www.usip.org/pubs/specialreports/sr89.html.

77 Gerd Nonneman, 'Rentiers and Autocrats, Monarchs and Democrats, State and Society: The Middle East between Globalization, Human "Agency", and Europe', *International Affairs*, 77, 1 (January 2001), p. 152.

78 For the case of the Taliban, see Christopher P. Freeman, 'Dissonant Discourse: Forging Islamist States in Secular Models – The Case of Afghanistan', *Cambridge Review of International Affairs*, 15, 3 (October 2002), pp. 533–47.

79 Sir Jeremy Greenstock, 'What Must Be Done Now', *Economist*, 6 May 2004, pp. 27–9.

80 Peter Galbraith, 'How to Get Out of Iraq', *New York Review of Books*, 13 May, 2004, http://www.nybooks.com/articles/17103.

81 See Tonny Brems Knudsen, 'From UNMIK to Self-determination? The Puzzle of Kosovo's Future Status' in this volume.

11 The future of international trusteeship

Conclusive reflections

Tonny Brems Knudsen and Carsten Bagge Laustsen

The essays in this book reflect on three main issues regarding the future of international trusteeship: the vicious circle of nationalism and revenge and how to break it, the securitization of international trusteeship, and the consequences of international trusteeship for the normative machinery of international society.

As argued by Laustsen, Kühle and Vetlesen, the pattern of nationalism, myth-making and revenge has taken on a seemingly permanent character in Kosovo. This was evident in the notorious memorandum published by the Serbian Academy of Arts and Sciences in 1986, in the attacks on and mass expulsion of the Albanian population in 1998 and 1999, and, following the intervention by NATO, in the revenge against the Serb population whose continued existence in Kosovo is threatened as evident also from the 2004 March Riots. Strikingly, the atrocities on non-Albanian groups were legitimized on the basis of a claim of a right of first possession to Kosovo, just as the atrocities on the Albanian population were justified in 1998–9.

Under such circumstances, inter-community reconciliation and integration appears to be wishful thinking. How can the vicious circle of myth, atrocities and revenge be broken? In the short and medium term, mutual toleration of separate existences protected by either international or national security forces seem to be the best that one can hope for. This is to some extent also reflected in the analyses of the educational system and local governance by Nelles and Baskin. In the longer term, however, it must be possible to proceed from guarded separation to mutual toleration among separated communities, and then to genuine reconciliation and integration. According to Vetlesen, there is some hope not least due to the intervention of third parties. The important task is to reverse the logic of genocide that is to relocate guilt and responsibility from a collective to an individual level. Unfortunately, however, the case against former President Slobodan Milošević is seen by many as just another stroke by NATO imperialists against a suffering Serbia. It is essential to counter this myth of suffering and victimization, and to force the players to acknowledge that there can be perpetrators and victims on both sides. This will allow the two groups to meet, for instance in trade, but it will not create a genuinely integrated multicultural society.

Arguably, such a society has never existed in Kosovo. After more than six years of trusteeship administration, much energy is still spent on enabling the remaining

Serbs to stay in Kosovo. This basically means building two separate societies, two educational systems and two systems of local government. This will solidify the divisions brought about by war and atrocities, and requires the ongoing presence of foreign troops, observers and administrators no matter whether the coming negotiations concerning the future status of Kosovo will lead to a final conclusion or not. The international administrators of the trusteeship of Kosovo have struggled hard, but until now largely in vain, to overcome the disintegrative and violent power of the vicious circle of myth, nationalism and revenge, and in one form or another, elements of trusteeship will have to continue for some time, even after a decision regarding future status has been taken.

Another major question rising from the contributions to this book concerns the securitization of international trusteeship. Has the revived trusteeship institution become an ideological and securitized project as indicated by Pugh and Freeman?[1] What drives international intervention and the reconstruction of war-torn societies following the end of the Cold War and '9/11'? Genuine humanitarianism informed by human rights? Pragmatic concerns informed by the need and obligation to continue from humanitarian diplomacy to the use of force when diplomacy has no effect, and from force to comprehensive reconstruction when the resultant damage is to be repaired? Rationalist concerns informed by a recognition that a stable international order requires states that function and collective measures to put out local fires before they escalate into regional and global ones? Or is it rather concerns for national security prompting great powers (usually in the West) to intervene in key and rogue states in order to increase their own security by responding to threats, and by attempting to transform troublesome states and regions into liberal democratic societies closer to the Western ideal?

The most accurate answer is probably (1) that intervention, peacebuilding and trusteeship have been informed by a mixture of all these concerns since the end of the Cold War, (2) that humanitarianism in cases like Iraqi Kurdistan 1991, Somalia 1992, Haiti 1994, Bosnia 1992–5, East Timor 1999 and Kosovo 1999 was (increasingly) accompanied by concerns of pragmatism and order as well as a desire for the spread of Western values in a broader sense, and (3) that humanitarianism, pragmatism and order have given way to strategic and ideologically informed national security concerns following '9/11' (the most relevant cases being Afghanistan and Iraq), not least in the minds and initiatives of the US leadership.

On the other hand, it can be argued that these are the main trends, and that the motives and politics of international intervention, peacebuilding and trusteeship have remained complex all along the way, leaving aside the war against Iraq in 2003. As a striking exception to the post-Cold War rule, this war and reconstruction has remained a predominantly American project motivated, by all indications, not by an acute fear of Iraqi weapons of mass destruction (even if we accept the pre-war doubts about the facts at face value), but by a relatively simple, but apparently also very clear and decisive, long-term strategy for a transformation of the Middle East and the broader Islamic world by means of the imposition and spread of liberal democracy by threat, force and a tough dose of societal reconstruction.[2] In all the other cases mentioned above, including Afghanistan, strategic and national security concerns have been accompanied by concerns expressed in the legal and institutional machinery of international society, including concerns about collective security and human rights. What is worrying, from an internationalist or 'solidarist' perspective based on international organization, collective security and human rights, is the thought that the pattern of war and societal reconstruction witnessed in Iraq from 2003 onwards might become the new order of the day.

However, even in a not so American and securitized version (meaning, instead, the UN-based and 'solidarist' one), the resort to international trusteeship might appear a bit of a nightmare to 'pluralist' international society writers. In his contribution to this book, Freeman argues that today, security policy extends to 'the penetration of the state, the socialization of its polity and the administration of its rule of law' and that 'constitutional pluralism is discredited by a core group of liberal states which use solidarism to legitimize the militarized replication of their political system'. Freeman's main target is Afghanistan and Iraq and thus international (or rather military) trusteeship under the post '9/11' anti-terror agenda, but his critical analysis of the liberal inclusion of failed and rogue states is directed against the UN trusteeships under the internationalist agenda of the 1990s as well.[3]

For his part, Robert Jackson has already warned, in the heated aftermath of the NATO intervention in Kosovo, that British Prime Minister Tony Blair's 'doctrine of international community' – presented in an important speech in Chicago in April 1999 during the air campaign against Yugoslavia – would become a slippery slope of Western values: a trail that would take Western-led international society from humanitarian intervention against genocide to intervention for liberal democracy, directed against dictatorships which would then make up a new second-class international community deprived of the legal rights and guarantees of first-class states.[4] Arguably, Jackson's critique was more correct with regard to the aspiration inherent in the thinking of Blair and other Western leaders than it was for the actual circumstances of the intervention in Kosovo, in so far that it could, as also recognized by Jackson, be defended as an intervention against atrocious conduct. However, if we move from the intervention and UN trusteeship in Kosovo to the war and military trusteeship in Iraq, Jackson's warning becomes more acute and valuable than ever.

In our view, however, it is important to stress that the most obvious target of this criticism is not the solidarist conception of international society and the UN-based model of humanitarian intervention and international trusteeship associated with it. To begin with, Blair's 1999 'doctrine of international community' went too far beyond defending the minimum standards of humanity in its value-based interventionism to deserve the theoretical category of solidarism. Following the legal and philosophical tradition championed by Hugo Grotius and Hersch Lauterpacht at different points in history, this conception of international society is first of all an internationalist vision of collective security, international organization and global human governance based on legal principle and a strong concern for international order as well as international justice. Moreover, when the doctrines of Tony Blair meet the ones championed by US President George W. Bush following '9/11' – including the right of preventive warfare, multilateralism defined as the coalition of the willing, and the transformation of dictatorships into liberal democracies as a just mission for the US and a cure against terrorism[5] – the solidarist and internationalist conception of international society is hardly recognizable any longer. Rather, we are talking about what might be called 'hyper-solidarism' (Blair's 'international community' doctrine) or an explosive and disruptive combination of realism and idealism (Bush's 'war-on-terror' doctrine).

The US national security strategy can thus be seen as a combination of hard security measures (preventive war), liberal strategies for a long-term peace (the spread of democracy which is, however, rarely recommended by means of force), and liberal moral values like human rights, democracy and freedom. Moreover, the war against Iraq and the resultant military trusteeship can at least to some extent be seen as an attempt by the US to implement or test its National Security Strategy of 2002. This is clearly at odds with the solidarist and internationalist conception of international society, where the duty to avoid war when possible, and to promote international order and justice by means of world organization and the respect of international law, remain central.[6] The 2002 US National Security Strategy, the war against Iraq and the concept of military trusteeship is thus bad medicine for the solidarist conception of international society. Neither international order in general nor the particular practice of trusteeship can be built on unilateralism, coalitions of the willing, imposition of democracy and wars of choice. At a minimum, trusteeships must be based on a humanitarian necessity which is not self-created, or which is a consequence of a use of force which could not be avoided unless basic principles of humanitarian law were abandoned.

It is essential for the acceptance of international trusteeship that it is not burdened by private objectives and contested projects. The legitimacy and success of such arrangements furthermore depend on the reestablishment of law and order, and sensitivity towards local cultures and traditions during the rebuilding of societal key elements like local governance, the economy and the educational system. This is the less imperialist, more pragmatic and more restrained model of trusteeship advocated by Freeman, Baskin and Pugh in their contributions to this book. It is tempting to call this 'light footprint' the pluralist approach to international trusteeship with reference to what Robert Jackson has on several occasions referred to as the 'pluralist restraint'; a formula for calmness, tolerance and prudence when it comes to reform of the fundamental institutional machinery of international society on the scale of the 'Kosovo experiment', as Søbjerg calls it in her contribution to this book. However, trusteeship is an inherently solidarist activity, as it is embedded in the belief that international society has a responsibility for its constituent parts including not only states, but also nations, minorities, and populations.

Does the critique raised by Jackson, Freeman and Pugh not affect the solidarist and UN-based model of international trusteeship of the 1990s? Yes it does, in so far that what the UN administrators and their partners have aimed for in cases like

Kosovo (more or less uncompromisingly) is really Western and liberal standards for the economic, social and political organization of domestic society – the 'good life'. At the same time, most observers agree that there has been a degree of pragmatism behind the decisions to resort to *de facto* trusteeship arrangements in recent years in cases like Bosnia, Kosovo and East Timor. In the case of Kosovo, it is difficult to see what else could be done following a background characterized by ethnic violence, crimes against humanity, civil war and international intervention. Kosovo could hardly be governed by Belgrade due to Belgrade's 1998–9 record of crimes against humanity and mass expulsion. Likewise, the Albanian side could hardly be trusted to rule over the Serb minority as evident from the forced displacement of Serbs following the turn of fortunes at the end of NATO's bombing campaign and again during the 2004 March riots. The UN trusteeship was an obvious solution. It is, furthermore, difficult to see, how a territory and a population can be ruled, and a society reconstructed, without a set of principles. There has to be some sense of direction regarding the society that is going to emerge from the international trusteeship arrangement, and democracy is hardly the worst model around. But as forcefully argued by Pugh and Freeman, the question remains whether new trusteeships have to be run on the basis of a specific version of Western liberal democracy based on a free-market economy and a low degree of central interference and redistribution? There is always room for manoeuvre regarding the involvement of local constituencies as argued by Baskin, the control of the market as argued by Pugh, and the respect for local traditions as argued by Freeman with reference to the involvement of the Loya Jirga in the reconstruction of Afghanistan, a move in which he sees some hope for the dawning of a more culturally informed and participatory approach.

Turning to the third main question rising from the contributions to this book, the return to international trusteeship and other solidarist institutions like humanitarian intervention and war crimes tribunals arguably threatens the consistency of the normative and institutional framework of international society. The relationship between humanitarian intervention, international trusteeship and the right of self-determination is complicated and full of political and moral pitfalls including the ones of defining the 'self', dismissing the sovereign, and resorting to paternalism.[7] But the question relating to international trusteeship is whose self-determination has been infringed: the self-determination of, for instance, former Yugoslavia and Indonesia which was more or less openly put aside by the UN and the international community, or the self-determination of the great majority of the peoples of Kosovo and East Timor who were subjected to atrocities and oppression before the resort to humanitarian intervention and international administration? If self-determination belongs to the people and not to the state, then the establishment of trusteeships in Kosovo and East Timor was arguably a protection of the principles of self-determination rather than a negation of it.

However, this argument only serves to underline the point raised by Kristensen that the normative machinery of international society is in need of renewed consistency. Under the present circumstances, trusteeships like the one in Kosovo may, as argued by Kristensen, at times find it difficult to reconcile its two main purposes: to fill a governance vacuum and to solve a territorial dispute. When it is clear from the beginning that independence is the goal, as in the case of East Timor, contemporary international trusteeship takes on much the same quality as envisaged under the mandates system of the League of Nations and especially the UN trusteeship system, namely to prepare a territory and its people for independence. When there is no clear answer to the territorial dispute, and the future status of the territory under international administration is therefore unclear, as in the case of Kosovo, the trusteeship must concentrate on filling out the governmental vacuum without having a clear idea of how to assist in building up local and national structures of government and without having a clear idea of the kind of political association that these structures must later be a part of.

Clearly, there is still no international enthusiasm for the right of national self-determination in these cases, and for good reasons it could be argued with reference to the historical and potential turmoil associated with this doctrine.[8] Thus, even when state authorities have abused their own sovereign powers in the extreme – and it can hardly be denied that the Yugoslav authorities were guilty of that in the case of Kosovo 1998–9 – there remains a clear international reluctance to hand over sovereignty to the victimized people even when central questions concerning demography and borders are less problematic than in most cases. In the case of Kosovo, Kristensen's call for more consistency in the international normative framework can lead to the following two points: first, it can be argued that when atrocities and mass expulsion triggers humanitarian intervention and trusteeship to protect people and society, self-rule and independence should not be ruled out automatically;[9] second, it can be argued, as Kristensen has done, that if international society was more open to various alternative models of national self-determination, there would perhaps have been no reason for the Kurds of Iraq in 1991 and the Albanians of Kosovo in 1998 to resort to a rebellion which could hardly succeed in itself, but might possibly lead to self-determination and independence with humanitarian intervention as a calculated stepping stone.

The cure for the turbulence associated with the return to earlier solidarist practices of humanitarian intervention, trusteeship and war crimes tribunals is not to put these back into the museum as dated international institutions. The cure is, rather, to complete the solidarist modernization of the institutional machinery of international society, for instance by embarking on a more flexible approach to claims for national self-determination, and by improving the relevant organizational machinery, as the 2005 UN World Summit has attempted with the decision to establish a Peacebuilding Commission. At the same time, however, it is imperative that the Western world gives up the idea that war-torn societies, failed states and contested territories must necessarily be reconstructed in its own image.

Notes

1 This theme is also addressed in the discussion of military trusteeship in the introductory chapter and, as an international security device used for the solution or containment of territorial disputes, in Chapter 8 by Kristensen.

2 Tonny Brems Knudsen, 'Denmark and the War Against Iraq: Losing Sight of Internationalism?', *Danish Foreign Policy Yearbook 2004* (eds. Per Carlsen and Hans Mouritzen) (Copenhagen: Danish Institute for International Studies, 2004), pp. 69–73 and 80–85.

3 On the distinction between trusteeship under the neo-internationalist agenda of the 1990s and the anti-terror agenda following '9–11', see the introductory chapter.

4 See Robert Jackson, *The Global Covenant: Human Conduct in a World of States* (Oxford: Oxford University Press, 2000), pp. 355–360; 366–368. On the distinction between 'solidarism' and 'pluralism' see also the introduction to this book and the chapters by Søbjerg, Kristensen and Knudsen.

5 We refer to the White House, 'The National Security Strategy of the United States of America' (Washington: September 2002), and successive State of the Union speeches by George W. Bush. See also Knudsen 2004 (n. 2 above), pp. 69–73 and 80–85 and the discussion in the introductory chapter.

6 For a forceful solidarist critique of the war against Iraq and US foreign policy following '9–11', see also Tim Dunne, 'Society and Hierarchy in International Relations', *International Relations,* Vol. 17, No. 3, pp. 303–320.

7 See Jackson (n. 4 above), pp. 301–315 and William Bain, *Between Anarchy and Society: Trusteeship and the obligations of power* (Oxford: Oxford University Press, 2003), pp. 140–154.

8 See James Mayall, *Nationalism and International Society* (Cambridge: Cambridge University Press, 1990).

9 On the future status of Kosovo, see also Chapter 9 by Knudsen.

Index

Printed in the United States
123267LV00002B/206/A

9 780415 459587